The Dance of the Rose and the Nightingale

Gender, Culture, and Politics in the Middle East

Leila Ahmed, Miriam Cooke, Simona Sharoni, *and* Suad Joseph, *Series Editors*

The Dance of the Rose and the Nightingale.

The Dance of
the Rose and
the Nightingale

Nesta Ramazani

Syracuse University Press

The paper used in this publication meets the minimum requirements of
American National Standard for Information Sciences—Permanence
of Paper for Printed Library Materials, ANSI Z39.48–1984.∞™

Library of Congress Cataloging-in-Publication Data
Ramazani, Nesta, 1932–
The dance of the rose and the nightingale / Nesta Ramazani.—1st ed.
p. cm.—(Gender, culture, and politics in the Middle East)
ISBN 0-8156-0727-X (alk. paper)
1. Ramazani, Nesta, 1932– 2. Dancers—Iran—Biography. 3. Women
dancers—Iran—Biography. 4. Iranian American women—Biography. 5. Iranian
Americans—Biography. I. Title. II. Series.
GV1785.R34 A3 2001
792.8'028'092—dc21
[B]   2001054940

In memory of my mother,
Winnifred Burton Shahrokh,
whose courage and fortitude made it all possible

and to my grandchildren
Ariana, Gabriel Bijan, Allegra, Annika,
Anthony Kaveh, and Cyrus Louis,
that they might know their heritage.

Nesta Ramazani is an independent scholar who writes and lectures extensively on the Middle East. Her latest book is *Persian Cooking: A Table of Exotic Delights.*

Contents

Illustrations

Acknowledgments

HAD IT NOT BEEN for the persistent persuasion and encouragement of my friend Farzaneh Milani, I would never have undertaken the joyous yet demanding task of writing this book. Without her unerring conviction that I had a singular story to tell, her unfailing confidence in my ability to narrate the tale, and her determination that I *would* narrate it, this story would never have been told. She also gave generously of her time to read and critique various versions of the work as it progressed. I am forever indebted to her.

When Caroline Rody started reading my early chapters, helping to mold and give direction to a work that was still raw and unformulated, she was not yet my daughter-in-law. I am happy to say that before the work reached completion, she had become a family member—the wife of my youngest son, the mother of my first grandson. For her sure guidance, her unerringly accurate assessments, her penetrating and candid criticism I am deeply grateful. Without her encouragement I might not have had the confidence to see the work to its conclusion.

I am also grateful to Joyce Colony, who tirelessly edited many versions of various chapters; to Toni Rhoades, whose sharp editorial pencil pointed out many flaws in an earlier version of this work; and to Rebecca Saunders, whose unwavering support and guidance at a time of doubt and uncertainty saved the day and convinced me of the value of this narrative. I am indebted to my son Jahan, who set aside a busy schedule to read parts of the manuscript and brought to bear on it his expertise, his ear for the right turn of phrase, and his keen eye for detail. Mary Selden Evans, at Syracuse University Press, was particularly helpful in seeing this book to completion, as was Annie Barva, who meticulously and expertly copyedited the manuscript.

And I am most grateful to my husband, who is a major figure in this tale—the nightingale to my rose—for everything he has always meant to me, for his intellectual encouragement, and for awakening in me a deep love of Iranian culture. I thank him also for always supporting me in my literary endeavors. He was the first to express confidence in my writing abilities. Without his encouragement, support, and forbearance there would have been no book.

Introduction

IN A DANCE STUDIO in Virginia I sometimes play a recording of a Persian folk tune. Its pulsing rhythms electrify my students. Suddenly they are all attention and concentration as the alien but evocative music invites them to enter another world. As I start dancing, they watch me and imitate what I am doing. Soon they are responding to the pulsing beat, their hands held high, their arms snaking around, their hips rotating gently, voluptuously, in a manner at once innocent and inviting.

That I teach them Persian dances does not surprise them. That I should also be teaching them movements drawn from ballet and jazz and theater dance is what mystifies them, for they know that although I was born in England and my mother was English, I grew up in Iran. This fact is why newcomers invariably ask, "Where did you study ballet?" expecting me to say Moscow, London, or even Virginia. "In Tehran," I answer. And there always follow expressions of disbelief. "In *Tehran?*" I explain that a White Russian émigré, having fled the Russian Revolution, opened a ballet studio in Tehran many years ago and that I had studied ballet with her. "And where did you learn to jitterbug like that?" some ask. And I answer, "From watching American movies." It surprises them that I could have grown up in such a remote and alien a place as Iran and yet have been exposed to the same musical and dance influences as they. Their astonishment only increases when they learn that as a teenager I was a member of Iran's first ballet company and that I performed on the stage.

I am not surprised at their surprise. After all, their perceptions of Iran are deeply colored by the Islamic Revolution of 1979. The images of Iranian women they carry in their minds are of chador-clad, fist-shaking, faceless black blobs, not young girls in tutus. Of course, they know I grew up long before the Islamic Revolution, in an Iran that was modernizing rapidly and whose ruler, Mohammad Reza Shah Pahlavi, was intent on remolding his country in the image of the West. But to have danced on the stage? Been a member of a ballet company?

Actually, they are not far off the mark, for in fact the opportunities for me to study dance were severely limited, and the prospects of my being able to pursue any sort of dance career in the 1940s in Iran were dim, in spite of its rapid modernization. But, thanks to the Russian Revolution, there was a ballet studio in Tehran. I was also lucky that my mother was English and encouraged my inclinations in that direction, and that my father's family were Zoroastrian, not Muslim, and somewhat open to new and modern ideas.

So a host of different variables entered into the unlikely equation. I was living in changing times. The war raging in Europe came to Iran's very doorstep, with unimaginable consequences. Great Britain and the United States started using Iran as a transit route to supply war munitions to the Soviet Union in its fight against Nazi Germany. As many as forty thousand American troops landed in Iran, bringing with them their easy informality, pop culture, and alien ideas. And the U.S. government, implementing Franklin D. Roosevelt's dream of helping to modernize Iran, sent to Tehran a woman who had a profound effect on my life, Nilla Cram Cook.

By then Mohammad Reza Shah was in power and, following in his father's footsteps, was vigorously enforcing a top-down modernization of Iran, a policy that introduced new ideas that inevitably collided with long-cherished beliefs and traditions. Popular attitudes of disapproval toward dance and music started to soften under the country's increasing exposure to Western movies, theater, music, and other art forms and ideas. Princess Ashraf—the Shah's twin sister, whose power rivaled or even exceeded that of the Shah—was pushing strongly for the modernization of Iran. When Nilla Cook proposed the formation of a national ballet company, the idea appealed to the princess, and she became the patron of the novel enterprise, supporting it with her exceptional resources and prestige.

And so Mrs. Cook's dream of an Iranian performing dance company, so at odds with ancient traditions, became a reality. Conceiving of the company as a blending of the East and the West, the traditional and the modern, the ancient and the contemporary, this singular woman skillfully accommodated herself to the taboos of Iran's indigenous culture, while at the same time drawing on that culture for themes and inspiration. She managed to overcome the objections of traditionalists by imaginatively showcasing Persian poetry, legend, and folk dance, even as she grafted these elements onto a foundation of Western concepts of dance as an art form buttressed by ballet training. And I, who had in all facets of my life combined different cultures into a kaleidoscopic mix, found it quite natural that we would interpret through dance the lyrics of Hafez, the grand epics of Ferdowsi, and the mystical verses of Jalal ad-Din Rumi. To me it seemed perfectly reasonable to blend Western ballet with Persian folk steps, to add an arabesque to a Kurdish dance, a *soutenu* turn to a mimed Gilaki wedding celebration, or a jeté to a Bakhtiari stick dance. I moved easily from performing a Zoroastrian temple dance to interpreting mystical Sufi poetry and to portraying the love of a rose and a nightingale.

Although the environment I grew up in was largely inimical to dance as a performing art, the artistic genius of Persian culture had nevertheless nourished my imagination, even as I was studying largely Western ideas and art forms. All my life I had been exposed to the luscious colors and intricate designs of hand-woven carpets, the delicate chiselling on silver vases and copper trays, the restfulness and beauty of exquisitely landscaped gardens, and the balance and harmony of ancient mosques covered with inlaid tiles glowing with brilliant colors. Ironically, it was my English mother who encouraged my appreciation for all these art forms.

From childhood I had heard quotations from the great poets, both English and Persian, allusions to mythical figures, snatches of prayer, and accounts of ancient legends. Persian and Western music formed equal parts of my musical exposure. Persian, English, and later French and Italian deepened my awareness of language and love of literature. The various schools I attended introduced me to different ideas of the meaning of life. Zoroastrian chants, Shiite mourning processions, and Catholic High Mass exposed me to rite, ritual, and pageantry and to the emotional impact of pattern, repetition, and dramatic punctuation. All these elements helped shape my creativity, and I was able to draw on them when Mrs. Cook encouraged me, young as I was, to apply my imagination to the choreography of our dances.

Later, my travels with the troupe introduced me to the great tribal and ethnic diversity of Iran's population, to the extraordinary richness of its literary heritage, to the sonorous beauty of its language, to the depth and breadth of its culture, and to the antiquity and variety of my roots. In addition, it introduced me to another rich Middle Eastern culture, that of Turkey. From all these experiences I would some day create a symbiosis of cultures in the dances I would choreograph for my own students, spinning magical worlds for them to enter.

Eventually fate brought me to the United States, my new country, where in time I would learn the excitement and spontaneity of jazz, tap, and theater dance. I would improve my touch at the piano and learn a different musical vocabulary, deepen and broaden my love of literature, earn an advanced degree in English, and become a writer and lecturer, addressing subjects that ranged from Persian cuisine to the status of women in Muslim societies. I would not only incorporate dance into my life as a source of personal satisfaction and creativity, but would undertake a career as a dance teacher, sharing my delight in the ethereal beauty of this art form with students of all ages.

These pages, then, depict my awakening to the richness of the exterior world as well as to the turmoil of an inner life of new emotions and ideas. They tell of encountering love and death, of dreaming impossible dreams, of enjoying unexpected triumphs and heartbreaking disappointments. They portray an intimate and personal slice of life that exemplifies the extraordinary fusion of cultures that has taken place throughout the long span of Persian history and that in part explains Iran's rich and diverse heritage.

In addition, these pages tell of the far reach of such American ideas as freedom of speech and the right to life, liberty, and the pursuit of happiness. They describe the sowing of the seeds of those ideas in distant lands through an American presence, whether by way of missionary schools, radio, cinema, consumer goods, or technical or military aid. And, finally, they tell how the strength of those ideas drew my husband and me to this great land, where we were able to find the freedom and the opportunities to fulfill our fondest dreams.

The Dance of the Rose and the Nightingale

Daring to Dance

For in and out, above, about, below,
'Tis nothing but a Magic Shadow-show,
Play'd in a Box whose Candle is the Sun,
Round which we Phantom Figures come and go.
——Omar Khayyam, *Rubaiyat*

NEVER BEFORE had a young girl from a good family danced in public. I was only dimly aware of the waves I was making, of the centuries of tradition and entrenched beliefs I was violating. For me, it was a simple matter: dancing filled me with joy. For Tehran society, however, it was scandalous. Good girls did not perform in public, baring their legs for all to see, putting themselves in the limelight to attract the lust of strangers.

In 1944, when the idea of forming Iran's first ballet company was just taking shape, the belief that "nice girls don't dance" was so prevalent that seven hundred boys—and no girls—showed up for the opening of Nilla Cram Cook's new studio in Tehran. Two years later when a few other young girl students and I were finally persuaded to join the nascent troupe, we at first gave recitals only in the Shah's palace and in the American embassy, and only to select audiences. When we eventually started dancing in public, where anyone could purchase a ticket and see us perform, we were violating ancient sanctities, for ever since Arab conquerors had brought Islam to Iran in the seventh century, dance and music had been considered corrupting frivolities that incite passion and so should be avoided.

In my case, innocence protected me—somewhat. But most of all my mother's being English helped, for everyone knew foreigners behaved differently and allowed their daughters outrageous liberties. My father's family name helped, too. A family of such standing and good repute could take the criticism. In addition, my paternal family was Zoroastrian, members of the ancient religion preached by Zarathustra (Zoroaster), more than two thousand years ago. Although in my days the Zoroastrians—like most Iranians—were unreceptive to dance as an art form, in ancient times under Hellenic influences Zoroastrian women had danced in public festivals and processions. Perhaps this historical fact made it easier for my relatives gradually to soften their initial opposition to my appearing in the spotlight.

Iran was in my time, as it is now, a Muslim country, where for centuries women had veiled themselves so as not to be seen by any man who was not a relative and thus to avoid arousing passion in their hearts. When Reza Shah banned the veil in 1936 in his drive to modernize his country, a few modernists greeted the decree with enthusiasm. But among the large masses of people, including women, for whom the veil was the foremost symbol of female chastity, the Shah's order unleashed a firestorm of anger, resentment, and resistance. Some women defied the ban and went out with their chadors on, only to have policemen savagely rip them off their heads.

I was barely four years old when the decree was issued, and I witnessed how brutally it was enforced. I clung to my mother's hand as we stood riveted to the sidewalk, alarmed at the sight of a woman frantically running down the street, her chador billowing out behind her, a policeman in full chase. Quickly overtaking the woman, the officer grabbed the end of her black covering and yanked it off her head, leaving her with a look of stunned horror on her face. She turned on him in a fury. "Son of a burned father," she screamed. "May God strike you dead!" The officer hesitated for an instant, but then with one tug ripped the chador in two. He had his orders, and no one defied Reza Shah.

Suddenly women were faced with having to go out in public unveiled. There were few options: either go out feeling "naked" or stay at home. Some women covered their heads with Western-style hats. Others wore scarves. But some found their sense of modesty so violated that they simply refused to go out and remained housebound for several years until the ban was lifted. Being from a modern family and a non–Muslim one at that, I wore a veil only twice, once in order to see the splendid tiles and mirror work of the shrine of Shah Abdul-azim in Rey, south of Tehran, and another time so as to watch a *ta'ziyeh,* a religious passion play.

Eventually, after Reza Shah abdicated in 1941 and his son Mohammad Reza Shah succeeded him, veiling became voluntary, but by then Iran was well along the path to modernization, and Western dress was commonplace among the upper and middle classes. The veil became the garment of the poor, the elderly, and the pious, whereas the young and the modern outdid Parisians in style and dash, often carrying to the extreme every fashion statement, with exaggerated décolletage, flashy fabric, and spiked heels in which they stumbled over the potholes in Tehran's pavements.

But attitudinal changes require more than a decade to evolve, and when I was in my teens, it was commonplace for unveiled young girls to be the targets of jeers and taunts and salacious comments, not to mention pinching and, occasionally, indecent exposure. I experienced more than my share. *"Keef mal-e kieh?"* "Who owns your pouch?" was the crude suggestion I frequently heard, accompanied by sighs and heavy breathing. Dressed in modern clothing, I was considered fair game by street urchins who believed I was "asking for it" by not hiding my blossoming curves under an all-enveloping length of fabric.

These ruffians had perfected the art of bottom pinching and I the skills of self-defense. Outmaneuvering them was a daily challenge, their ribaldry a perpetual gauntlet to run. On empty streets I often found myself crossing over to the other side to avoid passing a solitary man walking down the sidewalk. On crowded streets I frequently braced my arms, ready to strike at an intruding hand. Sometimes I succeeded in landing a hard blow with my fist or elbow, but most of the time those street-smart bums were too quick and, having managed a quick stroke of my breast or a pinch to my bottom, would dash away with a triumphant laugh and a jeer, leaving me fuming.

In his push to modernize the country Reza Shah shocked the sensibilities of his populace in many ways other than the dress code. He decreed mixed social functions where ministers and their deputies had to appear once a week with their unveiled wives. He introduced Western-style ballroom dancing and sought to institute mixed classes in the first four grades of elementary school. He ordered an opera house to be built and brought Western-style theater to the capital city, introducing the shocking new concept that men and women would sit together and watch plays in buildings specifically designed for that purpose. Translations of Molière plays became commonplace, and gradually women started performing in these productions and even occasionally dancing on stage. But the populace was slow to accept the notion that acting and dancing were forms of artistic expression or that "proper" women might pursue such professions.

It is not entirely clear why so many Shi'a jurisprudents throughout the ages have condemned music and dancing, for the Koran does not place prohibitions on either. And the interpretations of the hadith—the reports of the sayings or actions of the Prophet Mohammad—are ambiguous with regard to these art forms. But we do know that in the seventh century A.D. Caliph Omar issued a verdict against music, associating it with dancing girls, and Caliph 'Ali faulted the Mu'awiya for keeping singing girls. A twelfth-century scholar wrote of the "harmony" between singing and fornication. Centuries later, in 1694, the last Safavid shah, Sultan Husayn, issued a *farman* prohibiting music and dance at all weddings and even in separate receptions for males and females. Against such an entrenched history of the association of dance and music with the seduction of men by undesirable social elements, Reza Shah's modernizing efforts and later those of his son Mohammad Reza Shah, failed to make headway, and the society continued to frown on public performances by women.

Of course, in spite of the traditional condemnation of dance and music, they both existed in abundance. Every village and every tribe had its musicians and ceremonial dances, and some Iranian Sufi orders used dancelike whirling to intensify religious experience. There had always existed a highly regarded classical form of music that was philosophical and spiritual. The Porcelain Room of 'Ali Qapu, the sixteenth-century Safavid palace that overlooks the great square of Isfahan, was reputedly used as a music room. Exquisitely painted cutouts decorate the ceiling, behind which an air space serves to enhance the acoustics of the chamber. And the life-size paintings of women dancers on the walls of the Chehel Sotoon Palace in Isfahan attest that caliphs and shahs were patrons of the arts.

Among the general populace, at weddings or major feasts young girls have always been encouraged to dance to lilting musical rhythms, *reng,* with soft undulations of the hips and snakelike movements of the arms, while everyone else claps in time to the music. But a sharp distinction has always been drawn between dancing festively and *performing,* and those who entertain professionally at such festivities are called *motreb,* a derogatory epithet.

So it is not surprising that when as teenagers Aida, Wilma, and I first made our appearance on the stage, we sent shock waves through the community. As the curtains rose, the three of us—girls from good families—lay with our heads resting on one arm. Behind us a play of lights on the curtain simulated the dawn—three sleeping village girls awakened by the sun's rays. We rose, we stretched, we set about various tasks. Through pantomime we conveyed such activities as sifting flour, kneading bread, washing clothes, and playfully splashing each other with water. Our work finished, we beautified ourselves, preening while coquettishly swinging one hip. Picking up our chiffon handkerchiefs, we coyly twirled them overhead or from side to side, occasionally flipping them into the air, while spinning rapidly around and around.

Unlike the dress of real village girls, our bodices were brief, revealing a bare midriff, and garnished with baubles and bangles that glinted in the stage lights. Our head scarves were made of transparent pink tulle that dropped to midcalf and covered all, but hid little. Our skirts were a gossamer layer of shimmering blue over a layer of deep pink. The effect was of a blur of lilac as we pirouetted, dipped, and leaped, while the orchestra played a folk melody and a voice sang out, "Touch not my kerchief; it is made of silk." The bells on our ankles jingled as we occasionally stamped one foot. As the music shifted to a faster tempo and the lyrics rang out, "I am drunk—drunk with love of you," our pace quickened while we flirted with village boys, sinuously snaking our arms, raising and lowering our eyebrows and swishing our skirts to reveal bare feet and ankles.

Recalling the ancient nomadic shadow play *khaymeh sayeh-gardoon* at the end of our dance, we slowly made an exit behind a massive backdrop on which the shadows of our silhouettes played, while the famous lines from Sa'di rang out: "O caravan of life, go slowly, slowly. For the tranquility of my soul is ending."

To my dismay, in spite of their progressive attitudes in all other spheres of life, my father's family shared the nation's traditional disapproval of dance and did not like the idea of my performing in public—at least, not at first. But my mother steadfastly dismissed what she considered to be "narrow-minded" attitudes and encouraged both my dancing and my performing. She had left England and come to Iran as an eighteen-year-old bride, learned to speak Persian fluently, and adapted remarkably well to a strange land and alien people. But there were certain aspects of Persian culture that she totally rejected and on which she permitted no compromise. She knew perfectly well what was "proper" and "improper" behavior, and *no one* was going to tell her that there was anything improper in my dancing. So when an American woman of exceptional talents came to Iran to set up Iran's first ballet company, she encouraged me to join the enterprise.

I was barely fourteen when my fellow ballet student, Aida, took me to meet Nilla Cram Cook. On the way, she told me a little about this singular American woman who could speak Persian fluently, could recite Hafez and Sa'di like any native Iranian, and was intent on creating a ballet company that would highlight Persian legends, poetry, music, and dance.

Mrs. Cook, Aida said, was a former dancer who had gained much experience in theater work when married to George Cram "Jig" Cook of the Provincetown Playhouse. But, having broader interests and ambitions, she had abruptly left her husband, taken her only son with her, and gone to India to immerse herself in the study of Oriental arts and literature. There, according to rumor, she had shaved her head and become a follower of Gandhi. It was whispered she had also had some romantic liaisons with powerful Indian princelings. In 1941, when she went to Iran to continue her research, she had gained an extraordinary mastery of Persian language and literature, and had become an impassioned admirer of the great Sufi poets and philosophers. After traveling a year or so in Afghanistan, she had returned to Iran in the fall of 1943. "They say she is a spy," Aida whispered. Now, Aida continued, Mrs. Cook had set up a dance studio with the objective of ultimately creating a dance company. The Shah had requested a command performance to take place the following month in his palace at a dinner to be held in honor of the American ambassador. Mrs. Cook had already started choreographing some dances for the occasion, and Aida had been rehearsing with her, but they needed more girl dancers. "I have told Mrs. Cook about you, and she is hoping you will join us. Wilma is already learning her roles, and we would love to have you on board. You know the three of us can work well together. Please—won't you come to a rehearsal and meet Mrs. Cook and let her tell you about it herself?" A chance to perform! In the Shah's palace! My heart beat fast at the thought, and I agreed to go with Aida to a rehearsal to meet Mrs. Cook.

Much later, I learned that Mrs. Cook had come to Iran on behalf of the U.S. Office of War Information. Initially, as an employee of the Iranian government, she had taken over as chief censor of Iranian theaters and cinemas, a position of power that earlier occupants had used mainly to stifle criticism of high government officials and incidentally to line their pockets. But a new climate of freedom toward the end of World War II as well as Mohammad Reza Shah's administrative policy of the moment favored a display of liberalism, giving Mrs. Cook leeway to draft new ordinances and regulations that enlarged the scope of what was permissible on stage or screen. Under the protection of the minister of the interior, she was able to fight off the intrigues organized against her by commercial and political interests and to lighten considerably the heavy hand of censorship, allowing writers to poke fun at municipality, court, and cleric. Numerous skits and plays appeared in the theaters at this time, freely satirizing every aspect of social life, from villainy and intrigue at court to government corruption at all levels. Subsequently, the Ministry of the Interior gave this foreign woman the awesome responsibility of founding a department of theaters and organizing a national opera and ballet.

What none of us knew was that Mrs. Cook was part of a grand design Franklin D. Roosevelt had dreamed up to help shape the postwar world. With the war over, Iran was to be an "experiment station" for his policies, which aimed at stabilizing and developing underdeveloped areas. The idea was that the United States would pursue an "unselfish" policy that would help Iran develop a pattern of self-government and free enterprise that would raise its standard of living and help it resist the machinations of Britain and Russia. Mrs. Cook's mission was to help restore Iranians' sense of pride in their own culture—an endeavor that would also advance American influence. In establishing Iran's first ballet company, she was attempting to create a repertory that integrated Persian dance forms, literary motifs, and music. This approach fit in neatly with the Iranian government's commitment to modernization. Such an artistic venture would represent a blending of the traditional with the modern and a fusing of Western with Zoroastrian and Islamic cultural elements. Mrs. Cook's knowledge of the Persian language and its literature as well as her experience with the theater uniquely qualified her for the task, but in other ways she was, to say the least, an odd agent of the U.S. government. Mummy and I laughed at the notion that Mrs. Cook might be a spy and dismissed it as "conspiracy theory" paranoia.

What neither of us realized at the time was that in participating in this bold arts project, we were unwittingly being used as instruments of both U.S. and Iranian government policies.

In trying to establish a dance company, Mrs. Cook was up against a major impediment—at first she could find no girl dancers willing to perform on stage. As I mentioned earlier, when in 1944 she advertised for dancers to audition for parts in a Persian ballet, no women responded, and among the several hundred young men who flocked to her studio, not one was a trained dancer. All were acrobats, bodybuilders, or athletes of various sorts. Of these applicants she first selected sixty to put through a course of classical ballet training, finally whittling them down to four, whom she set about training to perform her restorations of the ancient war dances of the Achaemenid and Sassanian eras.

Mrs. Cook cast about for girl dancers and, after much cajoling, finally succeeded in pressing into service one young woman trained in Persian and Caucasian folk dancing, and then she discovered Aida, who was half Russian and the star of the only ballet school in town. Aida finally joined the enterprise, but Mrs. Cook needed more girl dancers, and Aida, she hoped, would help her find some.

Of course, Aida did not need to explain to me why it was so difficult for Mrs. Cook to find girl dancers for the company she hoped to create. For years Aida, Wilma, and I had been studying ballet with Madame Cornelli, and the only performances we had ever given were the ballet school's annual recitals held at the end of each school year.

I must have been eight when Mummy had first walked me over to Mme. Cornelli's ballet studio. I had had little idea where we were going, but had climbed the stairs with her to the second floor and stepped for the first time into a dance studio. A large, airy room, it was completely bare except for an upright piano in one corner and two long bars running along the walls. I had found myself in a magical world. That day, as I took my first hesitant steps, formed my first awkward five positions of the feet, raised my arms and legs at odd angles, I had felt transported, lifted on the wings of music into a whirl of motion, a lightness of being, a sense of freedom, and a delirious happiness.

Mme. Cornelli, a White Russian émigré forced into exile by the Russian Revolution, had established the first ballet studio in Iran and had already been teaching there for many years when I first met her. A stern woman with a forbidding demeanor, she demanded—and received—unquestioning obedience.

No one dared to arrive late or to whisper or talk during her classes. She meant business, and anyone who did not like it could leave. Disdaining to learn Persian, although she had lived in Iran for years, she conducted classes in a mixture of her native Russian and fluent French, exposing us not only to the principles of ballet but to snatches of those languages. *"Ras, dva, tri, chtiri,"* she would count in Russian during class, or *"Ochin kharasho,"* she would say when giving approval or encouragement. But when it came time to end the class, she would call out, *"Reculez, s'il vous plait. Alors, on va faire la reverence,"* as she directed us to back up in preparation for end-of-the-class curtsies.

Three days a week, including part of each weekend, we would spend hours in class, stretching, bending, leaping, and twirling. After the bar and center work came the dances. Classes were long, often lasting a couple of hours, and we spent much of our time on character dancing, in particular Russian folk dancing, with its high leaps, fast turns, and foot-stomping, intoxicating bravura. In addition, we learned a lively Italian tarantella, a heel-clicking Hungarian czardas, a knee-bending Russian *lezginka,* a tiptoeing Chinese dance, a castanet-clacking Spanish zarzurela, as well as a clown dance, a sailors' hornpipe, and an "Oriental" fantasy, all accompanied by pantomime. An elderly woman played the piano tirelessly, adjusting the music to Mme. Cornelli's specifications, cutting here, adding there, speeding up where Madame—not the composer—ordered it, or slowing down far beyond what was indicated by the musical notations.

Mme. Cornelli no longer danced. She directed the classes mostly with gestures and words, demonstrating with the help of the more advanced students. She had once been a beautiful woman and had danced on the stage. When I knew her, however, she was well past her prime and had lost her svelte dancer's figure. She would clutch at her heart whenever she made the slightest exertion. Only rarely would she dance to a few measures of the music, then stop, panting and out of breath, with her hand clutching her chest. We would watch, wide-eyed, adoring, our hearts full with the certainty that her skill and grace were without parallel.

Preparation for our recitals would take weeks of extra classes and much waiting around for one's turn, but we lived for those recitals. Performances would be on one night only, usually in a rented theater that would *not* be open to the public that evening. Tickets were sold only to friends and relatives of Mme. Cornelli's students, and the theater auditorium was always packed with doting family members and uncritical, enthusiastic friends.

It was in dance class that I had met Haideh Akhundzadeh, whom we called Aida, and who spoke Russian and Persian fluently. She had long straight hair that fell to her waist like a jet-black waterfall. Her eyes were slightly slanted, giving her a Tatar appearance that was enhanced by her proud posture, full, pouty lips, and look of slight disdain. Striking rather than beautiful, she danced exquisitely and had a plasticity that was the envy of all. She could do a full backbend to the floor with the greatest of ease and, whenever a dance required it, could curve her back in a graceful arc reminiscent of the arched backs of prancing horses in a Persian miniature painting. I envied but also admired and respected her.

Then there was Wilma Protiva, whom I loved and hated at the same time. In terms of appearance, a greater contrast to either Aida or me could not be imagined. Wilma was as fair as we were dark—blue-eyed, light-skinned, and obviously foreign. Her parents were Czech, but they had lived in Iran for many years, and Wilma had grown up in Tehran. Like me, she went to the American Community School and was bilingual.

No wonder I had mixed feelings about Wilma. She was bossy and pushy and apt to take control in all social situations. There was the time, for instance, when we were playing Cinderella at my house with Aida, and right off Wilma took charge. She designated me as Cinderella and herself and Aida as the ugly sisters. I was pleased at first, thinking I had drawn the best role. I was not going to be an ugly sister. I was going to be Cinderella! We pulled some of Mummy's old dresses out of a dilapidated trunk in the attic and dressed up for our roles. Wilma extracted a moth-eaten fox fur stole with a real head, pointed snout, and artificial eyes, and wrapped it triumphantly around her shoulders. But as the morning wore on, the story line of our *Cinderella* never developed beyond the sweeping, cleaning, washing, and cooking stage. It began to look as though I would never go to the ball! I put up with being bossed around for a while, but then, when Mummy brought us some juice and cookies to eat and Wilma forbade me to have any, I revolted and put an end to the game.

To be perfectly candid, I felt a sense of rivalry with Wilma that I did not feel with Aida. Of the three of us, Aida was clearly the best dancer, and I knew full well I would never be as good as she. Wilma and I, however, were more evenly matched and apt to compete for the same roles. We vied for the upper hand in dance class and for the more spectacular role in school plays. Whereas she could do magnificent arabesques, I had to struggle with extension. But whereas I had

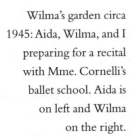

Wilma's garden circa 1945: Aida, Wilma, and I preparing for a recital with Mme. Cornelli's ballet school. Aida is on left and Wilma on the right.

natural grace and moved with great fluidity, her arms were gaunt and sticklike, her movements precise but stiff.

When Aida recruited me to join Mrs. Cook's group, the three of us were excited at the chance to perform for royalty, and all our parents agreed to let us do so. None of us at that point really expected that a full-fledged dance company would emerge from this tentative beginning. Our parents made clear from the start, of course, that every rehearsal and performance would have to be chaperoned to protect our good names. Most of the time it was Aida's mother who did the chaperoning.

Mrs. Cook was rehearsing her students when Aida and I arrived. At the far end of a cavernous, dimly lit room devoid of furniture I saw a large woman on a bar stool, calling out instructions while tapping a rhythmic beat with one hand on a table-high drum that she straddled with her legs, her flabby thighs exposed where her straight skirt had hiked upward. Her ample flesh spilled over the sides of the stool. She seemed to be carrying a balled-up fur coat in her other arm, but as we came closer, I realized she held a miniature poodle. As we approached, she immediately stopped tapping on the drum and came forward to welcome us. I found myself face-to-face with a woman whose voluminous bulk, plump face, and double chin gave her a friendly and amiable appearance. Clearly, she was a foreigner, with her watery blue eyes and fair complexion. Her long blond hair, swept upward off her forehead, hung loose over her shoulders in a youthful manner at odds with her matronly figure. The bright pink lipstick gleaming on her lips matched the flushes of pink generously brushed over her cheeks. She greeted me with a coy, almost girlish smile, a limp handshake, and a gush of words that outlined in glowing terms her plans and my part in the whole project.

Propelling me forward, Mrs. Cook introduced me to several young men who were working out in the center of the room, tumbling, doing backbends, leaping, twirling, and displaying much agility, flexibility, and athletic prowess. It was obvious that they were acrobats, not dancers. They stopped what they were doing, shook hands with me, then went back to their exertions with renewed vigor and some self-consciousness now that they knew I would be watching. There was only one other girl besides Aida and myself, a tiny Armenian with smooth black hair and long, silky eyelashes, who was practicing an Azerbaijani folk dance. She was fluttering and batting her eyelashes to enormous effect, while simultaneously raising alternate eyebrows with a skill I could never hope to match. Her arms sinuously circled her head or snaked through the air with extraordinary grace. I did not know it then, but I would soon be taking her place.

Mrs. Cook picked up her drum, started tapping on it, and told me to dance to its beat. Sweeping aside my objections, she began singing, "La-la la-la-la la-laaa la," without a trace of self-consciousness. I was taken aback. I felt painfully shy in front of so many strangers, and I was not even dressed in appropriate clothing because I had not expected to be dancing there that day. But her insistent yet friendly manner induced me to follow her instructions. She kept on with her "la-las," interrupting them only to call out instructions: "Step, step, arabesque, turn, and hold. Good. Now, lift up, arch back. One more time. Two sautés—a little higher. That's it. Good girl." And before I knew it, she was telling me what role she had in mind for me. I was to be one of three village girls dancing on the Bridge of Isfahan in *Caravan,* and perhaps I might also do a solo, a dance about a nightingale in love with a rose. I would be the rose.

We would be performing for the royal family and their guests. The American ambassador and his wife would be there, as well as the French ambassador and other important people. Mrs. Cook would need to take my measurements so that Mrs. Sadeq could make my costume—a full-length layered skirt, a bare midriff, and a jeweled brocade sleeveless bodice. A long transparent veil would hang down my back, and my feet would be bare, with bells around my ankles.

"Oh, you will look lovely in it," she gushed. Our performance was to be in three weeks' time, and, as if that were not excitement enough, Mrs. Cook announced that we had been invited to attend a ball at the palace the next week. "Of course, your mother is invited, too," she added.

That afternoon, when I told Mummy about the rush of events, I could barely contain my excitement. Her reaction was more restrained than mine, but she raised no objections to either proposition, and I soon found myself caught up in an intense schedule of rehearsals. Mrs. Cook had put together a perform-ance program of roughly half an hour, appropriate for a soiree at the palace. I think she conceived of it as a divertissement in the tradition of performances by musical and dance ensembles in the palaces of Europe's monarchs in a different era. She would be bringing "Persian ballet" into the royal halls and eventually into the public arena.

In order to cut through the tangle of obstacles that she knew she would en-counter, she had gone directly to the principle source of power and decision making in the country—the royal family, who, as I have mentioned, were pro-moting modernization in every conceivable way. She was breaking taboos, so strong backing was important. The royal imprimatur on her enterprise would assure it a reasonable chance of success, but she was also banking on the promi-nence of our families' names, the ethnic nature of our performances, and the lyrical quality of our dancing to drive home the serious purpose of our enter-prise. She wanted to make sure that we were not taken for "dancing girls," but seen for what we were—artists. She was counting on the royal stamp of approval to sanctify the endeavor as one that not only was respectable, but would advance the cause of nationalism and be a genuine source of pride for Iranians.

Winged Gods

Shoot the arrow straight
And tell the truth
—Persian proverb

OF COURSE, had my mother not been English, I would not have learned to dance, or if I had, I certainly would not have been able to dance on the stage. In those days it was highly unusual to be half this and half that, to have one foreign parent and one Iranian parent. Things have changed now, of course, but back then the floodgates had not yet opened and marriages between Iranians and foreigners were infrequent, to say the least.

Whenever I asked Mummy how it all started, she would sigh and say, with a trace of sadness in her voice, "He was tall, dark, and handsome, and I was young and foolish," a hint of regret hanging like a whisper in the air. She was barely eighteen when she married. One of seven sisters, she was the daughter of the postmaster of the city of Manchester. Her name was Winnifred Burton, Winnie for short. But because the Persian alphabet lacks a *w* and the short *i,* for the rest of her life she answered to "Veenee."

Her mother and father had died in an automobile accident when she was just sixteen. A single faded photograph of them stood on the mantlepiece. I would often pick it up and stare at it. Looking stiffly back at me was a young man, fair, of unremarkable height, with an impressive handlebar mustache, a formal dress coat in the Edwardian style, and hair parted in the middle. Seated next to him with billowy floor-length skirt draped over the photographer's chair was a diminutive, fair woman with a wasp waist and ruffles at her neck—Mummy's mother, a grandmother I would never know.

I wonder now whether my mother had any inkling of what life would be like in that distant land to which she was going, blindly placing her trust in a man she hardly knew, who was from a land and culture about which she knew nothing. She had never before traveled outside of England. Was it a sense of adventure that led her to plunge headlong into the unknown? Was it the romance of the East that thrilled her, as it had so many English travelers before her? Did she think love would overcome all obstacles? I can only guess at what went through her mind, but I do know that when she tied her destiny to my father's, she dramatically changed the course of her life—and the lives of her future children.

Mummy often told me that when she met Daddy, Manuchehr Shahrokh, in Manchester, England, she had never even heard of the Zoroastrians, but the family she married into was not only a Zoroastrian family of some renown, but was headed by Arbab Kaykhosrow Shahrokh, the leader of the community, a man of great prestige, the political representative of the Zoroastrians in the newly established Parliament, the Majlis. And here was the son of that leader violating one of the most basic tenets of the community by marrying outside the religion. Although the tenets of the faith do not actually forbid interfaith marriages, this minority group, out of a need for self-preservation, had developed a strong tradition against marrying outsiders. My parents' marriage, I gather, created quite a stir.

In time other members of the family followed suit, three of my uncles and two of my aunts also marrying foreigners. Eventually even my grandfather broke the rules and, after having been widowed for some years, married a Bahai, a member of a religious sect considered heretical by the majority Shi'a Muslims of Iran. But that would not happen until later. My father was the first of the family to break tradition. Perhaps it was inevitable, for he was one of the first to go abroad for higher education and encounter Western women—so fair, so bold, so different. Later generations saw thousands of aspiring young men—and eventually women—flock to European and American universities, but in Daddy's day it was a rare privilege. He was studying textile technology in Manchester, England, when he met my mother, some time in the 1920s.

A petite woman who stood no taller than five feet and two inches, she had eyes as blue as Tehran's skies and light brown hair the color of honey. Fair hair was a rarity in that land of predominantly dark-haired people, and in Iran she was considered blonde. Her appearance loudly proclaimed her to be a foreigner, at that time an asset because the antiforeign sentiment of later years had not yet emerged. Western men and women were treated with great respect and were indiscriminately considered to be better educated, more knowledgeable, and more advanced than the average Iranian.

Her exuberant personality, open and unabashed, also attested her being a *farangi.* For this she was both admired and criticized, as Iranians tried to sort out their feelings toward the new outspoken, independent image of woman they encountered in American movies, in magazines, in trips abroad, and in women like my mother who had come to live in their midst.

Mummy was widely admired for her looks in a land where fair skin was a primary mark of beauty, where poets had long sung the praises of skin "like marble" and "peachlike" cheeks. By contrast my complexion was olive and would become so darkened by the relentless sun that our maid, Naneh, would tease me and call me Blackie. *"Siyah,"* she would call in her taunting way. She did it good-naturedly, but it still made me sulk. My fondest wish was to have Mummy's blue eyes and light hair, but instead a black mass of unruly curls topped my head and sometimes fell into my dark brown eyes. I had a British mother? You could not tell by looking at me—except for an occasional gold streak bleached into my hair by the sun. My brothers had even darker hair and eyes than I. A stranger would have been hard put to tell that we were our mother's children.

I imagine Mummy's integration into the Zoroastrian community could not have been easy. Had she thought that marrying into one of the first families of the Zoroastrian community would be only a privilege? If so, she must have soon learned that it was also a liability, for being part of that family meant that her every word and every move would be monitored closely for its impact on the family's honor.

The family in Iranian society is the center of social life, a support system, an extended network of relatives who help each other out in hard times. But as Mummy must have found out early on, families meddle, too, and this family meddled often. They did not quietly accept any odd behavior on Mummy's part just because she was from England, for there was the matter of honor, which was why they kept trying to make clear to her that she must never do anything to

With Mummy and
brother Parviz.

tarnish the Shahrokh family's good name, that she was expected to conform to
certain standards, respect rules of behavior, accommodate, and comply. It
seemed she learned this lesson only gradually and painfully over the years, and
much of the time she refused to conform, for what the family felt was dishonor-
able conduct she considered normal, acceptable behavior.

There was the matter, for instance, of laughing out loud in the movie theater.
In those days English-language movies were not yet being dubbed into Persian.
Instead, the film would be stopped every few minutes and a translation of the
earlier dialogue would appear on the screen, which many in the audience would
read out loud, for the benefit of those who were illiterate. So the general public
would then laugh at the humorous dialogue that had taken place a few minutes
earlier when Mummy's singular bell-like laugh had rung out all by itself,
prompting heads to turn and stare at this shameless woman who was making a
spectacle of herself. Of course, Mummy could not help it if she was the only person in the theater to understand English, but that was one of the things that made
her an embarrassment and marked her as being different from everyone else.

Coming from England, Mummy probably thought that getting married was
a private matter between two individuals. But no, not here. Here it was a family
affair, and the grand patriarch of the family would normally expect to have a say

in matters of who marries whom. Daddy, of course, must have known there would be opposition to his marrying a foreigner. I gather the young lovers married secretly in England and only then wrote to Grandfather, facing him with a fait accompli. In his letter Daddy simply announced that he had married an Englishwoman, that they were expecting their first child, and that they would be returning soon to Tehran.

When Mummy told me of their elopement, she did not say what Grandfather's reaction was, but in the family apparently resentment and bad feelings persisted for a long time. Some whispered that perhaps Daddy had married this Englishwoman because she was pregnant. Ironically, even though it was Daddy who had broken the rules, the family vented its frustration and venom largely on Mummy—the foreigner, the outsider—but in time they came to accept her, although some petty grumblings, gossip, and occasional bad-mouthing behind her back continued throughout her life as she balked at the restrictions everyone seemed to want to place on her.

Mummy quickly learned to speak Persian, to shop in the bazaar, to direct the domestic help, to cook on kerosene stoves, and to live without electricity. She could haggle and bargain as well as any Iranian housewife, although prices rose whenever vendors saw her blue eyes and heard her foreign accent. But she learned all the tricks. "What?" she would say, raising her voice in disbelief, "Five tomans a kilo for these worm-eaten apples? They are not even worth two tomans. But I'll give you that out of the goodness of my heart. There are plenty of other apple vendors in the marketplace." And she would walk away, knowing full well the vendor would call her back before she was out of earshot.

Mummy's bargaining skills were honed out of necessity, for she had to conserve her resources carefully. Daddy had set up an import-export business in textiles, but he was not the most astute of businessmen. In addition, he was extravagant outside the home, giving money to charity, even when we were all short of basic necessities. This extravagance was in part a matter of *ab-e roo,* saving face, and in part a matter of Zoroastrians having a strong tradition of philanthropy. If there was a need, Daddy would give, even if he didn't have it to give.

Pregnancies followed one after the other. Mummy's first child was a baby girl who was born blind, with hydrocephalus, and who died when she was two months old. Two healthy sons followed, raising Mummy's status in the eyes of a society that valued boys above girls. I came next. Because Mummy was in England at the time of my delivery, I was born a British subject, and she named me after a Welsh princess—Nesta, a diminutive of Agnes, meaning lamb of God, or innocent.

Being the only girl and for a long time the youngest, I held a privileged place in our family, and my parents seemed more partial to me, sometimes showing preferential behavior toward me. Whenever Parviz and Iraj misbehaved, Daddy would strip the leaves off a slender willow branch, dip it in cold water, and give them "a good thrashing," but he never raised a hand against me, with the result that my brothers resented me and teased and bossed me around mercilessly. "Stop playing that gramophone *this minute*. I'm trying to study." "No, you cannot join in our game. You're just a stupid little girl." And sometimes, "Go play with your dolls and stop bothering us." Of course, at times we got along reasonably well, and Parviz, who was only fourteen months older than I, did occasionally play with me. Iraj was five years older and more remote.

How it was that Mummy's younger sister, Doris, came to be living with us, I do not know. It was not uncommon in those days for families to have close or even distant relatives stay with them, in particular unmarried or divorced female relatives, and as far back as I can remember, she was there, another gentle presence in the house, one to whom I could turn with a bruised knee or a nosebleed or a question. She was young and unmarried. She would sometimes help me bathe, and I still remember the soft feel of her delicate hands gently soaping my back. She had more time to fuss over us than my mother did, and I would occasionally ask her to read to me or tell me a story if Mummy was busy in the kitchen.

When I was eight years old, Mummy became pregnant again. I watched with fascination as her stomach grew larger and larger. How on earth did the baby get inside her? I wondered. In response to my questions she said, "Little girls must pray to God to give them the number of children they want to have when they grow up." And so I prayed, "Dear God, please give me one boy and one girl when I grow up." Neither Mummy nor Daddy ever discussed sex with us, and I knew it was a taboo, hush-hush subject. I suppose they believed it was important to maintain our innocence as long as possible and that we would eventually learn the facts of life from our peers. And although Mummy denounced prudery in every form in which she encountered it in her adopted country, she never taught us the accurate English names for male or female genitals, which I learned only at puberty, when I started reading books on sexuality. For my brothers' private parts she used the Persian *dooley,* and for mine she came up with the imaginative *coskawiski.* Where that word came from I shall never know. Of course, my Persian sexual vocabulary was rich by comparison because I was early exposed to direct and graphic sexual words and sounds as I made my way through the instructive streets of the capital city.

I pondered Mummy's belly and soon was demanding to know how the baby would get out. Mummy's evasive answer and the way she quickly changed the subject signaled that it must have something to do with the private parts we never spoke of, though exactly what, I did not know. But I figured it all out easily enough after the delivery, when I saw traces of blood on the sheet beneath my mother and realized the baby must have come out from between her legs, although I still did not know how he had gotten inside her.

The baby was a boy, and they named him Kaveh after the heroic smith who, in Ferdowsi's epic poem the *Shahnameh,* made a banner of his old apron, led the Persians against the tyrant Zahhak, and defeated him.

Kaveh was like a ray of sunshine, spreading joy and happiness throughout our household. Every day when I came home from school, the first thing I would do was drop my books on the floor and run to find my baby brother. I would take him up in my arms and play with him, bouncing him on my lap or playing "pat-a-cake" and "this little pig went to market," and burying my face in his little round belly to make him laugh. Kaveh was my delight. Happily, I had no crystal ball to tell me of the misfortune awaiting him—and us.

Mummy liked to say that when she first came to Iran, there were no paved roads, not even in Tehran. She said that before Reza Shah came to power, one could sink knee-deep in mud in the streets of the capital city. Fortunately, it did not rain often.

Iran had once been a great empire and had given birth to a great civilization, but it had stagnated over the centuries, drawn in on itself, and been left behind by the Industrial Revolution. Waking up as if from a long sleep, it was trying to pull itself together and accommodate its culture to the altered circumstances of a technologically advanced world.

Reza Shah, the ruler of Iran at the time, was determined to draw his people

into the twentieth century. Born in 1878 in the Caspian province of Mazan-
deran, a young Reza Khan advanced to a high command in the Persian Cossack
Brigade by virtue of his forceful personality. In 1921 he effected a coup d'etat. In
1925 he made himself shah and established the Pahlavi dynasty, ending the rule
of the Qajars. Those who met him were invariably impressed by his command-
ing presence, buttressed by a haughty demeanor, ferocious eyes, and imposing
height. Mummy met him once, under peculiarly memorable circumstances.

Grandfather worked closely with Reza Shah in his modernizing efforts for a
number of years. The Shah entrusted him with overseeing the building of a
mausoleum to honor Ferdowsi on the occasion of the millennium of the great
poet's birth, and Grandfather had worked long and hard to bring the project to
fruition. At a reception held in Tehran to celebrate the official opening of the
mausoleum Mummy stood in the second row, along with other members of her
extended family and numerous foreign scholars and dignitaries who had been
invited to attend. As Reza Shah paraded slowly by with Grandfather and other
Majlis deputies, the hushed, restrained guests watched and listened, awed at the
stern look Reza Shah cast on them. Only Mummy was not intimidated. Hearing Reza Shah ask Grandfather why his sons had not come to the celebrations
and feeling entitled to represent her absent husband, she stuck out her gloved
hand—an unthinkable breach of etiquette—and to the dismay of her relatives
called out in a loud voice, *"Salaam aleikom."*

A gasp of collective horror, I am told, could be heard from various family
members, for *no one* ever addressed the Shah without numerous honorifics and
elaborate titles and without first having been addressed by him. But the deed
was done; there was no way of retracting it or covering it up. To Mummy's delight and everyone else's relief, Reza Shah was bemused at the effrontery of the
foreign daughter-in-law of the Zoroastrian deputy. He took her gloved hand in
his, bowed to her, and replied, *"Aleik-om-o-salaam."* That moment of mixed embarrassment and triumph was burned into the consciousness of the Shahrokh
family, and for years afterward they spoke about it, the tale growing in relish
with the passage of time.

Reza Shah had only the most rudimentary formal education, and some even
claim he was illiterate. Yet he recognized the tragic contrast between the glory of
Iran's past and its present state of decline, and set about almost singlehandedly—
and by force—to industrialize Iran and to foster national unity and a renewed

sense of pride among his countrymen. His methods were ruthless and his rule dictatorial, but he built factories and schools and constructed the Trans-Iranian Railway as well as thousands of miles of new roads. Determined to end the rapacious interference of outside powers in Iran's internal affairs, he ended the humiliating system of capitulations that placed foreigners beyond the reach of the national judicial process, set up a customs system, and brought semiautonomous areas such as Khoramshahr under the control of the central government. His style was paternalistic, and he seemed to believe that his ends justified the harsh means he employed, but he did get things done—sometimes, though, at the expense of anyone who got in his way. One of his victims was my grandfather.

Arbab Kaykhosrow Shahrokh

Guardian of the Flame

Now the New Year reviving old Desires,
The thoughtful Soul to Solitude retires,
Where the White Hand of Moses on the Bough
Puts out, and Jesus from the Ground suspires.
—Omar Khayyam, *Rubaiyat*

I AM SORRY I did not know my grandfather better. He had gentle eyes, a kind expression, and a dignity that comes naturally to born leaders, but I was too young to understand any of this. To me he was simply "Baba-joon," my father's father, toward whom I felt affection mixed with a liberal dose of awe, for although kind and loving, he was the grand patriarch of the family, and I sensed the reverence in which he was held.

It was not until many years later that I realized the full extent of his reputation and his accomplishments: that he was an educator, merchant, and leader, who represented his people in the second Parliament, the Majlis, through twelve sessions, from 1909 until his death in 1940; that he was well known as a pro-Western liberal and modernizer; and that it was through his efforts that the Parliament first acquired a printing press. I was in my teens when I first read *The Strangling of Persia,* a book written by the American financial adviser to Iran, Morgan Shuster. I glowed with pride as I read his assessment of my grandfather: "a man of the most pleasing personality," who exhibited "both inflexible integrity and unfailing courage under the most trying and difficult circum-

My grandfather, Arbab Kaykhosrow
Shahrokh, member of Parliament and
leader of the Zoroastrian community.

stances." And I soon became aware of the instant respect *I* could garner by making it known that I was Arbab Kaykhosrow Shahrokh's granddaughter.

Much later, when I learned how humble his beginnings were, I was even
more amazed at Baba-joon's accomplishments, for in a land where privilege, titles, and power were normally inherited, he was a self-made man. Born in Kerman in 1874 during Naser ed-Din Shah's reign, he never knew his father, who
died before his birth. His nineteen-year-old mother, widowed and impoverished, was barely able to support her two sons and herself on the meager wages
she earned as a weaver. The fatherless boys went to a one-room village school
for only two years—just long enough to learn to read and write, after which
they were sent out to work. A few years later, however, upset over their mother's
remarriage, they left home and went to live with an uncle in Tehran. There they
studied for four years at the Tehran American School while working part-time
at the American hospital.

For Baba-joon there followed a year of study in Bombay, where a large
community of Parsis lived, descendants of a small contingent of Zoroastrians
who had landed on the coast of Gujarat in India in A.D. 916 after fleeing persecution in Iran. But the climate did not agree with my grandfather, and he was

frequently sick, so although he was an outstanding student and received several awards, he left Bombay after only one year and returned to Kerman to accept the position of principal of the Zoroastrian School. He was seventeen. By this time he was fluent in English and also knew a little German and Russian, could play the *tar,* a stringed instrument, and loved poetry, which he occasionally wrote. A year later he married Firoozeh, to whom he remained devoted until her death thirty-two years later. They had seven sons and four daughters. My father was their third son. They named him Manuchehr, "heaven-faced," after a great ninth-century Zoroastrian leader. Mummy called him Mano.

Baba-joon's return to Kerman marked a turning point in his life. He became the representative of the Zoroastrian Amelioration Fund, an organization set up to give assistance to needy members of the faith. Perhaps this appointment helped shape his mission in life, or perhaps it simply provided him the means to implement goals he already had in mind, but from that moment on he dedicated himself in a myriad ways to improving the lot of his fellow Zoroastrians.

One of the first things he did was to raise funds to renovate and furnish the Zoroastrian village school in Kerman, which was then a single room of mud brick, with unplastered walls, a dirt floor, neither carpet nor chairs, and for boys only. At a time when the idea of educating girls was considered dangerous and subversive, Baba-joon raised funds with which to build three girls' schools. He then built three more boys' schools in Kerman before eventually moving to Tehran, where he established more schools.

I remember perching on his lap not long before he died, while he looked affectionately into my face, asking me how old I was, what games I liked to play, and how I was enjoying school. Even at the age of six I was aware of the extreme respect everyone showed him and could not quite feel at ease in his presence. It is the only such intimate moment I remember; otherwise, he was a rather distant figure.

This moment with my grandfather took place at Norooz, the Persian New Year's Day, when the entire extended family had gathered at his spacious house for the annual spring celebration of the vernal equinox. It was a time for visiting family and friends, for this was the most important festivity of the year. There had once been seven devotional feast days spread throughout the year linked to Zoroastrian teachings about the seven creations, but six of these feast days had been long forgotten, and only Norooz survived, a great national holiday that all Iranians, not just Zoroastrians, celebrated.

My grandfather, Arbab Kaykhosrow
Shahrokh, and one of his four daughters.

I had only recently returned from two years in England and, for me the upcoming celebrations held the heightened excitement of novelty. I took much
pleasure in the increased activities going on around me, for the house cleaning
and baking and sewing and planting of green sprouts were all tinged with happy
anticipation. We were going to have thirteen days of celebration, of visiting and
receiving visitors, and then on the thirteenth day, known as *seezdah be-dar,* we
would throw all the greens we had sprouted into a stream of running water,
which would surely bring us good luck for the rest of the year.

On the first day of the Norooz celebrations, we went to Baba-joon's home
to pay our respects and to celebrate the arrival of the new year. As the patriarch
of the family, he, along with my stepgrandmother Katayoon, would be "at
home" the first few days of the thirteen-day holiday to receive visitors and to
hand out gifts of tiny gold coins to the children and money and clothing to servants and anyone else who provided services for the family.

We arrived to find all my cousins already there—Pari, Katayoon (whom we
called Kitty), Pooran, and their brother Shahrokh, all half Indian; Shirin and her
two younger brothers, half German and already fluent in three languages; and
Firoozeh, a younger cousin. Shirin and Pari were closest to me in age, and I
looked forward to playing with them. Just a few days earlier, the three of us had

With my cousins Shirin *(center)* and
Pari *(right)*, at about three years old.

spent Chahar Shambeh Soori together, celebrating the eve of the last Wednesday of the old year by jumping over a big bonfire.

We were all wearing new clothes, as was the custom. My aunts usually had
dressmakers come to the house and stay for several days or weeks at a time, to
transform bolts of silk, taffeta, and English wool into new outfits for the entire
household. But Mummy could not afford such a luxury and made a new dress
for me out of a pretty white cotton organdy, with puffed sleeves and a big bow
at the back, to my mind a dress fit for a princess. I could hardly contain my excitement when it was finished and I was finally able to wear it. Watching the
skirt flare out as I twirled around in front of the mirror, I thought it was the pret-
tiest dress in the world.

We entered the enormous living room of Baba-joon's house and went
straight up to him and my stepgrandmother to offer our New Year wishes. I
knew I must keep quiet while the grown-ups went through the usual greetings,
but I became restless and wandered off and joined my cousins. Pari and I started
to play tag, but our parents sharply reprimanded us. "Where are your manners?"
they admonished. "Come and wish Baba-joon a happy Norooz." And they lined
up Pari and me along with my brothers and other cousins in front of Baba-joon
to wish him a happy new year. We all knew we must approach him with defer-

ence. We stood there in a row, all twelve of us. He remained seated while each of us greeted him with a "salaam," followed by "*'Ayd-e shoma mobarak,*" displaying the proper respect the younger generation must show toward their elders by greeting them first. He talked to my cousin Kitty, then to Pari, then let his gaze rest on me for a moment. He leaned over, picked me up, and put me on his lap. He spoke gently to me, while I looked up at him with wonder. "What bushy eyebrows," I was thinking. "And his mustache is all white." I was a shy child, and I imagine my answers to his questions were barely audible, but they must have been enough to convince him I was relearning the Persian I had forgotten while in England, and after a while he set me down, patted my head, and, giving each of us a shiny little gold coin, sent us off to play.

"Come see the *haft-seen* table," Pari cried, grabbing my hand and leading me to a display table set up in front of a large bay window. As I caught sight of it, I came to an abrupt stop, for it seemed like something out of a fairy tale. "Oh, how beautiful!" I thought. A cloth of deep wine red embroidered with blue, green, and gold had been spread on the table. Candles flickering in rose-colored globes threw pink highlights onto a bowl of eggs sparkling with gold and silver glitter. An ornate gilt-edged mirror set between the candles caught their reflection and doubled their dancing flames. A copy of the holy Avesta lay closed on the table, its cover decorated with scrolls of red, blue, and green. Spread around were platters of assorted sweets, a tray of rose-red pomegranates, and a goldfish in a bowl. "He will signal the moment of the arrival of the new year by turning," Pari said confidently.

She proudly explained to me the significance of the *haft-seen* table, the table of the seven *s*'s. "That is the *sabzeh,*" she said, pointing to a platter of dark green shoots of wheat set in the center of the table. "And," she said, parroting the explanation she had heard many times, "it symbolizes spring and rebirth." She pointed out six more items, all of them having names beginning with the letter *s*. "See, this is *sombol, seeb, somaq, seer, senjed,* and *samanoo*" (hyacinth, apples, sumac, garlic, fruit of the jujube tree, and a confection made of wheat germ). Pari was pleased with herself, for her recitation had been flawless.

"Why seven items starting with an *s?*" I asked. Pari looked at me with a blank stare and shrugged her shoulders. "I don't know," she said. Just then Daddy came up behind us. "It is just a tradition," he said, but Aunt Farangis gave another explanation. "They represent the seven good angels that bestow life, health, happiness, prosperity, joy, and beauty on mankind."

I looked around the spacious room with its high ceilings and crystal chandeliers and saw rows of straight-backed chairs set against the walls of the room so that no one would sit with his back to another, which would have been considered unforgivably rude. Small tables placed in front of the chairs at regular intervals were mounded high with the choicest of cookies and confections: baklava sweetened with rose-water syrup; rice-flour cookies topped with poppy seeds; chickpea cookies flavored with saffron; melt-in-your-mouth cotton candy from Yazd; and *gaz,* a white pistachio-filled nougat from Isfahan; as well as *ajeel,* a mixture of walnuts, hazelnuts, roasted chickpeas, pumpkin and watermelon seeds, raisins, and dried mulberries. Fresh European pastries from the local bakery had been arranged pyramid style on silver platters with raised stems.

In the old days all the traditional baked goods would have been made at home, with housewives spending days making their own rice flour and chickpea flour, which would have necessitated first cleaning the rice or chickpeas in huge copper trays, picking out the debris, soaking it until it was soft, spreading it out to dry in the hot sun, and finally pounding it into flour to use in preparing the mouth-watering delicacies. But now all these treats could be bought ready-made.

Servants offered the guests tea in *istikans,* narrow-waisted miniature glasses set in delicately carved silver holders, as well as *sharbat* in tall glasses—cool, sweet drinks made of cherry, strawberry, or pomegranate fruit syrup mixed with water. I could happily have gorged myself on the chickpea cookies and on the dried fruits and *ajeel* piled high in hand-chiseled silver bowls, but I knew that no matter how many tempting delicacies were spread out in full view I must never reach for anything until invited to do so. *"Befarmaeed"* was the ritual invitation to take a cookie as the servants or one of my aunts passed them around. I knew I must refuse politely and wait to have it offered to me again. *"Nah, merci,"* I replied, waiting for the second offer. Because I was a very young child, it was all right for me to decline only once. My older, more polite cousin Kitty declined two or three times before finally taking a cookie.

Suddenly, a cannon boomed, announcing the exact moment of the vernal equinox, the arrival of the new year. While the grown-ups got up and embraced their relatives and offered good wishes, I dashed to the *haft-seen* table to see the goldfish turn, but it simply floated lazily around the bowl. "Why didn't it turn?" I asked Pari. "You said it would turn." "Well, it did," she answered. "You just weren't watching closely enough."

By now it was two o'clock in the afternoon, and dinner was served. I had already ruined my appetite, for in spite of my "no, thank you's," I had already had my fill of goodies. Spread out on the dining table were large platters of pan-fried white fish and aromatic herb rice dotted with specks of dill, parsley, spring onions, and coriander, the traditional Norooz dinner, the green herbs symbolizing spring. A fragrant aroma filled the room, and I was sorry I had ruined my appetite. There were huge mounds of saffron-colored rice, bowls of different kinds of aromatic meat stews, and bowls of thick, creamy yogurt mixed with cucumbers, mint, and dill. Interspersed among these dishes were platters of a thin bread called *lavash,* accompanied by chunks of feta cheese and fresh basil, tarragon, and spring onions, with radishes adding a splash of bright red.

I had picked out an extra-large piece of *tah-deeg,* the crust of rice known as "the bottom of the pan," and contentedly munched on that, while merely picking at the fish and the yogurt Mummy had put on my plate. After dinner, fruits appeared, arranged fancifully in great copper or silver serving trays—golden oranges verging on bronze, thin-skinned tangerines sweet as honey, bright red apples tinged with gold, and smooth-skinned yellow, sweet lemons, as large as grapefruit, as well as crisp little cucumbers, which were served and eaten as fruit. In addition, there were bowls of pomegranate seeds, enticingly succulent and sweet, sparkling like rubies. Tea was then served in *istikan*s with lumps of hard sugar.

In the dining room over the mantle was a large portrait of Grandmother Firoozeh, whom I had never known because she had died some years earlier. My inquiries about her often had been met with silence or whispered exchanges, then an obvious change of the subject. It wasn't until much later that I found out that she had died of breast cancer, not only a calamity but also an embarrassment because the disease had attacked her breast, an anatomical part it was not proper to mention or discuss, except in private.

Of this huge gathering of relatives, some I knew well and some I hardly knew at all. Except for me, everyone had historical Persian names. Everyone except immediate family referred to Baba-joon as Arbab Kaykhosrow, even though Reza Shah had abolished the title *arbab* when he was stripping nobles of their former power and prestige. My grandfather was named after the great Sassanian king, Khosrow Anushiravan the Just.

Family names were relatively new in those days. In his drive to modernize Iran Reza Shah had simply directed all Iranians to give themselves family names, instead of being known simply as sons or daughters of their fathers. People were free to choose whatever name they wished. My grandfather's family name became Shahrokh (Kingface), after a fifteenth-century king, fourth son of Tamerlane and one of the most cultured of Iran's monarchs, whose capital, Herat, became the intellectual center of middle Asia. In many ways Shahrokh was an appropriate name, for by the standards of the day our family was highly educated and had many artistic and cultural interests.

At this time, too, women started acquiring their husband's family name when they married, giving up their maiden names for the sake of modernization—an ironic twist. Although this practice would later change and many women would go back to retaining their maiden names after marriage, during my childhood all the women who married into Baba-joon's family were known as Khanom-e Shahrokh, Mrs. Kingface. So it was that many Shahrokhs were gathered together for the Norooz festivities at the home of Arbab Kaykhosrow. And so it is that my strongest memory of my grandfather is that of him presiding over these elaborate celebrations.

Another strong "recollection" I have of Baba-joon, however, is of an event I did not actually witness, but in my mind's eye I can see it clearly, so vivid was Daddy's wrenching account. Grandfather's body is stretched out on the side of the road. He lies still and does not move. He does not breathe. He has been assassinated by one of Reza Shah's henchmen. The event is imprinted on my mind like a snapshot.

Baba-joon had gone to a wedding, a grand celebration attended by many dignitaries. After dinner he was seen leaving the room with one man on either side of him. What happened after that, his family could only guess because it was the last time anyone saw him alive. His body was discovered early the next morning on the pavement near the *joob,* the water conduit. There were no marks on it. The keys to his house and to the press office of the Majlis were still in his pocket, his wallet untouched. Clearly, the motive had not been robbery. Reconstructing what must have happened, family members concluded that he must have been hustled outside and jabbed with a lethal injection of air, a method of assassination much used by Reza Shah's cohorts to eliminate men whom the king perceived as potential threats to his absolute rule. Perhaps it was inevitable that Baba-joon's liberal democratic ideas would ultimately bring him into conflict with Reza Shah, whose growing dictatorial powers and anti-intellectual, antiliberal leanings were opposed to everything my grandfather stood for.

"Why would anyone want to kill Baba-joon?" I asked, teary-eyed and sad. I was only eight years old, and this incident was my first encounter with death, let alone assassination. Daddy, his eyes red from crying, did his best to explain in terms I could understand, "Reza Shah is a dictator and gets rid of anyone who stands in his way." I am not sure I fully understood, and even today it is not entirely clear to me why Reza Shah should have wanted to eliminate Baba-joon, but the Shah had a track record of disposing of statesmen on whom he had once relied, but whom he perceived as having become too powerful. Perhaps he felt threatened by Arbab Kaykhosrow's increasing popularity and prestige based on his impeccable integrity. Baba-joon himself laments in his memoirs that the all-powerful Shah seemed to have turned against him and had refused permission to his bank to send him money for medical treatment while abroad. He was not sure why but speculated that perhaps rival statesmen, jealous of his influence, were conducting a campaign of vilification behind his back that eventually succeeded in poisoning the Shah's mind against him.

Some time after my grandfather's death, when historical accounts were written of the assassination, a version of the event emerged that suggested that poison had been placed in Baba-joon's after-dinner coffee at the wedding. The exact circumstances of his murder continue to be debated, but many believe that Baba-joon paid with his life for his democratic beliefs and for his criticism of Reza Shah's heavy-handed, autocratic tactics.

The Fire Worshipers

The secrets of eternity are beyond us
And these puzzling words we cannot understand.
—Jalal ad-Din Rumi, "The Bliss of Union"

SOUTH OF TEHRAN, on an abandoned and unforgivingly barren desert escarpment, one can still see the vestiges of a Zoroastrian funerary tower. Before the Muslim conquest of Persia there must have been hundreds of such "towers of silence" scattered across the country, always outside the city limits. Stark and gaunt, their patterned brickwork soared upward like giant candles, sinister reminders of man's ultimate destiny. Gateways to the shadowy other world, they were appropriately devoid of any color or frivolous ornament.

At the top of these *dakhmeh,* on stone slabs on a circular platform approximately twenty feet in diameter, Zoroastrians placed the corpses of their deceased so as not to pollute the earth, one of the seven creations. There, vultures stripped away the flesh from the bones. After being left to dry in the sun, the skeletons were thrown into the pit at the center of the tower. Eventually, as the pit filled, the bones were collected and stored in ossuaries or buried. Occasionally rock-hewn chambers set in the side of a mountain held the bones, principally of royal personages, such as those at Naqsh-i-Rustam, where the sepulchers of King Darius and three of his successors can still be seen. More common were terra-cotta caskets, sometimes beautifully ornamented with carvings and decorations that paid homage to the dead.

When Baba-joon passed away, however, his body was not placed on top of a funerary tower, but buried in a tranquil *aramgah,* a "place of rest," a graveyard bright with flowers and marked by burial stones. Not long before he died, he had introduced to the Zoroastrian community this radical reform in funerary custom, holding that the use of *dakhmeh* did not correspond with the teachings of the Prophet Zoroaster, but had its origins in primitive rituals. He believed that the practice was unhygienic and unsuited to modern life. Such was his stature and standing that there was very little opposition to this drastic change. To make the reform as compatible with Scripture as possible, appropriate measures were taken to prevent contamination of the soil. Coffins were used, which were placed in graves lined with cement. This practice stood in marked contrast to the Muslim custom of placing a shroud-wrapped corpse directly into an unlined grave, with no coffin. From then on the Zoroastrians of Tehran buried their dead in graves marked by headstones in a cemetery whose site Baba-joon helped establish. Two years later an *aramgah* was also instituted in Kerman, although the *dakhmeh* there was not totally abandoned until the 1960s. The Zoroastrian community in Yazd followed suit in 1965.

When Mummy and Daddy took me with them to place some flowers on Baba-joon's tombstone, I took it for granted that he was buried in the ground, for that was the practice with which I was familiar. I had never even seen a *dakhmeh,* but I was perplexed by a number of things. How was his soul going to be reunited with his body on the Day of Resurrection? How at the end of time, when there was nothing left of his body but a skeleton, would it and its former flesh be resurrected and reunited with his soul? Daddy assured me that the Saoshyant, the Savior, was all-powerful and would bring about the unimaginable miracle in preparation for the fiery ordeal at the Last Judgment, when everyone must pass through the great flow of molten metal that would pour over the earth and purify it of all evil. "He will resurrect Baba-joon's body. And because Baba-joon was such a good man, the fiery river won't burn him, but it will feel like warm milk." "But wicked people," he went on, fixing me with a penetrating look, "will burn and suffer for a long time until they are purged of all their sins." He let this tidbit sink in for a while and then reassured me that in the end even they would be saved.

According to family lore, our family were descendants of the Sassanid king Bahram-e Goor, so named because he hunted *goor,* the wild ass. Famous for his knightly deeds and hunting skills, he was immortalized first by Ferdowsi and later by the twelfth-century poet Nizami. In this latter poet's romances

Bahram-e Goor discovers seven portraits of seven extraordinarily beautiful princesses in a secret chamber in his castle. Soon afterward, having succeeded to the throne, he demands and obtains these seven princesses in marriage. Each one is lodged in a separate palace, and Bahram visits each of them on seven successive days. Each princess tells him a story. The fourth story became the prototype of Gozzi's *Turandot,* later adapted by Schiller for the stage and still later by Puccini for the opera.

I was enchanted to think that I was a descendant of the great king and one of the beautiful princesses, although I am not at all sure this bit of family lore had much effect on my behavior. Of course, what Daddy was trying to instill in us was a sense of the glory of our Persian heritage. Yet he made little effort to inculcate in us a belief in the tenets of Zoroastrianism, although he did make my brothers memorize long passages of the Avesta in the ancient Avestic language. I remember Iraj walking up and down the garden with an open book in his hands, reciting out loud, *"Asham vohi vaheshtam."* His eyes were glazed over, for he did not understand a word of what he was memorizing, and Daddy never bothered to explain to him the meaning of the sacred text. *"Asti oshta ahdi oshta,"* he droned on. I watched and listened but was spared the effort of memorizing the Avesta, for by the time I was old enough, Daddy seemed to have given up the effort.

Except for some incidental knowledge I picked up along the way, I grew up knowing little about my ancestral religion. I did know, of course, that Ahura Mazda, the force of good, and Ahriman, the force of evil, were locked in eternal combat for the possession of each human's soul. And once, when showing me the ruins of Persepolis near Shiraz, Daddy explained that the Throne Hall bas-relief of a king plunging his dagger into the stomach of an upright bull represented Ahura Mazda killing Ahriman, symbolizing the ultimate victory of the force of good. I was familiar also with the old Zoroastrian saying, *Pendar-e neek, goftar-e neek, kerdar-e neek:* good thoughts, good words, good deeds. But that was about all I knew. Even though we sometimes heard Daddy speaking Dari, the Persian dialect spoken by Zoroastrians that had roots in the language of the Medes, neither my brothers nor I ever learned to speak it. Occasionally we went with our parents to ceremonies at the temple on special feast days, but, to be honest, what we looked forward to on these occasions was seeing our cousins and eating *seerok,* a sweet fried bread served at such times.

It was not until fairly late in my life that I learned that Zoroastrianism was probably the first religion to posit a belief in a force of good and a force of evil, in life after death, and in a day of judgment. It was the first to teach that a savior would come, the Saoshyant, who would be the divine World Savior, but also a man, born of human parents, conceived of Zarathustra's own seed, miraculously preserved in the depths of a lake where near the end of time a virgin would bathe and become with child by the Prophet. I also learned that many scholars believe that all three of the world's monotheistic religions—Judaism, Christianity, and Islam—have their roots in Zoroastrianism.

The links I discovered between Zoroastrianism and Christianity, specifically Catholicism, surprised me. Christian theology, during its early formative years, was greatly influenced by St. Augustine, who was for a number of years a convert to Manichaeism, a corrupted form of Zoroastrianism founded by Mani, a visionary Persian prophet of the third century A.D. St. Augustine, in formulating his own theology, which dominated Christian thought for at least a thousand years, was influenced by his exposure to Manichaeism—whether in his absorption of Manichaeistic ideas or in his ardent rejection of them.

What I was even more surprised to learn, however, was that Grandfather, like my brothers, had memorized the Avesta without understanding its meaning and without any religious instruction. How, then, had he become such a fervent upholder of this faith? As related in his memoir, his years in the American School in Tehran had instilled in him such a strong Christian belief that when an English priest settled in Kerman, Baba-joon attended mass every Sunday. One day a member of the Muslim clergy came to the church to observe the mass, and his nationalistic sensibilities were apparently offended at seeing a Zoroastrian—a true Persian—attending a Christian church. He took my grandfather aside and suggested that Baba-joon might do well to follow his own religion, which was at least an authentically Persian religion, not a foreign import. He even offered to help my grandfather learn its doctrines. Baba-joon, deeply disturbed by the mullah's words, mulled them over for several days.

A few nights later, before going to bed, he prayed to God to give him guidance, went to sleep, and dreamed that his house was on fire; the flames rose above the roof, but nothing burned. He saw himself kneeling in the middle of the fire dressed in white, reciting the Avesta. The following morning he asked his wife Firoozeh to fetch his *sedreh* and *koshti,* the Zoroastrian white shirt and ceremonial cord, which he put on after having bathed. From then on he began an ardent study of the Zoroastrian religion. The more he studied it, the more he became convinced of the essential truth of the central principles of Zoroastrianism, although he remained respectful of other religious systems.

In the temple a fire burns constantly. Long ago, Zoroastrians built their *ma'bad* over natural gas fissures that fueled the sacred flame. Their zeal in not allowing the fire to die out earned for them the epithet *fire worshipers,* a misnomer based on misapprehension of the meaning of the fire.

This practice was one thing that Daddy took pains to explain to me. The significance of the fire, he said, lies in its relationship to the birth of Zoroaster. According to some ancient texts, at Ahura Mazda's command the Prophet's *khar,* his heaven-sent glory, was brought to the hearth of his maternal grandfather, where the fire burned perpetually from then on, without fuel. This *khar* enveloped a young woman who then gave birth to Zoroaster, the perfect man. My imagination was fired at this explanation, and in my mind I could see the *khar* wrap around a young woman like a pillar of fire, but of course without burning or hurting her. Because I was blissfully ignorant of how babies were made and of what was meant by a "virgin" birth, the story made perfect sense to me. Daddy said that after Zoroaster's miraculous birth, "he was always surrounded by a divine radiance," which produced a perfect picture in my mind of Zoroaster with a halo shimmering above his head.

The fire, then, is a symbol of the Prophet's divine grace, a call to the faithful to practice spiritual cleansing and purity. During the years of persecution by Turkish, Mongol, and Afghan invaders Zoroastrians kept the sacred fires in small mud-brick buildings that looked like houses and even then often had to hide the fires in tiny rooms with obscure entrances that looked like cupboard doors. Not until the twentieth century, when they enjoyed state protection, were they able once again to build handsome temples.

Although I was never formally initiated into the Zoroastrian religion, I did attend the initiation ceremonies of relatives. One I remember particularly well. It was a sort of first communion, a solemn occasion followed by feasting. Three *mobed* in white robes stood in a semicircle around the sacred fire. In front of its flickering light, a distant relative—a young boy—stood, his eyes fixed on the flame. His arms were stretched before him, and in his hands he held a *koshti,* the ceremonial cord. He also wore the pure white *sedreh;* at its neckline was stitched a tiny cloth purse. He started reciting words I did not understand. The liturgical incantation rose and fell rhythmically. The meaning of the unknown language flowed through me like waves, penetrating to my soul. I did not need to know the words. The *mobed* joined in the chant; their voices rose in unison. There was a pause, then the priests recited, and the boy responded in antiphonal counterpoint. As he resumed his incantations, he tied and untied the *koshti* around his waist in loose knots. Three times he passed it around his waist, knotting it in front and then in back, his eyes fixed on the fire. He prayed continually. Incense, intermittently thrown on the open flames, enveloped us in smoke. Its sandalwood scent was overpowering. Overcome by the smoke and by the mystery of the proceedings, I felt dizzy as my senses vibrated in communion with a myriad souls who, in centuries past, had sought in ritual and prayer the answers to questions about life and death and good and evil.

As Daddy explained it to me, the cord the boy tied around his waist was a "sacred girdle," which every believer puts on at maturity. The initiate ties the knots himself to signify that he takes full responsibility for his own conduct. After this first ceremony he must repeatedly tie and untie the rope while reciting prayers five times a day for the rest of his life. The threefold cord exemplifies the threefold ethic of Zoroastrianism, with its emphasis on good thoughts, good words, and good deeds. The cloth purse at the neckline of the white shirt reminds the initiate to fill it constantly with good deeds.

In times of persecution the *koshti* became a liability because it marked a person as being Zoroastrian. Arab tax collectors in the eighth century would sometimes mock Zoroastrians for wearing it and would rip it off, hanging the cord around the necks of the beleaguered faithful.

When Islam swept across Persia in the seventh century, it subjugated a people who were largely Zoroastrians. Although Zoroastrianism, unlike Judaism and Christianity, is not mentioned in the Koran as an accepted religion, the hadith tradition has it that both the Prophet Mohammad and the leading Shi'a Imam 'Ali considered it to be a monotheistic religion like the other two and therefore a valid, accepted religion. Nevertheless, the Zoroastrians faced varying degrees and forms of oppression, including the *jaziyeh,* a heavy tax on non-Muslims. Zoroastrian sources record the method of exacting this tax as designed to humiliate the *dhimmi,* the taxed person, who was compelled to stand while the officer receiving the money sat on a high throne. Upon receiving the payment, the officer gave the *dhimmi* a blow on the neck and drove him roughly away. The public was invited to watch the spectacle.

Such instances of persecution did not start immediately after the Muslim conquest. During their early centuries as a minority in a Muslim land the Zoroastrian communities enjoyed enough protection from their conquerors that they were able to survive and sometimes even to prosper. By the tenth century, however, under mounting persecution, large numbers of them felt compelled to flee Iran, but it was not until the Seljuk and Mongol invasions that they faced almost total annihilation. When the Seljuk Turks, zealous converts to Islam, swept out of the steppes of Central Asia in the eleventh century and onto the Iranian plateau, they exterminated or forcibly converted those who did not profess their newfound faith. Slashing and burning everything in their path, they built towers of skulls of the men, women, and children they slaughtered.

In the thirteenth century the dreadful Mongol invasions followed, led first by Genghis Khan and then by his grandson Hulagu. Sweeping across Iran like a swarm of locusts, they put to death entire populations. In Nishapur they beheaded every man, woman, and child in the city and then systematically cut open their stomachs, for that was the Mongol custom. Stacking the heads into pyramids, they piled around the bases the bodies of dogs and cats they had also killed. Plundering and pillaging other cities lying in their path, they spared the lives only of those they wished to keep as slaves. The rest they encircled like a herd of cattle and shot with arrows. In the countryside large numbers of people suffered death from famine and starvation, for these conquerors from the steppes not only destroyed the life-giving *qanats*, the irrigation works essential to life on the arid plains, but salted the land around them so that nothing would grow. It took seven hundred years for the population to recover its pre-Mongol levels. Not only was the loss of life without precedent, but also the loss of property and culture, for the Mongols destroyed the last great collections of Avestas as well as the fire temples, which previously had been protected by treaty with the Arabs.

The Zoroastrians who managed to survive regrouped and settled just north of Fars, in Yazd—famous for its satins, velvets, and silks interwoven with silver and gold metallic thread—and in Kerman, known for its exquisite carpets. These oasis cities are located on the edges of the inhospitable deserts, Dasht-i-

Lut and Dasht-i-Kavir, both notorious for their harsh climate. Yet even here the Zoroastrians were pursued, as the Safavid kings of the sixteenth century sought to compel them at sword point to accept Islam. The rivers ran red with the blood of those who refused.

Today, the gutted remains of a Zoroastrian ghetto near Kerman can still be seen, with its humble homes and temples outside the city walls. It was destroyed by Afghan conquerors in the eighteenth century. But in a small village near Yazd two of the greatest sacred fires of Sassanian Persia are still burning. Brought here for safekeeping, the fires were joined together and are said to have been burning continuously for more than two thousand years.

Persecution of the Zoroastrians finally eased during the last decades of the nineteenth century. The burdensome *jaziyeh* tax on non-Muslims was lifted, and through hard work and scrupulous honesty the Zoroastrians were able to prosper. Down the centuries they had maintained reputations for husbanding the earth and for being upright, peaceable, and devout. Now they also became known for their mercantile skills and their magnificent gardens as well as for building, in Yazd, one of the first Iranian schools for girls.

Even so, Zoroastrians living under the rule of the Qajar kings still faced some forms of discrimination. As late as the early part of the twentieth century they were not allowed to ride horses, donkeys, or mules in a time when there was no other form of transportation (a proscription common at the time for *dhimmi* throughout the Ottoman Empire as well). What is more, they were not allowed to wear overcoats but were compelled to wear long robes called *qaba* and cotton *geeveh* on their feet even in the winter. As my grandfather described their plight in his memoirs, "Zoroastrians were often attacked and beaten by Muslims in the streets. When they shopped in the bazaar, they were not allowed to touch any food or fruits." Zoroastrian men in Yazd would carry a large shawl that they would place under their feet when visiting a Muslim's home so as to prevent the carpet from being polluted.

When Baba-joon returned to Kerman from Bombay as principal of the Zoroastrian School, he vowed to himself that he would change this intolerable situation. "For me, life has no meaning without a strong will to overcome odds," he declared. And upon landing on the Iranian coast, at Bushehr, he defiantly bought a donkey to transport him to Kerman, where he arrived astride the beast, wearing a long cloak, trousers, a hat, and boots, all forbidden to Zoroastrians.

The next day he was summoned by Prince Farmanfarma, the governor of Kerman. Against the advice of his friends and associates, who were sure he was endangering his life, Baba-joon rode to the governor's mansion on a horse, wearing the forbidden garments. Then, to everyone's consternation, instead of standing deferentially at the back of the reception hall, he walked up to the governor and shook his hand. But to everyone's surprise, instead of denouncing Baba-joon for his brash behavior, the governor invited my grandfather to become his English tutor. From then on Baba-joon rode horseback to the governor's mansion, refusing to be intimidated by numerous threats he received.

Not until 1923, however, was the general proscription against Zoroastrians' riding horses and donkeys lifted, after Baba-joon pleaded the case of his coreligionists in an audience with Reza Shah. He pointed out to His Majesty what hardship Zoroastrians had to endure in not having transportation and how unjust it was for them to suffer such privation simply because of their religious beliefs. They were, after all, human beings and, indeed, true Iranians. Reza Shah, visibly moved by my grandfather's plea, summoned his commander in chief and instructed him to send out cables to all the provincial governors ordering them to lift the restrictions on Zoroastrians.

Baba-joon published two books on the Zoroastrian religion and Iranian history that have been credited with helping to moderate the attitudes of Muslims toward Zoroastrians in the early part of the twentieth century. His *Mirror of the Mazdayasnie Religion* was published in 1907, and all seven thousand copies printed were distributed free. Similarly, all seven thousand copies of his *The Light of Mazdayasnie* were distributed free between 1908 and 1920. He received congratulations and commendations for his writings from many teachers of Islamic theology, a number of clergymen, and others, all attesting to how these works had helped them gain greater insight into the Zoroastrian religion and greater respect for its followers.

And so the fortunes of the Zoroastrians gradually rose under Reza Shah in the first decades of the twentieth century, and eventually they were allowed to dress as they pleased. What is more, my grandfather persuaded his fellow deputies in the Majlis to pass a bill allowing Zoroastrians to have their own religious codes in cases of marriage, divorce, and inheritance, a document that he helped to draw up.

As Iran started to modernize, many Zoroastrians moved to the new capital city, Tehran, where there was more opportunity for advancement, and there they built temples, hospitals, and schools. In 1906, after eleven years in Kerman, Baba-joon moved his family to Tehran, so that is where Daddy brought his English bride and where the couple established their home. By the time I came along, the Zoroastrians were a highly respected, well-educated, relatively prosperous community. Growing up in Tehran at that time, I could not help being aware of the general good will toward them. In fact, many Muslim Iranians went so far as to say that the followers of this ancient religion were the "authentic" or "true" Iranians, so I felt twice blessed—once for being Zoroastrian and once for being half English. Oblivious to the past sufferings of the members of my father's faith, I simply took for granted the privileged status I enjoyed not only as a member of the community and the granddaughter of Arbab Kaykhosrow, but also as the daughter of an English mother. I was *do-rageh:* I had the blood of two distinct peoples coursing through my veins, which, with no effort on my part, enabled me to speak two languages and to blend two cultures effortlessly into my very being.

Unlike members of many minority groups throughout the world who feel marginalized, stereotyped, and looked down upon, I sensed nothing but respect on the part of Muslim fellow Iranians when they learned I was Zoroastrian or when they learned I was half English. How unusual an experience that was for a member of a minority I did not fully realize until much later. I was, it would seem, in the right place at the right time.

Two Worlds

Why, all the Saints and Sages who discuss'd
Of the Two Worlds so learnedly, are thrust
Like foolish Prophets forth; their Words to Scorn
Are scatter'd, and their Mouths are stopt with Dust.
—Omar Khayyam, *Rubaiyat*

FROM THE BEGINNING I had my feet in two worlds. I spoke English at school and with my family at home, but Persian with the servants and outside the home. At one point in my life, though, I came close to growing up in an entirely English environment. When I was four years old and Parviz five, my parents, following a long-established British tradition, decided the time had come to send the two of us to a boarding school in England for "a good British education." This they did at great cost and much sacrifice, for they fervently believed they were doing the best possible thing for us. So it was that my parents took us on a long journey by boat and train, stopping on the way in Berlin for the 1936 Olympics, whose historic significance was completely lost on me. Our destination was Brighton in the south of England, where Parviz and I became boarders at Taunton House School. Within a short period of time, I forgot how to speak Persian, and although Mummy and Daddy came the next year and took us to the pebbly Brighton Beach, it was a brief visit, and I quickly forgot my parents, —even what they looked like.

One might imagine that I would have felt frightened or abandoned or lonely, but I do not remember feeling that way. How could I miss parents about whom I remembered nothing at all? Besides, my brother Parviz was there. He was only one year older than I, and we were rather close. What is more, all the

With Mummy at the 1936 Olympics. I knew nothing, of course, of the rise of Hitler and the triumphs of Jesse Owens.

children in the school were boarders, and so it seemed to be the norm for children to live away from their families. The only difference was that our parents lived much farther away than most, and we could not visit them on holidays.

But, luckily, we did have family nearby with whom we spent the long English holidays, for my mother's sister, Aunt Stella, lived with her husband and two children in Liverpool. Our cousins, Pauline and Max, were just about our ages. They were as blond and blue-eyed as Parviz and I were brunette. We must have made quite a contrast. Aunt Stella would come and fetch us from the school, and we would ride home with her by train, becoming part of her household several times a year. As was apparent in photographs of her, Aunt Stella resembled my mother and was also a beautiful woman. I think she enjoyed having us visit because we helped keep our cousins occupied during the holidays, although we did, of course, have occasional scraps. We must have been quite a handful. Together we would go on family outings, one of which is captured in an old photograph I still have that shows us in a park, holding tight to the railings of a long, enclosed double settee strapped to the back of an elephant so large it dwarfs us.

Taunton House was a small school with a homelike atmosphere, and the principal had rather progressive ideas. In a photograph of my class spending a summer's day at the seaside, I am standing stark naked amidst a group of romping children, none of whom is wearing a stitch of clothing. We are totally oblivious to our nudity and unselfconscious about our bodies—an attitude

With Parviz on the beach at Brighton
in our school uniforms.

completely at odds with the supersensitivity about exposed flesh I would encounter upon returning to Iran and, surprisingly, also at odds with the puri-
tanism I would confront years later in the United States, where at a public lake I
was instructed to "put some pants on" my naked one-year-old son "or else
leave!"

The teachers at Taunton House did their best to stimulate our artistic inclinations in imaginative ways and in me found a passionately receptive student.
Some evenings we sat before a blazing fire and made up stories based on what
we saw in the dancing flames. Often our teacher, whom I vaguely remember
was called Miss Penelope, gathered us around her at the piano to sing songs
while she played. Sometimes she gave us sheets of blank music paper, showed us
how to make quarter and half-notes, and instructed us to "compose" a song by
placing notes wherever we wanted on the lines. She would then play "the tune"
we had "composed." Occasionally she encouraged us to dance as she played.
That was the part I liked best. As her fingers tinkled out a melody on the piano,
I imagined myself a fairy princess and twirled around and jumped up and down.
I kept on even after she had stopped playing. "That's enough," she would say, but
I just kept on spinning around and around until I was dizzy and out of breath.

I was five when I learned to read and every day looked forward to the hour
of reading we were allowed before the lights were turned off and we had to go
to bed. I would select a book from the school's small library and lose myself in its
contents. I have never lost the habit.

On Sunday mornings we were obliged to write letters home. Having no

With Daddy and Parviz on the beach at Brighton.

recollection of my parents on which to draw, I felt it was a futile exercise. I had learned the opening formula, "Dear Mummy and Daddy, I hope you are happy and well," and started every letter the same way. Then, not having much else to say, I would go on, "Please send me some *gaz.*" *Gaz* was one of the few things about home that I still remembered. Sunday after Sunday I wrote the same letter, until one of the teachers finally lost her temper. "Can't you think of anything else to say?" she asked crossly. But as hard as I tried, I could not, which is not surprising because I had no real idea with whom I was supposed to be communicating. I doubt that the letters were ever sent. In any case I never did receive any *gaz.*

What I disliked most intensely at Taunton House School was not the rigid schedule, the rules, or the uniforms, but the lumpy, unrefined, brown porridge we had to eat every morning. We were not allowed to leave even a spoonful in our bowls, but were obliged to eat every last bite of it, even though it tasted awful. I dreaded the daily ordeal. I would hold my nose, drink water, and swallow, almost gagging on the horrid stuff.

And there are a few other unpleasant memories that linger on, such as the time I was falsely accused of getting red paint on a classmate's collar and punished for it. Or the time the teacher thought it was I who was whispering after the lights were out and, ignoring my protestations of innocence, made me stand alone in the cold, dark hall for what seemed like ages. And the time the princi-

Taunton House School, Brighton. I am third from right, and Parviz is
in the center of the front row of the boys in the background.

pal administered a spanking because I had wet my bed at night. I sobbed at the
humiliation of it all. As if I had done it on purpose!

I remember how terrified I was when they started fitting us with gas masks
at school in preparation for war, for there were rumblings of great disturbances
afoot in Europe. I imagined myself diving under the desk with my mask on
while enemy bombs dropped all around, with explosions and mayhem everywhere. Fortunately, I was spared the experience, for long before Chamberlain
went to Munich, declaring that he had ensured "peace in our time," my parents
decided that it would be wise to bring us home.

It had been two years since I had last seen my mother, and I had not the
slightest idea how I would recognize her. In fact, I did not; my teacher had to
point her out to me. "That's your mother," she said, pointing toward a petite
woman with fair hair and blue eyes coming toward us. Without hesitation I ran
up to her with arms outstretched, crying, "Oh, Mummy, I'm so fat I can't run."
She smothered Parviz and me with kisses, put us in a taxi, and started the long
trek home. From the very first moment of reunion I felt comfortable with her
and very quickly got to know her again as though there had never been any separation. I can't speak for Parviz, but for me the rebonding was instantaneous,
perhaps because I had never felt that I had been sent away to school as an

Spending the holidays with my English cousin Pauline.

unloved child. I always knew my parents loved me and that they had sent me away because they wanted me to have a British education.

From Dover we went by ship to Calais, across France by train to Berlin, where we visited the magnificent Berlin Zoo and where I learned to say, "Ein banana, bitte," and was reluctantly and tearfully photographed sitting next to a baby lion. Then we went on by train across Germany, where the trains were always on time, and across Russia, where they were always late, to Baku on the Caspian Sea. By ship we proceeded to Rasht on Iran's Caspian coast. Then came the final stretch, by train, over the lofty Alborz Mountains, through which Reza Shah had carved long tunnels, to Tehran and what from now on would be home. As far as I remember, I made the transition with relative ease.

It still amazes me to think how different my life would have been had it not been for the clouds of war menacing England. Parviz and I might have stayed in Brighton and grown up in Great Britain. I might never have bathed in a *hamam* or ridden a *doroshkeh* or lived in our house outside Government Gate or learned to speak Persian. I certainly would never have known Grandfather or any of my Iranian cousins. I might not even have known my parents—at least not very well. As things turned out, however, I was reunited with my family and was able to grow up in a bicultural situation. For the rare gift of being able to slip in and out of sometimes diametrically opposed cultures, I have always been grateful.

Not long after our return Mummy explained to me that I would soon be

At the Berlin Zoo,
terrified of the baby lion.

going to school. I would be entering the first grade and Parviz the second. At first delighted, I burst into tears when she told me I had been enrolled in an American school. "But I can't speak American," I wailed. Mummy laughed and, putting her arm around me, reassured me. "Don't worry," she said, "Americans speak the same language as the English, but with a funny accent. You will get used to it." I was so relieved I stopped crying instantly.

I loved Community School from the very first day I stepped into its walls. Built by Presbyterian missionaries some decades earlier, it was the only primary English-speaking school remaining open in Tehran. Enclosed in a large shady compound along with the homes of the American missionaries and their church, it was a coeducational school strictly for foreign, English-speaking children. It had an international student body, with Americans in a clear minority.

Before 1886, when Presbyterian missionaries first built a school for girls in Tehran, most Iranian girls were entirely illiterate, except for a select few who were tutored at home. Boys attended traditional religious schools, known as *madreseh,* where they studied the Koran, theology, and mathematics.

At first only Zoroastrian, Armenian, and Assyrian (Nestorian) families sent their daughters to the missionary school, for in the Muslim community the notion of sending girls outside the home for several hours a day and exposing them to foreign influences was outrageous. Girls had to be prepared for marriage and motherhood. Education, it was believed, would only make them rebellious. Gradually, however, attitudes began to change, and a few Muslim families ventured to send their daughters to the school.

By this time Reza Shah had started building public schools and was trying to educate a largely illiterate populace. The ethnic diversity of the country was a challenge to his attempts to unite the country because many children grew up speaking Turkish, Kurdish, Armenian, or Arabic rather than Persian. He made instruction in the Persian language compulsory throughout the land, and gradually young people all over Iran were able to speak and read Persian.

As attitudes toward education for girls modified, the missionary school slowly gained acceptance and American missionaries were able to establish the Alborz College for boys and the Sage College for girls. By 1919 there were approximately five hundred boys and three hundred girls in the Tehran mission schools. Besides educating and converting their young charges, the missionaries sought to instill in their pupils the idea of patriotism and service to their country. But despite this philosophy the mission schools soon came up against a major obstacle—nationalism and Reza Shah's drive to free his country of foreign domination.

By the time I was ready to enter the first grade, there had already been much acrimony between the government and the mission schools. By 1940, when I was in the third grade, Community School alone among all the mission schools remained open. It stood as the premier Presbyterian school in Iran until the Iranian Revolution broke out, and it was seized by the Islamic Republic in 1980.

Had we not been half English, Parviz and I would not have been able to attend this school, but our English mother and our knowledge of English were sure entry tickets. I was happy there. All my classmates were of mixed or foreign parentage—English, French, Iraqi, Armenian, Swedish, Belgian, and American sons and daughters of the many foreigners living in Iran at that time. Most of them were multilingual, some knowing as many as four or five languages—Armenian, Russian, Persian, English, German, and sometimes French. Most of them had traveled widely. It was a stimulating environment. Our daily Bible classes would turn out to be an advantage years later when I decided to study English literature.

Unlike Taunton House School and the public Iranian schools where uniforms were mandatory, we had the freedom of wearing clothing of our choice. What is more, we had no sense of competition about our clothes, brand-name garments being unknown to us because there was no clothing industry in Iran back then. My wardrobe consisted entirely of home-made skirts, blouses, or

Community School, Tehran. I am in the center of the front row, the one with the plaid skirt and sleeves. I am seven or eight years old.

dresses. At most I had two outfits per season and thought nothing of wearing the same dress several days in a row.

In Iran in those days it was highly unusual for a young girl to attend a coeducational school. Although there had been some traditional *maktab*s, or schools, run by women in which prepubescent girls and boys studied together, such mixing was quite rare. And although Reza Shah had experimented with coeducation in the primary grades, the experimental schools were abandoned when he abdicated in 1941, and coeducation existed only at the university level. So to grow up associating freely with boys in and outside of the classroom during puberty was most irregular. It was one of the many ways in which my upbringing was different.

Persian was not part of the curriculum back then, so although my brothers and I could speak Persian, we were growing up without a knowledge of the written language. Daddy hired a tutor to come to the house to teach us to read and write Farsi, or Persian. Although an Indo-European language and thus with a close affinity to European languages, Persian is written in a modified Arabic script and goes from right to left.

Even in the summer I was expected to practice my Persian penmanship under Daddy's supervision. I would sit resentfully in his office and struggle laboriously to make smooth strokes and curves sweeping from right to left in imitation of the elegant strokes in the book. I succeeded, however, only in reproducing inelegant and inexact facsimiles, definitely not promising of calligraphic talent. I did not want to do the assignment and pouted and sulked, but

Daddy was firm. He did not allow me to leave until I had finished writing the entire page.

The house of my early childhood was one of the first to be located outside the old city walls. There had once been twelve city gates, but there were only four left. Ornately decorated with colored tiles, these gates used to be locked at night to protect the residents living within, but by the time we moved to Darvazeh Dowlat, Government Gate, there were no city walls, and a large boulevard had rammed its way through the space once occupied by the stately eastern entryway, which was already only a memory.

Our roomy brick house had two stories and several wings, four capacious bedrooms, two large verandas, two salons for entertaining, a dining room, a kitchen, a cellar, two small servants' rooms, and wide and spacious hallways through which I was forever jetéing, pirouetting, cartwheeling, and forgetting what it was I had been sent upstairs (or downstairs) to fetch. Mummy, too, made use of the expansiveness of the rooms and hallways, and often tuned the radio to the BBC and fox-trotted around the house for exercise, disregarding the raised eyebrows or censoring looks of the servants.

Houses were solidly built in Tehran because labor was cheap and stone and bricks plentiful. A brick-making kiln south of the city, one of Reza Shah's innovations, provided an abundant supply of inexpensive bricks. Not only were the walls of our house thick, but even the internal walls were built of brick covered with plaster, which Mummy frequently had whitewashed. The electric wiring ran along these walls, snaking across the plaster in full sight. The rooms were airy, with high ceilings edged with chalk faience carved with arabesques, whose curlicues and delicate lines I loved to follow with my eyes.

Tehran was then a sleepy city of five hundred thousand residents. It had one foot gingerly placed in the present and the other firmly planted in the past, as if holding a balletic fourth position, but uncertain whether to step forward or back. Although it was actually being transformed at a dizzying pace, to those of us living there at the time that change was not yet apparent.

Situated at the foot of the towering Alborz range, the city offered air that was crystalline in its purity and breathtaking views that could be seen from any point. In spite of the aridity of the surrounding wilderness large plane trees cast dappled shade along the grandiosely broad city boulevards that revealed the measure of Reza Shah's ambitions. Planted alongside the *joobs*, roadside ditches that carried life-giving water to the city from the snow-capped peaks, the roots of the trees were soaked at regular intervals, and they flourished, even though their leaves were always covered with a fine powdery dust. The wide avenues of upper Tehran were blissfully free of motorized traffic.

Clip-clop, clip-clop, clippety clop-clop-clop. The principal traffic noise we heard was that made by hooves hitting the pavement with the rhythmic precision of tap dancers as we rode *doroshkehs* through the grand boulevards built to accommodate grand processions and luxurious motor cars. These horse-drawn carriages were the taxis of the day. Their name, borrowed from the Russian, reflected the proximity of the Soviet Union, which shared a 1,200-mile border with Iran, as well as centuries of Russo-Iranian cultural and mercantile interchange.

Parviz and I would giggle as the horses farted while straining to draw the carriage and its occupants along, and somehow we thought it enormously funny that the horses pulling our *doroshkeh* would defecate while trotting. But I did not laugh when I once crashed into a dung cart and found myself covered with horse manure. I was about nine years old.

At that time professional street cleaners, *sopoors*, swept up the droppings of the horses that pulled the *doroshkehs* along. Pushing a small cart, with broom and dustpan in hand, they walked the streets of Tehran to collect the refuse left by the horses. As usual I was riding my bike to school, quite oblivious to how outrageous that must have seemed to passersby. Because it was indecent for girls to wear pants, I wore skirts, totally indifferent to how much leg I was showing while flying down the invitingly broad avenues. I coasted past the Bank-e Melliye Iran, the National Bank of Iran, in front of which stood two majestic marble lions that reminded me of the ones I had seen in Trafalgar Square in London. I was going fairly fast, for it was all downhill on this stretch of the road, and there was virtually no traffic.

Without warning a young *sopoor* thrust his dung cart into the path of my bike, sending me sprawling against his vehicle and onto the pavement, my dress caked with fresh manure. He stood there laughing while I picked myself up and brushed off the filth as best I could, smearing it and getting it on my hands in the process. Cursing, I picked up my bike and pedaled away fast before he could inflict any further indignities on me. I arrived at school sobbing and was taken in hand by Mrs. Fisher, the wife of the principal, whose house was next to the school, inside the mission compound. Drying my tears and comforting me, she helped me clean up, lent me one of her daughter's dresses, and had her maid wash and iron mine, ready for me to put back on before returning home. Years later in Virginia, when I was taking a seminar in medieval English literature and came upon Chaucer's description of a "dung cart" in the "Nun's Priest's Tale," it struck me that I was probably the only person in the class who had ever *seen* a dung cart, let alone collided with one!

Although the natural habits of the horses amused us, my brother and I mostly felt sorry for the poor animals. How on earth could they see where they were going with such large blinkers blocking their side vision? Covering the sides of my eyes with my hands, I would try to imagine what it would be like to be able to see only straight ahead. The gay trappings festooning their harnesses—the bells, the tassels, and the bright blue beads to ward off the evil eye— could not camouflage their misery. Underfed and overworked, maltreated by masters who were themselves underfed and overworked, the sad creatures were so emaciated that they responded only fitfully to the lashings their frustrated masters laid on their backs. Their braided tails bore mute testimony to the restricted nature of their existence. They could not even flick away the flies that swarmed over them.

A ride in a *doroshkeh* was never smooth, for we would be jolted from side to side. In the summer we rode in the open air, with the black hood of the carriage folded down in the back, like a giant accordion. When it rained or snowed, the hood was pulled up for protection. Like a huge umbrella, it was adequate against the wet but did not keep out the cold. The driver, of course, had no protection at all from rain or snow or sun or cold. I was well into my teens before automobiles or buses became commonplace in Tehran, and most of the time I either rode my bicycle or walked.

Later, as Tehran grew and as distances increased, buses careened around the city with reckless speed, often racing each other so as to pick up the largest number of passengers. There were no traffic lights and little in the way of schedules. Waiting at a bus stop, all I could do was to hope that a bus would arrive within a reasonable amount of time and that it would stop. Often it went flying by without a pause, either because it was too full or because it was too empty and was trying to get ahead of a rival bus. Much later, after I had left the country, traffic lights were installed, and buses ran more or less on schedule, but by then most middle-class people owned cars, clogging the roads, honking horns, and ignoring all traffic rules.

Bus etiquette in the early days represented a peculiar attempt to wed ancient traditions with the modern world. Following custom, anyone sitting toward the front of a bus paid the fare for acquaintances seated further back, who would go through the motions of protesting. On another day the roles in this delicate minuet would be reversed. As Tehran grew and buses became more and more packed with strangers, such customs gradually died out.

When the city buses first began to run, it was impossible to predict how long it would take to arrive at a given destination, but time never had been highly valued in the Persian scale of things, and arriving late was the norm. Invited for six o'clock, dinner guests knew better than to arrive on time and might show up at eight or even nine. Naturally, everyone knew the rules, and the hosts were perfectly well aware that their guests would not arrive at six. A leisurely pace ranked high on our scale of values, and I think that was one aspect of life in Iran that Mummy genuinely appreciated. It meant, for one thing, that when I was little, she read to me a great deal.

Of course, I could read perfectly well myself, but I loved having her read out loud, for she did it with feeling and expression and wonderful dramatic flourishes. I remember sobbing as she read the account of Robin Hood's death—by bloodletting, a health measure familiar to us because it was still practiced in Iran at the time, and many of my relatives carried the resultant razor scars on their upper backs between their shoulder blades.

A large table stood at the center of the spacious dining room that opened onto the garden. Sunny and light, it was where we gathered to study or to play. Here Mummy helped us with our homework in our early years or mediated our quarrels or, while we studied, sat and darned socks, lost in her own thoughts and occasionally sighing.

Here Aunt Doris would sometimes help to soothe ruffled feelings or tend to one of us while Mummy was occupied. Sometimes my aunt would lead us in singing songs, usually English ballads. Daddy never joined in. According to Mummy, he was tone-deaf and had no sense of rhythm, although he seemed to enjoy listening. Perhaps he was simply enjoying watching Aunt Doris as she sang. Daddy always had an eye for the ladies, and Aunt Doris was unusually pretty.

My father joined us in the dining room principally for the midday dinner, the main meal of the day, after which he would take a nap before returning to the office. He was a stickler for table manners. In a country where the bulk of the population sat on the floor around a *sofreh* (table cloth) and ate with their hands, he insisted on the correct use of each table utensil. And in a culture where reaching for food was more polite than interrupting another person's meal Daddy insisted on the correct English form: "Please pass the butter," or "Pass the bread, please." We had many a scene at the dinner table over sloppy or incorrect table manners, and we children had trouble understanding what all the fuss was about. Whereas Mummy and Aunt Doris instructed us by example, Daddy taught by precept, violations of which annoyed him beyond measure.

Occasionally Daddy supervised our homework, but otherwise he had little to do with our daily routine and left the entire care of the house, home, and family to Mummy, Aunt Doris, and the servants. He was sometimes very affectionate with us, and he used to laugh and joke with Aunt Doris, but most of the time he just left us alone. He seemed to live in a world of his own.

Every afternoon Mummy had high tea spread out on the dining table for us when we came home from school. It usually consisted of fresh flat bread—either *sangak* or *taftoon* or *sheer-mal*—with butter, assorted jellies, feta cheese, and tea.

Sometimes, if the servants were too busy to fetch fresh bread from the baker's, Mummy would send Parviz and me to buy some. It was one chore we did not mind. Handing us a couple of rials, with admonitions not to dawdle along the way, she would send us off. "Hurry home," she would say, knowing full well that *nothing* could be hurried along in that country at that time. Parviz and I would then go to the nearest baker's, where the aroma of hot, fresh bread greeted us. A blazing furnace in the back of a dark cavernous room lit up the silhouettes of the bakers, who seemed to be dancing. Their rhythmic movements blurred as they rapidly and repeatedly placed a ball of dough onto the wide, flat head of a long-handled paddle, flattened it out with a thin stick for a rolling pin, stretched it over a large round mold covered with a wet cloth until it was paper thin, then slapped it onto the hot upper surface of the wide mouths of deep furnaces spewing forth fire and heat like legendary dragons.

I was intrigued at how the dough stuck, upside down, to the hot surface and fully expected it to obey the law of gravity and fall off, but it never did. It quickly turned golden brown and crisp, and the baker would reach into the glowing oven with a long pole topped by an iron pick, spear the golden prize, and pull it out. After tossing it onto a board to cool, he would fold into our string shopping bag the number of loaves we had asked for. Parviz and I would argue over who would carry them home. "Let me carry them," I would plead. "No, you goose," Parviz would reply, yanking the bread out of my reach. "I know you; you'll just eat it all up. I'll carry it." So Parviz would carry it, tearing off pieces as we walked along—big pieces for himself and little pieces for me. By the time we reached home, we had usually devoured at least one of the loaves, but Mummy did not seem to mind.

After supper we would study until dusk, when the daylight grew more and more feeble, and the room darker and darker, and it became increasingly difficult to see what we were reading or writing. Then suddenly the light overhead would come on, and everyone would cry out, *"Shab be khayr"* (May the night go well), a phrase that also means "good night." It was always a celebratory moment, for we could never be sure the lights would come on, and we felt privileged to have electricity, even if we only had it from dusk till about midnight. We knew that large parts of the city had none. Sometimes the lights did not come on, and then Naneh, our live-in maid, would get out the kerosene lamps. Mummy would often sigh as she spent inordinate amounts of time trimming the wicks of these sometimes smoky, frequently malfunctioning vessels, but she never complained.

Managing the Servants

Come wealth or want, come good or ill,
Let young and old accept their part,
And bow before the awful will,
And bear it with an honest heart.
—William Makepeace Thackeray,
"The End of the Day"

MANAGING THE SERVANTS was a perpetual challenge to my mother in her efforts at running a large household. Housework was time-consuming because labor-saving amenities were nonexistent or inadequate at best. Our only "appliances" were an icebox, brooms, mops, charcoal-heated irons and samovar, kerosene lamps, cooking stoves, and large tubs in which our clothes were washed by hand—making a great deal of back-breaking labor for the servants.

Every day Mummy would go shopping for food or send Mashd Mahmad, our manservant, to do it. Naneh and Batool, who was Mashd Mahmad's wife, spent hours preparing meals, carefully washing and chopping the green herbs so abundantly used in Persian cuisine and carefully picking over and cleaning such foodstuffs as rice and lentils. Because of the desert climate, the servants had to sweep and dust the entire house twice a day to keep at bay the fine white powder that settled on the furniture. Otherwise, within a matter of hours you could have traced your name on the banisters. The heavy copper pots and pans that were so marvelous for cooking they had to carry outside to the yard to scour with mud to make them gleam.

The servants were, on the whole, illiterate and knew nothing about hygiene. Not knowing what a germ was, they had difficulty understanding why tea glasses had to be washed in soapy water, not just rinsed out, or why each member of our household needed to have a separate towel. Mummy spent years training them, yet it was often a losing battle. Even so, it would have been impossible for her to run the house without them.

Mummy was ever on guard against petty theft and the padding of bills. She kept everything in the house under lock and key, including the refrigerator and nonperishable food items, for in the eyes of the servants, who were so poor, our household must have seemed rich beyond belief, and the temptation to steal often irresistible. Mummy was lucky to have found Naneh, who knew how my mother wanted things done and was also totally trustworthy. She was that rare creature in Muslim societies, a spinster—rare because the Islamic religion encourages marriage. What is more, girls from poor homes had few alternatives and were often married off even before they had attained puberty—anywhere from age nine to fourteen—a custom not banned until 1967, when the marriage age was legally set at sixteen for girls. It was reduced again, however, following the 1979 revolution.

I don't know why Naneh had never married. Perhaps her family had not been able to afford a dowry for her. Perhaps she was too plain or too skinny. She lived in our house, far from her village. She always wore a scarf over her head, but in our home she never wore her chador, even around my father and Mashd Mahmad, except when we had "outsiders" visiting. Even then she would put her chador on without drawing it across her face, but would wrap it around her waist so that her hands were free. She was bony, and her skin was sallow, but she had brilliant black eyes that radiated intelligence, and I felt very close to her. She seemed to have a special fondness for me, which I reciprocated, and I don't ever remember her being cross or short-tempered with me. She was in many ways a substitute mother much of the time.

I would sometimes go looking for Naneh and often found her in the kitchen, sitting cross-legged on the floor, bent over a large copper tray of rice or lentils or yellow split peas. "Come sit down," she would say, smiling. "Would you like me to tell you a story?" And, with her fingers deftly picking out bits of gravel, straw, or other debris, she would tell me stories about Khaleh Sooskeh— Aunt Roach. She did not know that some of these stories frightened me because I was afraid of insects, and Khaleh Sooskeh was, after all, a *roach!*

Sometimes she would recite a proverb, and if I were lucky, she would illustrate it with a tale to press the point home. Her favorite pearls of wisdom were: *Kam bokhor, hamisheh bokhor,* "Eat little, that you may always eat," or *Bad makon ke bad ofti,* "Do no evil lest you be ensnared by evil," loosely translated. Her version of "Don't count your chickens before they are hatched" went something like this:

Once upon a time there was a poor blind man who owned nothing in the world other than a *koozeh,* a clay water jug. One day as he sat by the roadside begging, it occurred to him that he could probably make a lot of money by selling his *koozeh.* "I could sell it to Gholam Hassan for ten rials," he thought to himself. "And with that ten rials I could buy some Homa cigarettes. I know Ali Aqha will let me have some cheap. Then I could sell those for a profit and buy a china cup and saucer that I could sell for an even greater profit. Gradually I'll have enough money to buy a donkey and a saddlebag, and I'll be able to buy fresh fruit and cucumbers wholesale from the bazaar and sell them uptown for a huge profit. Before long I'll be a rich man, and I'll be able to buy myself a house, and I'll even be able to hire a servant to do the work for me. And if that servant doesn't obey me, I'll let him have it. I'll take my walking stick and beat him over the head with it." And with that, the blind man picked up his walking stick and started flailing around, accidentally hitting his *koozeh* and smashing it to pieces.

And Naneh would laugh out loud.

It was largely from the servants that I learned something of the practices and beliefs of the Shi'a sect of the Muslim religion. Naneh, for instance, had me memorize the principles of her faith. From time to time she would ask me to recite them in order. "How many principles are there? *Osool-e din chantast?*" she would ask, proud of having taught me such important basics. And I would dutifully recite: "First, the unity of God; second, justice, *aval—towheed, dovom—adl,*" and so on in numerical order, going through all five without any inkling of what they meant, but liking the sound of them anyway and taking pleasure in the delighted response my recitation would elicit from her.

And once, when I was eight or nine years old, Naneh took me to a *rowzeh* in south Tehran, where a singsong lament was being recited of the martyrdom of Hossein, the Prophet's grandson, who was killed in A.D. 680 in the Battle of Karbala. As the *rowzeh-khan* began the lamentations, a group of women wrapped in black chadors and a separate group of men, all seated on thin, pile-less *gelim*s in the small courtyard, smacked their heads with the palms of their hands, beat their chests, or wept out loud, calling out "Ya Hossein." I watched, dry-eyed, while Naneh wept.

Sometimes at home I would come across Mashd Mahmad and Batool saying their prayers. They performed the requisite five prayers a day by combining two sets of prayers twice so that they actually prayed three times, as is customary in Shi'a Iran. First came the *vozoo'*, the ritual ablutions, after which they would roll out a small prayer rug on the floor and place at the top of it a *mohr*, a small disc made of clay from one of the holy cities of Mashhad or Karbala.

In stockinged feet they would stand, raising both hands to the side of the head, and recite the *shahada*, with its reverent *"La illaha el-Allah,"* there is no God but Allah, adding, as Shi'a Muslims do, that Mohammed is his Prophet and 'Ali his deputy. With closed eyes they would pray, their hands held in front with upturned palms, as if in supplication. They seemed transported to another world. Alternately standing and kneeling and touching their foreheads to the *mohr*, as if performing a slow and stately dance, they seemed to be in a reverie and oblivious to my presence. I was fascinated as much by the movement as by the melodious recitation of prayers.

What I did not learn from the servants was how to cook. Except for occasional visits with Naneh I kept away from the kitchen, for that was the servants' and Mummy's sphere, and I was not expected to help. Cooking was an all-day affair. Chickens did not come in neatly packaged cellophane wrapping. No, indeed. Mashd Mahmad would return from market with a squawking chicken in one hand, its legs trussed, its wings flapping. He would take it out to the courtyard and wring its neck to decapitate it, and the bleeding, headless creature would flap around in its death dance until it finally grew still. I was so used to the sight that it did not particularly bother me. I was more curious about how the chicken could flap its wings and dance around the yard even though headless. Then came the dunking in boiling water, the plucking of the feathers, and the cutting up of the carcass into pieces, before it was sautéed with onions and saffron and immersed in a walnut-pomegranate sauce. It had to simmer for hours, for chickens, although flavorful, were scrawny and tough. Years later, when American agronomists taught farmers in Iran how to raise plumper, more tender chickens, housewives found these "American chickens" too tender and likely to fall apart when cooked. "I can't fix a decent *fesenjoon* any more," they would complain.

Looking back, I am amazed at the sumptuous meals that emerged from our primitive kitchen, for all of the cooking was done on kerosene-fueled stoves. I marvel even more at the effort that went into preparing meals when I recall that Daddy was not particularly interested in food; he seemed to prefer smoking another cigarette, which he did almost all day long. The fingers of his right hand were stained and darkened from the tobacco, accustomed as he was to smoking cigarettes down to their stubs. Mummy would sometimes coax him into eating, for he had a habit of drinking on an empty stomach. "How about some saffron rice with *fesenjoon?*" she would ask, but most of the time he barely touched his food. His lean frame reflected his lack of interest. The rest of us more than made up for his abstinence, eating with gusto and relish everything that was put before us. Mummy was an accomplished cook and could prepare European or Persian dinners with extraordinary skill. Her repertory ranged from poached salmon, *salade d'olivier,* and assorted bombes and mousses to *baqali pollo* flavored with dill weed or *istanbolli pollo* laced with well-spiced tomatoes and green beans, as well as various *khoreshts* to pour over aromatic, fluffy rice.

My brothers and I often argued over whose turn it was to have the *sar-sheer,* the thick skin that would form overnight on top of our milk, which had to be boiled because it was not pasteurized. The cream would separate and form a creamy, mouthwateringly tasty treat. Sometimes Naneh, being partial to me, would scoop it off and give it to me secretly. "Sorry, but the cat got the cream last night," she would explain to Parviz and Iraj, while I licked my lips in quiet satisfaction.

A staircase at the back of the kitchen led down to the *anbar,* a dark, damp cellar that provided storage for melons, quinces, apples, onions, potatoes, and other fruits and vegetables Mummy had purchased in bulk from vendors who brought their produce-laden donkeys right to the door. I found the cellar spooky and would resist Mummy's requests to go down and fetch something. "Send Mashd Mahmad," I would insist, "I have homework to do." And I would quickly traipse off before she could scold me.

I mostly kept my distance from Mashd Mahmad. A slip of a man, his shirt hung loosely from his hunched shoulders, and his baggy cotton trousers flapped around his ankles. He always wore a felt *kolah-e namadi* over his thinning hair;

crevices lined his face, and he was cranky and bad-tempered. His name indicated that he had made the "little pilgrimage" to Mashhad, a holy city in northeastern Iran that is the site of the Shrine of Imam Reza, the eighth imam.

Many years younger than her husband, Batool had a round, full face and jet-black eyes. I thought she was very pretty. I sometimes saw Daddy's gaze lingering on her, so I guess he thought so, too. Married when she was nine, she had started bearing children with the onset of puberty and had given birth to seven, but only four had survived. She had accompanied her husband to the big city to work and send money home, where her children were being raised by her sister back in the village.

It was Mashd Mahmad's task to prepare the hot coals needed daily for the iron and the samovar. Twice a day he would place a few lumps of charcoal in an *atesh-charkhoon,* a little wire basket that had a long handle with which it could be spun around; then he would daub the coals with kerosene and light them with a match. Standing in the yard, he would swing the basket around and around, faster and faster, as the coals turned red hot, glowing, giving off an acrid odor and tiny sparks, like sparklers. The red-hot coals would turn into phosphorescent globes suspended in orbit, like planets in space, magically held there only by centrifugal force.

When the coals were glowing hot, Mashd Mahmad would place them in the central funnel of the samovar, which he kept going all day with a small pot of strong tea sitting on top, ready to serve to the family or guests, who often dropped in unannounced. The tea was served in tiny *istikans* because tea cups had not yet become fashionable. Parviz and I drank ours *dishlameh,* that is, sipping the tea through a hard lump of sugar held between the teeth. Even the sugar lumps involved labor because they were chipped off sugar cones into bite-size pieces. When precut sugar lumps became available, they seemed to us a great luxury.

The hot coals also served to heat the iron. A heavy contraption made with a compartment to hold the glowing lumps and a knob to keep the lid firmly in place, the iron was not amenable to controlled gradations of heat, and it singed, burned, and ruined many a shirt and sheet. Yet ironing was one of the household chores I liked best to help with, for that was when Batool would tell me stories while I sat by and watched or sprinkled water on the things she was about to iron.

Batool could neither read nor write, but like many illiterate people she had an extraordinary memory and an amazing store of tales and lore to recount. Story-telling was her principal pastime. Steeped in folk tradition, her tales were invariably about animals and taught the listener good moral conduct: not to lie or cheat, to be honest and truthful, and, above all, to beware of the chicanery and duplicity of outsiders. Sometimes she told tales of Mullah Nasrodin, a mythical folk hero whose imaginary exploits enabled Iranians to laugh at their government, their leaders, or themselves. Somehow I never found these stories as funny as she did. Perhaps I was too unsophisticated to get the point. There was one, though, that I did find amusing. This is how it went:

> Once upon a time Mullah Nasrodin was riding his donkey to town. Alongside him walked his young son. Passersby shook their heads at the sight and reprimanded the old man for riding while his young son walked. So Mullah Nasrodin got off the donkey and walked, letting his young son ride. Pretty soon another group of passersby were shaking their heads and wondering at the spectacle of a strong young man riding while his father walked. "Young man, aren't you ashamed to be making your poor old father walk while you ride the donkey?" The young boy was embarrassed and insisted that his father should ride, but Mullah Nasrodin decided that the two of them should ride the donkey. This time the passersby upbraided them both for being cruel to the hard-working donkey, who was obviously tired and overburdened, so Mullah Nasrodin got down, helped his son down, picked up the donkey, and started to carry it. Passersby then chided the old man for being a fool to carry the donkey, who is a beast of burden and should be used as such. Mullah Nasrodin finally learned his lesson. "I am a fool," he said, "for listening to people." He put the donkey down and climbed up onto him once again, letting his strong young son walk beside him and deciding once and for all not to let others' opinions influence what he did.

Batool also knew a smattering of Persian poetry, and her conversation, like that of most of her compatriots, was sprinkled with brief passages from the great poets. She would occasionally sigh and quote a quatrain from Omar Khayyam, which was her way of saying she wished she could change her destiny:

> Ah Love! could thou and I with Fate conspire
> To grasp this sorry Scheme of Things entire,

> Would not we shatter it to bits—and then
> Re-mould it nearer to the Heart's Desire!

Sadly, she knew—with Khayyam—that she could not.

Some household tasks required specialized skills, and once a year Mummy would hire a *pambeh-zan* to come and refurbish the mattresses. I stood by and watched as he unstitched the mattresses, emptied them, and fluffed up the compacted cotton into gossamer mounds with a harplike one-stringed contraption that he strummed all day with a wooden mallet, its incessant thump, thump, thump resonating in every corner of the house. He would then stitch the cotton back into the striped-ticking cases, restoring the firmness of the mattresses.

And every summer Mummy would have all the carpets collected and taken to Cheshmeh-ye Ab-e 'Ali, a large, spring-fed watering hole where the rugs would be totally immersed in the cold water, stomped on with bare feet, scrubbed clean, then spread out on the rocks to dry, creating a jumble of brilliant patterns and colors on the craggy bank.

Every morning the iceman would announce his arrival, crying *"yakhee, yakhee,"* and he would appear at our door with his doleful donkey, who staggered under a heavy load of ice. A creature with mournful eyes, equipped with a bridle covered with bright blue beads to ward off the evil eye, the donkey would patiently stand still while the *yakhee* removed chunks of ice from the salt-packed saddlebags slung over its back and weighed them on his simple portable scales.

He and his donkey made the trek early in the morning from Tochal, in the south of town, where melting snow, trapped and frozen in a huge man-made lake shaded by an enormous wall, yielded large chunks of ice to the *yakhee*'s icepick. It remained for Mashd Mahmad to crack these chunks into smaller pieces for use in the icebox and to cool our drinking water. The ice was full of sand, dirt, and debris, but we were used to impurities in our water and made no fuss about it. It would be years before an ice factory was built in Tehran, providing us with the ultimate luxury of smooth, clean blocks of ice delivered daily by truck, signaling that our world was changing.

Although our house did have piped water, what came out of the spigot was the impure water that ran downhill from the mountains, through the *joob*s. It was water that had been used by people along its course for every conceivable purpose—to wash clothes, to water donkeys, to bathe young children, or to scrub pots and pans.

The distribution of the *joob* water depended on an intricate system that channeled it to specific areas of the city on certain days of the week, with carefully controlled timing of how long it was allowed to run into each district and into each house. To control the flow, the man in charge of water distribution would block and unblock the canals that ran from the *joob*s to the houses. Once a week he would stand at the head of our *koocheh,* lane, in the grey of the predawn to direct the precious commodity into our *ab-anbar,* the cistern where we kept the water. Like a grouchy sentinel, he would stand there scowling, making sure no one diverted the water for their own use and seeing to it that we received our allotted supply before he moved on to the next house. This water we used for washing clothes, for scouring pots and pans, for cooking, for cleaning, and for flushing the toilets.

Our drinking water, on the other hand, was delivered daily by horse-drawn carriage and poured by the *abi* into our special drinking-water barrel. Clean potable water was precious, and we used it sparingly—only for drinking, brushing our teeth, and washing fresh vegetables and fruits, which Mummy meticulously disinfected by soaking in permanganate crystals, for in those days human waste, euphemistically termed *night soil,* was widely used to supplement animal manure as a source of fertilizer. None of us knew that permanganate crystals were in fact ineffective against many of the pollutants that contaminated our produce.

The *joob* that ran along our street was particularly wide and edged with stately plane trees. The water gurgled as it flowed over smooth rocks and boulders so that it had all the bucolic charm of a natural stream. One warm summer's day, when it was flowing and full, Mummy took off her shoes and stockings, hiked up her skirts and went wading in it, barefoot and barelegged. "Come on in," she urged, laughing girlishly. "It's such fun," but I hung back, embarrassed, wishing she would come into the house. She couldn't comprehend what all the fuss was about when Daddy angrily accused her of humiliating him and besmirching his good name. His family—and the neighbors—talked about the incident for months. Although I could understand that Mummy saw nothing wrong with wading in the *joob,* I was also acutely aware that what she was doing was viewed here not as an innocent pastime but as an act of indecency, and I blushed inwardly.

Our "European" toilet upstairs had a ball-and-chain pull that frequently broke, so, except for Mummy and Aunt Doris, most of us preferred the Persian-style toilet downstairs that never got clogged and didn't need fragile mechanisms for flushing. A simple porcelain square on the floor with a hole in the middle and two slightly raised footrests for squatting answered our needs. Next to the water spigot stood an *aftabeh* with a long spout, which we would use to wash our extremities. Next to that stood the toilet paper, mute witness to the way we combined cultures in every aspect of our lives.

We seldom used our porcelain tub with ball-and-claw feet, for the water-heating system was cumbersome and time-consuming. It was simpler just to go to the public bath once a week. The *hamam* we frequented was a modern version of the traditional bathhouses that still existed in south Tehran: it had a clothesline outside strung with large red cotton *longue*s and a bulbous domed roof set with round glass bubbles. But it had no large central chamber, as was customary in the older *hamam*s south of town, or a *khazineh* in which people could dip for the final rinse. Rather, it had separate tiled rooms, with showers and plenty of hot water. Along one wall ran a *sakoo* on which Mummy and I could sit or recline while being pummelled and scrubbed by the *dallak*, who for a small fee would come in and scrub us down with a coarse goat-hair *keeseh*, sloughing off the dead skin and leaving us squeaky clean. As I advanced into puberty, Naneh would sometimes counsel me not to sit on the *sakoo* when I went to the bath, predicting dire things could happen, but never quite spelling out what. "Don't ever sit naked on the *sakoo*," she said. "After all, men have been bathing in this same room." I finally figured out she was intimating that some male customer might have spilled sperm onto the platform, which might impregnate me if I sat on it. I was not sure in my own mind whether this was, in fact, possible, but I was not going to take any chances, so from then on I spread a towel underneath me whenever I sat on the *sakoo*.

Many of the old bathhouses remained in use in southern Tehran, where bathing was still an all-day affair for women. It was a time not only to get clean, but to socialize, with all the women in a family going together, as well as prepubescent boys. Once boys reached puberty, they would accompany male relatives to the men's *hamam*s. The women often took fruits and sometimes more substantial repasts to the bath for refreshment. There, amidst the steaming, soaking, and scrubbing, they would eat, chat, or gossip with family or friends and sometimes use the occasion to look over the physical attributes of a prospective daughter-in-law.

In between our weekly baths we limited ourselves to washing our hands and faces with cold water in a washbowl. Occasionally we would dab at our underarms with cologne, but mostly we accepted body odor as a natural fact of life.

In spite of the brilliant sun winters in Tehran were bitterly cold and central heating virtually unknown, but we managed to stay comfortable by congregating in a single room of our house kept cozily warm with a portable kerosene heater. For most of the winter we spent much of our time in our large dining room, where we children studied, played games, read, and occasionally got into fights and arguments.

Parviz and I shared a bedroom. It was unheated, and we took hot-water bottles with us to bed at night to keep our feet warm. In the morning our room was so cold we had to dress practically under the covers. To go to the bathroom we put on overcoats. In school we seldom removed these coats and sometimes even kept our gloves on. But we were used to all this and did not think to complain.

I will never forget my astonishment when one winter, in my midteens, I passed by the newly opened U.S. Information Service library and saw a sight that brought me to an abrupt stop. There behind the large plate-glass windows were two female employees dressed not in bulky sweaters, but mere blouses—in the dead of winter. It was snowing outside, and I was wearing several layers of warm woolen clothing, all of which I would keep on inside buildings, too. I stood there for a few minutes, transfixed at the miracle of central heating.

One of my classmates, Toori, had an old-fashioned *korsi* in her home, a traditional heating method consisting of a brazier of hot charcoals placed beneath a low table, over which were draped coverlets. Although she lived in a large house with plenty of kerosene heaters, and although her mother was German, the family kept a *korsi,* for the very fact that it was old-fashioned and traditional. Inexpensive and efficient, it had been at one time the principal method of heating and was still widely used in rural parts of the country. At Toori's house, however, it was a memento from the past. Sometimes I would stretch my legs out under it, enjoying the pleasurable inertia it induced. No wonder it was known as "the lazy house." Reclining against plump cushions, Toori and I would read, knit, crack pumpkin seeds, or sip tea, while keeping comfortably warm in an otherwise un-heated room. In the homes of poor people, where the *korsi* was still the only source of heat, family members would also sleep around it.

Tehran did not yet have a metropolitan sewage system, and our house, like other houses in the capital, had its own *chah,* where household waste collected, the liquid part of it eventually draining off into the porous, sandy soil. A stand-ing joke in those days held that Tehran could never have a subway system be-cause of all the cesspools that perforated the substratum of the city. This joke was usually accompanied by dire predictions that some day the pit-marked ground underlying Tehran would give way, and all the buildings would collapse into the *chah*s. These cesspools occasionally needed to be cleaned out, and Mummy would have a professional *moqanni* come in to perform this distasteful job. He would haul out the waste with buckets, while I pondered the fact that there were people so poor as to be willing to do such work. Not until the early 1950s did Tehran enjoy the luxury of a piped sewage system.

It was also in the 1950s, after I had left Tehran, that a piped-water system was installed. When I saw the city again in the late 1960s, clean drinking water was available in most houses and apartments, at least in northern Tehran, and there was warm water in abundance. The upper and middle classes now had private showers in their homes and no longer went to the public *hamam*s.

In a Persian Market

How long, how long, in infinite Pursuit
Of This and That endeavour and dispute?
Better be merry with the fruitful Grape
Than sadden after none, or bitter, Fruit.
— Omar Khayyam, *Rubaiyat*

MUMMY HAD A SPECIAL KNACK for dressing up old or worn furniture. With fresh braiding, an extra coat of varnish, or new upholstery fabric she performed miracles, converting run-down and dingy couches, chairs, and hassocks into smart-looking, elegant furniture. With scissors and fabric, a hammer and tacks, she often worked long after we were in bed, cutting, fitting, and hammering away. She single-handedly covered all the upholstered furniture in the house.

Opting for traditional Persian fabrics and designs, she hunted through the bazaars for just the right *termeh* to cover a chair or hassock. Among the treasures she rooted out was a handsome length of hand-painted silk taffeta that she framed and hung on the wall above the dining-room buffet. Our tablecloths were all hand embroidered or hand blocked and came from Isfahan, the ancient capital of Iran, the center of its most illustrious architecture, artwork, and handicrafts.

Her passion for Persian handicrafts was evident in the many hand-tooled silver vases, copper serving trays, or brass bowls that decorated our house. Ornamented with roses and tendrils and legendary kings astride arch-necked horses, with drawn bows and arrows shooting at gazelles or lions, these artifacts were for me an endless source of fascination. Many times I dreamily traced with eye and finger the figures around a vase or bowl, wondering at the intricate detail. As the country and the population's tastes lurched erratically toward pseudo-

70

Western styles in house ornament and decoration, and even as many were discarding traditional Persian handcrafted artifacts for cheap china figurines and plastic flowers in glass vases, Mummy was combing the bazaars and handicraft shops for prize pieces of fine workmanship with which to adorn a shelf, table, or sideboard.

I sometimes accompanied her on her excursions into the labyrinthine alleys of the bazaar, where the din of small hammers and mallets striking against chisel and maw created a cacophony of distinct rhythms and musical pitches. While she bargained, I would stand just outside the shop door and watch as men on low stools hunched over trays of silver, brass, or copper and painstakingly etched sprays of flowers or leaping stags onto the once plain surfaces.

The shoemakers' shops added to the welter of sights and sounds so characteristic of the bazaar. Here I watched leather being cut, pounded, molded, and stitched into a shapely or ungainly shoe, and, finally, a heel hammered in place. I stood transfixed as the makers of *qalam-kar,* hand-blocked prints, dipped their wooden molds in dye—blue, red, or green—then slapped them down on the undyed cloth, making a loud thud, in counterpoint to the *tap-tap, bang, clang* of the metalworkers, their movements as swift and rhythmic as those of a ballet dancer. Above the din peddlers hawked their wares, while I dodged bleating lambs being led to slaughter and braying donkeys carrying their goods through the crowds.

More often than not we were accosted by beggars of all sorts, men with gaping sores that oozed yellow pus, little children with twisted hands or a bent arm or deformed leg. A small boy no taller than myself, leading his blind mother by the hand, his other hand outstretched toward us, entreated, *"Khanom,* please give me one rial. As you can see, my mother is blind; in the name of your child please give me one rial. God will bless you." On and on he pleaded insistently until Mummy finally gave him the coveted rial. Most of the time she walked quickly on or shooed the beggars away or feigned indifference. She had learned to become relatively impervious to the pleading of beggars. It was the only way to cope.

The low prices in the bazaar for goods of all kinds made the trip to the south of town worthwhile for Mummy because uptown Western-style boutiques and shops charged a great deal more. Heavy traffic had not yet clogged Tehran's roads or made the trip to the south of town a veritable nightmare. For Mummy it was a quick and simple bus ride—no traffic jams, no parking problems.

The bazaar was a warren of interconnecting covered lanes, with unpredictable twists, turns, and sudden dead ends, each section having its specialty. I could not have found my way through it unassisted. Even Mummy had sometimes to stop to ask for directions. There was a section each for shoes; fabrics and tablecloths; copper work and brass ware; gold and silver; rugs and carpets; spices, condiments, dried beans, and dried fruits; and other items too numerous to mention. As we wandered around, jostled by the crowds, our eyes were inevitably drawn to the brightly colored scarves and fabrics hanging overhead, and our mouths watered at the smell of lamb being grilled over charcoal.

I was too young and apolitical, of course, to be aware that the bazaar was much more than just a place to shop. I had no idea it was one of the country's three major power centers, along with the monarchy and the mosque; that it had figured prominently in the Constitutional Revolution of 1905–11 and the nationalist movement of the early 1950s; and that some day it would also play a major role in the Islamic Revolution of 1979. To me it was just an endlessly fascinating, sometimes exhausting, but always rewarding place to shop as well as a place to eat, for the finest *chello kabab* restaurant in the entire city was located at one of the major entrances to the bazaar.

Daddy and Mummy once took me along when they were shopping for a large carpet for the living room. I must have been about nine. The din, dust, and crowds overwhelmed me as we walked past myriad shops piled high with rugs of different weave, style, and make, each with a display carpet hanging in the window. A few times we left the main passageway to enter a narrow alley lined with small shops and suddenly found ourselves in a spacious courtyard where carpets hung from balconies, creating a panoply of brilliant reds, blues, and indigos that dizzied our senses.

In one of the shops a man sat cross-legged in front of a loom, weaving. I watched, spellbound, as the man's nimble fingers passed the yarn through, looped it back, tied a knot, cut the thread, and then pressed the row of knots down to make sure it was even and straight and tight. Daddy said it would take years for him to finish the carpet. Although the labor of large numbers of women and children sustained the carpet industry, their work was done largely at home or in small workshops. In a public place such as the bazaar naturally a man would be doing the weaving. Eventually, in 1968, a child labor law would be passed making it illegal to employ children under the age of twelve as weavers, but before that happened, it was the norm, and we did not think to question that fact.

That day we saw simple Baluches, with their natural, undyed wools in beige, white, and brown; Kermans in red and gold, with their central medallions and intricate borders; Isfahans in blues or greens or orange, with their *boteh,* almond or paisley, patterns; and Kashans in all colors, with varieties of *gul* scrolls and arabesques carrying the eye from flower to leaf, to tendril and half-medallion, to varieties of borders and guard stripes framing the whole splendid pattern. And we saw Tabrizes, Abadehs, Sarouks, Hamadans, Shirazes, Feraghans, Joshagans, and delicate Nains made of the soft wool from baby lambs, their spandrels and rosettes sometimes edged with silk. My head was starting to swim and my feet to ache.

Although Mummy was partial to tribal rugs, with their stylized geometric designs and relative simplicity, she agreed with Daddy that the formal living room required a more sophisticated rug, so they finally narrowed down their search to Isfahans and Kashans with their curvilinear designs. Each time we slowed down in front of a shop to get a better look at the carpets on display, the storekeeper would press us to enter. *"Befarmaeed,"* he would urge. "Please come in. No obligation, of course. Just take a look. You might find something you like. I will give you a good price." And almost before we had one foot in the door, he and his helpers had unfolded several rugs and spread them out for better viewing, pointing out their fine weave, their soft colors, their unparalleled quality. Daddy, of course, was a connoisseur of carpets and did not need the storekeeper to tell him about quality. He could tell a fine carpet from an inferior one. He would not be duped.

Just when I felt I could not take another step, Mummy and Daddy stopped at the shop of an acquaintance with whom they had had previous business dealings and finally agreed on a Kashan they both liked. They settled in for a protracted bargaining process. Mummy knew enough to stay totally out of this part of the proceedings, for her blue eyes, fair hair, and accented Persian would have doubled the price. Daddy put on his best *arbab* manner, aloof and condescending. He knew how to haggle, how to appear contemptuous of the price the storekeeper offered, how to storm out in a huff. It was not just a matter of getting a better price. It was a matter of principle—of not being taken for a fool. It was a way of testing one's mettle, of proving one's intelligence and skill. It was a game of chess, pitting one mind against another.

As was the custom, we were invited to sit down and have some tea. "Hassan," the proprietor called, *"Chai biar."* And a young boy appeared as if from nowhere with a small copper tray on which were tiny *istikan*s of strong tea and a small bowl of sugar lumps. All major business transactions started with the serving of tea. It would have been incredibly rude to refuse such hospitality, whether we wanted it or not, so we each reached for a glass and were soon sipping the reddish brown liquid slowly after sweetening it well with sugar. The proprietor made polite inquiries about the health of our relatives and other such small talk before he and my parents got down to the business at hand, the price of the carpet.

It took much bargaining, and several times Daddy feigned an indignant departure, but each time the shopkeeper called him back, going through the motions of offering the carpet to him gratis. "Take it, take it," he urged. "By Allah, I don't want a penny from you. Your patronage of our unworthy shop is worth a thousand such carpets." And so it went. The last time we walked out Daddy and Mummy were the owners of an exquisite Kashan, with beige background and blue and navy *gul* and *boteh,* an overall pattern and an elegant central medallion. They had paid one-half the original asking price and felt triumphant. Of course, it is possible that the rug merchant got the better of Daddy anyway, for he had spent his life learning the tricks of the trade while Daddy was off studying textile technology in Manchester. How could my father possibly match the rug seller's skills? Besides, Daddy was not a hard-nosed person, but he was pleased with his own performance and pleased with the purchase. From that day on the Kashan graced the formal reception room of our home.

It was a large room at the far end of the house, reserved for formal entertaining. Used infrequently, it provided me a sanctuary where I could give free rein to my imagination without fear that intruding servants or siblings might walk through with disapproving glances or teasing taunts. Unlike my mother, I needed privacy when I danced.

Mummy had furnished our informal living room in the European style, with chairs grouped in conversational clusters. But this more formal salon was arranged in the Iranian style, with couch and chairs running around the perimeter of the room and small tables set at strategic intervals where large platters of fruit, pastries, and tea could be placed within easy reach of guests. This arrangement left a large space in the center of the room just right for dancing.

At one end of this reception room hung a copy of Gainsborough's *Blue Boy,* which Daddy, a fairly accomplished amateur painter, had painstakingly reproduced. A large mirror with a wide gilt frame hung on another side of the room. It served me well because I could watch my image in it and observe my movements. Here, I would wind the crank on our little portable phonograph with its picture of a dog listening to His Master's Voice and play one of our odd assortment of records. They were 78s, of course, and scratchy, but they included some wonderful Caruso songs, the bell song from *Lakme,* arias from *The Magic Flute,* as well as "Sheherazade" and "In a Persian Market." I guess these choices represented Mummy's musical tastes because Daddy listened mainly to Persian music, which the rest of the family did not appreciate, finding its wailing, monophonic quarter-tones displeasing to ears more attuned to the Western harmonic system.

In the seclusion of this salon, stirred by sensuous rhythms and evocative harmonies, I would let my imagination run free and choreograph dance fantasies, leaping and gliding, twisting and turning. Roused by the colorful harmonies and evocative rhythms of Ketelby, I would arch and sway, dip and rise, my arms floating above and around, sometimes as a slave girl in the sultan's harem prancing through a fictitious Persian bazaar. Or, responding to the lilting melodies of Rimsky-Korsakov, I would twirl, slowly, slowly, as the beautiful Oriental princess who wins the heart and hand of the king. Then, with the rhythms coursing through me like liquid fire, I would quicken my pace and spin around and around in a frenzy worthy of a whirling dervish until I collapsed, breathless, on the carpeted floor.

The musical inspiration and the dance form were Western-Oriental, as were the Hollywood images that made up my fantasy bazaars and harems, more real to me than the real Oriental world outside our garden walls. Perhaps the real world was already too modern to fire my imagination; it was the romanticized Old World that caught my fancy. Or perhaps the real world held too much poverty, ignorance, and ugliness alongside its beauty and charm. The gossamer veils of Hollywood, seen through rose-tinted camera lenses, were far more romantic than the somber black chadors that represented reality. So, in spite of my familiarity with the real bazaars of southern Tehran, my longings and desires found expression through music and dance based largely on Western fantasy images of the East, images reinforced by my dance teacher, Mme. Cornelli, in whose choreography the Orient was represented as a magical land filled with flimsily clad dancing girls.

It would be some years before Mrs. Cook would introduce me to the beauty and richness of Persian tribal or village dances, urge me to seek in Persian miniature paintings and ancient figurines an authentic pose, hand movement, or head tilt. It would be under her tutelage that I would learn to extract ideas for dances from the *zurkhaneh,* in which ancient forms of Persian gymnastics were accompanied by intricate drumming and the verses of Ferdowsi; from the rapturous whirling of Sufi dervishes; from the circumambulation of the fire by Bakhtiari tribesmen in honor of the dead; and from all the pictorial imagery and spiritual insights of Persian poetry through the ages.

For the moment, however, Hollywood was my standard, movies my source of inspiration as, lost in an imaginary world, I danced to Ketelby's "In a Persian Market." It was ironic, indeed, that my introduction to Persia's rich cultural legacy would come not from my immediate environment but from an unexpected encounter with a strange American woman. But that was still in the distant future.

In a Persian Garden

In sleep an angel caused him to behold
The heavenly garden's radiancy untold,
Whose wide expanse, shadowed by lofty trees,
Was cheerful as the heart fulfilled of ease.
        —Nizami of Ganja, "Layla and Majnun"

OUR GARDEN was moderately sized and enclosed by walls that shut out the dirt and din of the outside world, creating for us children a tranquil oasis in which to play. Its centerpiece was an oval pool ringed with potted geraniums whose brilliant reds made a splash of color against the dusty flagstone of the adjoining terrace. Formerly used as a reservoir for household water, its function was now largely decorative. Four symmetrical *baghcheh* bordered the outer edge of the terrace with tiny boxwood in the European manner so much in vogue. On the smooth paved area we would ride our bikes or play hopscotch. When no one else was around, I would turn cartwheels on it or jump over the cracks with grand jetés, which I would practice over and over again.

The rest of the garden was an open space, paved with gravel and ringed with trees. The fashion of cultivating lawns that required frequent, wasteful watering had not yet taken hold. The legendary gardens of old had always been oases of shade trees, fountains, and running streams, with judiciously planted rosebushes gracing the edges of pools. The most famous were those built by Shah Abbas I in Isfahan in the sixteenth century, their reputations resting in part on the contrast they created with the harsh aridity of their surroundings. No wonder paradise appears in the Koran as a lush and verdant garden, so difficult to attain and so rewarding, and no wonder the walled-in green spaces that the Persians so revere

77

gave English its word for paradise, which derives from the ancient Persian term *pardis* for an enclosed garden: *pairidaeza,* which the Greeks modified to *paradeisos.*

The Persians like to refer to their country as "the land of the rose and the nightingale," for the rose remains the most popular flower cultivated in their gardens and the nightingale the most beloved bird. Down the centuries, the rose and the nightingale have appeared as metaphor for the beloved and the lover in countless permutations in the rich and varied poetry of this poetic people. Hafez, one of Iran's great lyric poets, has used the theme in a hundred different ways. The metaphor has become such an integral part of the language that a child who displays exceptional verbal dexterity is said to be *bolbol zaban*—that is, to have a tongue like a nightingale's—and in nursery-room parlance a male child's genitals are sometimes referred to as *bolbol.*

Our garden, however, had none of the elegance and beauty that inspired the outpourings of praise by the great poets. Mummy referred to the one nightingale that frequented our trees as "that damned nightingale," for she suffered from insomnia and its singing kept her awake at night. Our only rose bushes were a few scraggly ones that were much neglected and bloomed only sparsely. Except for these bushes and a couple of fragrant lilacs, the only other natural ornament was the ring of carmine geraniums around the pool, but the garden was peaceful and unpretentious, and we could play in it without worrying about trampling anything.

One summer Mummy tried to interest us in planting flowers, but Parviz and Iraj balked and refused to do "manual labor." That was servants' work, they argued. To me, however, it seemed magical that brilliant flowers might emerge from the nondescript zinnia seeds Mummy held in the palm of her hand, so I planted them and was delighted when they sprouted, but the heat of the summer was too intense, and my interest wilted along with the flowers.

There was nothing in my first gardening endeavor to indicate that years later, in another time and place, I would become an avid gardener and plant banks and banks of azaleas and rhododendrons on a terraced hillside in Virginia, with steps and meandering pathways leading to pools and fountains and little enclaves and shaded seats. For me and my brothers at this time in our lives the prevailing sentiment was laziness, and the overwhelming cultural attitude one of disdain for all physical work. Mummy, of course, being English and imbued with the Protestant ethic, knew that manual labor was honorable, but try as she did to combat local attitudes, she had lost the battle before she ever started.

We had few toys and fewer friends to play with, for distances between houses were great and transportation slow, and associating with the neighborhood boys who organized soccer games in the alley that fronted our house was out of the question. Once in a while Parviz and I would go to the movies together, but his tastes ran to dark horror films, so, because he controlled the purse, I saw more than my fair share of Dracula and Frankenstein movies, which gave me nightmares and intensified my fear of the dark.

Social events were largely confined to the extended family, and such visits were often impromptu. Every so often there would come an unexpected knock on the door, which I would run to answer with a joyous sense of expectation. *"Befarmaeed,* we are so pleased to see you. Welcome, welcome," we would greet visiting relatives, whose unannounced arrival automatically preempted any previous plans we might have had. After a decent interval Aunt Farangis or Aunt Edith or Aunt Manijeh or whoever else was visiting us would go through the motions of leaving, and Mummy, as custom prescribed, would urge them to stay for the midday meal. I would get to play with my cousins, Pari or Shirin or Firoozeh, with much of our time spent in the garden playing tag or leapfrog or jump rope. Or we would use pebbles to play "jacks" or build houses with cards, only to have them come tumbling down, which would make us collapse with laughter. We girls sometimes tried to climb trees or skip pebbles across the surface of the pool as our brothers did, but because these activities were difficult and we were given no encouragement to try harder at what were considered to be boys' games, we gave up easily.

Visitors were infrequent, so most of the time my brothers and I were thrown back on our own resources. We drew hopscotch lines on the flagstone, then rubbed them out with the soles of our shoes, or we played tag, calling and crying out, which would bring Daddy, a late sleeper, to the upper verandah to yell at us, "Be quiet! You know I'm trying to sleep!" Our compliance lasted for a few minutes, and then, of course, our voices rose once again. Parviz and I would often play our gramophone out on the verandah, but we once forgot to bring the records in out of the sun, and many of them were warped and ruined. Our games were often contrived from the raw materials at hand—twigs, stones, peb-

With my brothers Iraj *(left)* and Parviz *(center)* in our garden.

bles, acorns, and string. Cat's cradle, skittles, and bat the ball occupied us on many an afternoon. Much of the time we played with Suzanne, our thoroughbred Alsatian, who was our watchdog, companion, and playmate.

Unaware how unusual it was to have a dog as a pet, I simply took Suzanne's presence for granted, for she had been there as long as I could remember. Most pious Muslims, however, consider dogs to be *najess,* that is, unclean. Historically, dogs were a source of tension between Zoroastrians and Muslims, for Zoroastrians, in keeping with their respect for all animal life, were accustomed to keeping dogs as pets. In part in reaction to that custom Muslims deliberately fostered the idea of the dog as an unclean animal, and maltreating a dog became an outward sign of an "unbeliever's" true conversion to the Islamic faith. Hostility toward dogs became pervasive among Muslims.

But Suzanne was very much a part of our family, although the servants did not much like having her around. I would romp and play with her in the garden, never feeling any lack of companionship. I once made the mistake of imagining myself to be Lady Rowena and Suzanne to be my horse. I tried to ride her, sidesaddle, but she objected and refused to cooperate, yelping, throwing me off, nipping at my legs, and incidentally teaching me a lesson.

Every year she had a litter of six, seven, or eight wriggling, squealing little puppies no larger than a child's hand. It was from Suzanne that I learned "the facts of life." The first time I saw another dog trying to copulate with her, I thought they were fighting, for Suzanne was moaning and resisting as the other dog tried insistently to mount her. I thought she was in pain. To my astonishment, when I yelled at them and tried to shoo the male dog away, Mummy restrained me and made no attempt to separate them. "Leave them alone," she told me in a firm tone. Next came the swollen belly, the birth of the little puppies, blind at first, and then the engorged breasts and eight squirming little creatures vying for a free nipple and sucking away, while Suzanne lay patiently on her side. What information I managed to draw from this experience was rounded out by whispered discussions with schoolmates and friends.

Here in the garden Aunt Doris would link arms with me and kick up her heels as we skipped around each other, first in one direction and then another, or we would hold hands and alternately tap our toes and heels or simply go around in circles. Sometimes, when I was alone, I would pretend to be a whirling dervish and turn around and around until my head spun. Occasionally I would make necklaces of jasmine or forsythia blossoms, which brought out the "fairy princess" in me and prompted me to make up a "flower" dance. Once in a while I would lean over the edge of the pool so that I could see my reflection in it and wave my arms over my head in concert with the dancing nymph in the water.

Our lives moved at a leisurely pace, and I would often sit by the edge of the pool and read a book from our own fairly substantial home collection or from the school library. Later, when I was in my teens, the U.S. Information Service opened a library, providing a broader range of reading materials and filling me with wonder that such an institution actually lent books out to the public with the full expectation of having them returned. I read almost anything I could get my hands on—all the Tarzan and Oz books, but also Sir Walter Scott, Daphne du Maurier, Charlotte and Emily Brontë, William Shakespeare, Matthew Arnold, Charles Dickens, Oscar Wilde, John Steinbeck, and Ernest Hemingway. I also read Superman, Captain Marvel, and Popeye comic books, and I remember being impressed that American candy actually gave one energy—as the ad in the back of the comic declared—Hershey bars, if I am not mistaken.

I read so much that Mummy worried that I would strain my eyes, and Daddy became annoyed that I did little else. My copy of *A Child's Garden of Verses* was worn from use. Sometimes I would write little poems in a notebook I had for the purpose, taking my cue from Longfellow, and sometimes I would simply daydream. I was much given to daydreaming, so much so that the family teased me about it constantly, calling me Nes-Fes-Fes, *fes-fes* describing someone who dawdles and takes her time.

The most enjoyable hour in our garden was in the late afternoon, when, just as the sun's ferocity was finally abating, we would gather on the terrace for tea. A rosy glow, brushed with streaks of purple, fuchsia, or vermillion, would slowly spread over the sky as the sun slipped behind the craggy mountains. The entire populace of the city would come back to life after the afternoon siesta. Shop-keepers would undo the padlocks and pull up the shutters on store windows, while hawkers would once again bring their carts onto the main thoroughfares. Hordes of shoppers and strollers would fill the streets, bargaining, buying, doing errands, ambling, ogling each other, or merely enjoying the ambience and the cool of the evening until well after dark.

But before anyone went out, there was afternoon tea. To prepare the terrace and settle the dust Mashd Mamad first sprinkled it with water, which gave rise to a pungent earthy aroma and a sense of cool freshness. He set up a table and chairs, and brought out the fare. It was a time for us to gather around and talk or bicker or tease or argue, while enjoying hot bread and butter, with varieties of jams, and occasionally Russian piroshki or cream puffs or meringues. Sometimes Parviz and Iraj played pranks on me and on one memorable occasion paraded Suzanne onto the terrace wearing my new panties on her hind legs. I did not think it was funny, and Suzanne was not pleased, but Parviz and Iraj laughed at my discomfort and at the animal's hangdog expression and hobbled movements.

At the height of the summer, when sleeping indoors was no longer bearable, Mummy had the servants set up *takht* (wooden bed frames) in the graveled-over area of the garden. At night they laid thin mattresses and bedding over the wooden base of each bed and set up netting to protect us from the mosquitoes that would otherwise make it impossible to sleep outdoors. The beds were arranged in rows, dormitory style, the white gauze of the mosquito nets floating above us like eerie ghosts.

After dark it was luxuriously cool in the yard, and often, before falling to sleep, I would look up at the jewel-speckled canopy of the sky, where the brilliant stars were so large and close I felt I could reach out and pluck them. I would trace with my eye the Big Dipper, Little Dipper, and other constellations. Frequently, I saw a shooting star streaking through vast open spaces and made a wish, certain it would come true. When there was a full moon, it was so light I had trouble sleeping, so Parviz and I took turns telling each other stories, until Iraj yelled at us to keep quiet so he could get some sleep. At dawn, when the sun came up, harsh and bright, we emerged from the mosquito nets, one by one, and traipsed into the house, carrying our pillows, to crawl into our regular beds and try to sleep a little longer. By then the servants were already up and about and would roll the outdoor bedding up and put it away to protect it from the bleaching sun. Except for the wooden bed frames, the garden would look itself again.

In traditional Persian homes the garden pool was for special occasions transformed into a raised platform, called *takhteh-hosy,* on which a small group of hired musicians, actors, or dancers, known as *motreb,* would perform for the guests. Covered with wooden boards, spread with carpets, the pool became a sort of theater-in-the-round, the focal point for the evening's entertainment.

Only once did I ever see our pool covered in that manner, though. My parents were having a dinner dance and had a platform of wood placed over the pool to add dance space to the terrace. My memories of the event are marred by the scene that erupted between my parents.

As usual Daddy had had too much to drink, and his jealousy had been aroused because Mummy danced one too many times with the same good-looking English officer. Mummy was quite beautiful, and many men were moved to lavish their attentions on her. She was flattered, of course, and for her it was just a little harmless flirtation, but for Daddy it was an intolerable insult to his manhood and contrary to age-old Persian mores. He staggered unsteadily up to the dancing couple and yanked Mummy out of her partner's arms. "That's enough dancing for one night," he said gruffly. A silence came over the party as the other guests stopped dancing and looked at each other with embarrassment, wondering what to do. In a bellicose tone Daddy turned on the officer, "You can leave now," he said. "And don't come back!" The officer beat a hasty retreat, while Daddy pulled Mummy off the *takhteh-hosy* and pushed her into a chair on the terrace. Needless to say, she did not dance any more that evening, and the party broke up rather early.

In our home, we never hired *motreb* to perform for the guests; our methods of entertaining were much more Western. At the homes of relatives, however, I occasionally saw a *roo-hosy* performance, and I remember the one at Aunt Homa's wedding particularly well.

I must have been eight or nine years old. Aunt Homa was one of my father's younger sisters and was considered the most beautiful. She was marrying the only son of Arbab Goshtasb, a Zoroastrian patrician of great wealth whose other offspring were all daughters—six altogether. It was a grand affair, uniting the most eligible young scions of two of the most prominent families of the Zoroastrian community.

The *gavah-giri*—the formal exchange of nuptial vows, known as *'aqd* among Muslims—took place in the *ma'bad* in the afternoon. The table set before the bride and groom held the traditional mirror, in which in days gone by the couple would have seen each other for the first time, a custom newly interpreted as reflecting the truth of their vows. Two large candles set in ornately decorated candelabra softly lit the faces of the bride and groom, gently highlighting their youth and beauty. On the table were large bouquets of white flowers, bowls of seven dried fruits mixed with sweetened nuts, a bowl of pomegranates, and a copy of the holy Avesta.

Three *mobed* recited prayers and reminded the couple of their obligation to cultivate the land, to assist the needy, and to struggle daily to ensure the victory of good over evil. Burning incense enveloped the wedding party with its jasminelike scent. Custom dictated that out of modesty Aunt Homa not answer right away when asked if she would accept Fereydoon as her husband. After the third time she finally shyly answered yes. Seven witnesses observed the legal registration of the marriage. As Aunt Homa knelt, one of her sisters rubbed together two large cones of sugar over a white cloth held above her head by two other relatives to catch the sugar powder drifting down, symbolically infusing the marriage with sweetness.

The event was marked by a solemnity appropriate to a union that was meant to last a lifetime. The sacred numbers three and seven were repeated in the ritual, reminding the couple of the religious significance of the occasion. As usual it was Aunt Farangis who explained to me why everything was done in threes and sevens. "The sacredness of the number three," she said, "comes from Zoroaster's teachings about the three divisions of cosmic history: Creation, when Ahura Mazda created all material and spiritual life; Mixture, when Ahriman brought evil into the world, making it necessary for man to struggle against evil; and Separation, a time in the future when good will be separated from evil, when evil will be destroyed and men and women will live in eternal goodness and peace."

Her explanation of the sacredness of the number seven was a little difficult for me to grasp, but as best as I can remember, she said it came from Zoroastrian teachings about Ahura Mazda's evocation of six lesser divinities known as "Holy Immortals," who "mingled" with Ahura Mazda to form a heptad of divine beings with beneficent powers that they used to further the struggle of good against evil. "Together they created the world in seven stages, enacting the seven creations—stone, water, earth, plants, animals, man, and fire—all with the ultimate purpose of defeating evil."

The names of the young couple, too, resonated with historic significance. The groom, Fereydoon, was named after the legendary hero from the *Shah-nameh* who triumphed over the tyrant Zahhak, overthrowing his wicked rule. Aunt Homa was named for the juice used in temple rites that is obtained from pounding the stems of the ephedra plant—the mystical white liquid that resurrected bodies will drink at the end of time, making them immortal. The couple's family name, Goshtasb (Hystaspes in Greek), was that of Zoroaster's first convert, who became his royal patron and helped spread his teachings. Aunt Farangis was a goldmine of mythical and religious lore, and referred to the *Shah-nameh* with almost the same reverence with which she referred to the Avesta.

Sumptuous wedding festivities, the *aroosi,* were held that evening in the garden of the groom's family. The wooden boards over the pool were spread with colorful carpets, providing a central stage visible and audible from every corner of the garden. Dozens of naked electric light bulbs were strung throughout the yard, for both illumination and decoration. Straight-backed chairs had been set up, in front of which stood small tables piled high with fruits, nuts, and pastries. Dinner, as everyone knew, would not be served for several hours, and the guests were enjoying fruit and pastries, sipping tea and *sharbat,* and commenting on the appropriateness of the match.

As the bride and groom came through the living room onto the terrace, women whooped and ululated, breaking and augmenting the sound by clapping one hand rapidly over the mouth. Others clapped and cheered. Family and friends alike tossed *ab-shan* (oregano), *noql* (almond confections), and small silver coins over the heads and shoulders of the bride and groom, while children scrambled to find and eat the sweet white candy and keep the coins.

Aunt Homa, dressed in a full-length Western-style wedding gown, complete with bridal veil and train, looked stunningly beautiful, her face made up for the first time in her life. Her forehead along the hairline had not been plucked as was traditional because she had such a naturally high one, but her eyebrows had been slightly reshaped. The bridal chamber had been prepared, and the consummation of the marriage would take place right here in the home of the groom's parents. Evidence of the bride's virginity would be forthcoming in the morning.

For the evening's celebration the Goshtasb family had arranged some *roohosy* entertainment, and the guests seemed to find the *motreb* highly entertaining, laughing at their comic performances, watching their gyrations, and dancing to their music.

There was the traditional blackface performer, a *kaka siyah* who clowned around, poking fun at his master—a tradition dating back to the days when Ethiopians had been brought here as slaves. There were three male musicians and one female dancer who sang as she rattled and banged a tambourine. One man sat cross-legged on the floor, his nimble fingers rippling over the tight heads of finger drums, his palms and thumbs creating percussive whacks in extraordinarily intricate and diverse rhythms. His fingers moved so quickly they created a blur. Next to him stood a *tar* player and a violinist. As the intoxicating rhythms filled the garden, some little girls, younger than I, got onto the *takhtehhosy,* and started dancing there, arms held overhead, making me half wish I had the nerve to join them. Mother saw me watching and said, "Go on, you can do it, too." But of course I did not. I was too shy.

The musicians and dancer doubled as actors, and they put on several brief comic skits during the course of the evening. Their jokes were largely incomprehensible to me because I was too young to understand all the salacious innuendoes that everyone else seemed to find uproariously funny, and I did not know enough to comprehend fully the significance of the red handkerchief one of the men kept waving around. But I was intrigued by the pelvic gyrations of the woman dancer and amazed at how her breasts quivered as she shimmied her arms and shoulders. Occasionally one of the musicians would join in, dancing in front of her, hips suggestively thrusting forward and back.

Later, the guests danced to the repetitious beat. Men and women, young and old, took mincing steps as they circled their hips, their hands held aloft. The seated guests clapped their hands in time to the music and egged on the dancers, who clicked their fingers and gyrated. Young girls who had been sitting demurely, eyes lowered, rose at the urging of friends and relatives, and pulsed and shimmied in a most provocative manner. Some of the dancers, as was the custom, approached a seated person, arms spread out, and invited that person to join in. Several approached me, but I was embarrassed at their insistence and refused, although part of me desperately wished to get up on the *takhteh-hosy* and show off and be the center of attention. I remained seated, lifting my head and tchtching, in the Persian way of saying "no," declaring I did not know how to dance.

As I watched, bewitched by the sinuous movements, the images of lissome hip rotations and snaking arms buried themselves deep in my consciousness. They would emerge years later when I found myself repeating those very same movements on a gigantic wooden platform built in the garden of the American embassy. There, on a wooden stage much larger than a *takhteh-hosy,* with a thrust of the shoulder here, a lift of the hip there, and soft and fluidly snaking arms, I would perform a dance whose movements had their roots in the *roo-hosy* performances I had seen as a child.

Summer Escapades

[I]t should be a beautiful garden running with conduits of wine and milk and honey and water, and full of lovely women for the delectation of all its inmates.

—Marco Polo, *The Travels of Marco Polo*

SUMMERS IN TEHRAN cracked our skin and parched our throats. The heat sapped our strength, weakened our resolve, and made us listless and lazy. The trees that lined the *joob*s of the main avenues turned grey under a coating of dust, and the cool basement of our house was the only place that offered some relief from the relentless heat. Every noon, as the pitiless sun rose high in the sky, an eerie silence descended on the city, pierced only by the shrill buzz of cicadas. Shutters were pulled down and locked; the rattle and din of people, cars, and donkeys ceased; and the midday meal and siesta began.

We often escaped the worst of the summer heat by moving to higher elevations for a few months, and the summer following Aunt Homa's wedding we spent some memorable months in the Goshtasbs' garden. Because we were now family, we gladly accepted their invitation to enjoy the cool comfort of the considerable lands they owned in the foothills north of Tehran near the village of Vanak—which they also owned. The higher elevation and the abundance of leafy foliage made the air deliciously cool and bracing. Little did we imagine that the summer would eventually lead to a sealing of another relationship between our family and the Goshtasbs, one with considerable consequences for everyone.

The Goshtasbs' garden in Vanak was actually an extensive orchard of apple, peach, pomegranate, fig, and plum trees surrounded by fields of wheat. Like all

Persian gardens, it was enclosed by mud walls that in the summer were dotted with clinging but lifeless and hollow brown cicada shells. An open area at the center of the garden provided ample space for several tents, enough to accommodate a number of families. The Goshtasbs had already settled in, occupying a group of clustered tents. Fereydoon and Homa were away in Germany, where he was studying engineering, but his unmarried sisters were at Vanak, one of whom was particularly beautiful. Her name was Parvin. She was eight or nine years older than I—too great a gap for us to become close friends, yet small enough a difference for us to find some interests in common.

She had large black eyes rimmed with luxuriant eyelashes and jet-black hair that fell long and straight over her shoulders. I was flattered by her attentions and pleased that she would sometimes draw me aside for a chat. Steeped in a culture that places great value on the modesty of girls, she took every opportunity to praise my reticent behavior. "You behaved so well in front of our visitors the other day," she said. "You kept your eyes lowered and your skirt pulled down over your knees." And another time, patting me on the back to indicate her approval, "What a modest girl you are. You keep your voice low, and you don't speak to grown-ups until they first speak to you." All this approval of reticence, of course, was in sharp contrast to Mummy's efforts to instill in me a sense of boldness and assertiveness as well as a contempt for prudery.

Our tent was pitched near an enormous pool that reflected the grey, canvas structure in its murky surface. Although fed by spring waters, the pool's walls were covered with green algae. Rushes, harboring frogs and snakes, spiked up out of the water and swayed with the slightest ripple. Although I loved to swim, I found the pool spooky and kept my distance from it. Parviz and Mummy, on the other hand, sometimes ventured in, and occasionally Parvin would join them. Although Mummy did not know how to swim, she would brave the green waters in order to get some exercise. Clinging to the algae-covered edge of the pool, she would kick her legs for all she was worth. Because she did not own a bathing suit, she would go in wearing her underwear—another of the many acts for which the family criticized her. Except for the toothless old gardener and a couple of servants—who, in her mind, didn't count—there wasn't a soul to see her except her own children and the daughters of Arbab Goshtasb. Nevertheless, her behavior was a breach of norms that provided abundant material for gossip. Once again I found myself wishing Mummy wouldn't do such outrageous things and felt embarrassed when the dark rings of her nipples and the inverted triangle of her pubic hair started to show as her underwear got wet. I saw Parvin and her younger sister with their heads together, tittering and whispering behind cupped hands. I overheard the words *shameless* and *immodest,* and blushed. How I wished Mummy were not quite so unselfconscious about her body. I noticed how Parvin wore a swimsuit whenever she went in the pool and kept a large bath towel near at hand with which she quickly covered herself the minute she stepped out of the water.

Among the many Persian myths that tell of men spying from a distance on women bathing in rivers or streams, the most famous is the story of Manijeh, the Turanian beauty, whom Bijan spied on from afar. He later spoke soft words to her and set her "virgin passion aflame," as recounted in Ferdowsi's *Shahnameh.* Perhaps such myths spring inexorably from imaginations inflamed by a culture that keeps women's bodies cloaked and veiled and out of sight. Even though Mummy was then a thirtyish mother of four children rather than a Turanian beauty with "rosy cheeks, languorous eyes, and lips redolent of rose-water," and even though the servants and toothless old gardener were far from being "happy-starred warriors," her behavior was considered outrageous. Meanwhile, Daddy's uninhibited flirtation with the Goshtasb girls, in particular Parvin, was indulgently overlooked.

My days were spent reading or roaming the acres upon acres of fruit trees nearby, where I occasionally reached for a plum or a pear. Sometimes I stepped between the rows of cucumber plants and, searching under the leaves, found the tiniest, crispest cucumbers, which I picked and ate right there in the patch. My brothers and I had frequent stomachaches from eating so many plums and cucumbers or sore mouths and lips from eating too many figs.

Once in a while Mummy would send Parviz and me trudging across the plains to Vanak village to buy fresh eggs from the villagers. We would set out early in the morning with a basket and some small change. Passing through fertile fields, we would stop to watch as a man trudged behind a plough yoked to two emaciated oxen. He wore black cotton pants, with cloth *geevehs* but no socks on his feet, and a loose tunic that hung to midthigh and was caught at the waist with a belt. On his bowed head sat a brown felt hat. Intent on his work, he did not stop to wave to us. At other times we would linger to watch a man poking two oxen with a long stick as they drew his crude thresher along. Next to

him on the plank that served as a seat was a young boy. As the oxen monoto-
nously circled a pile of wheat and the thresher blades ground it up, another man
with a simple pitchfork kept drawing wheat out of the stack down into the path
of the blades. We would also pause to observe men winnow wheat, lifting the
precious grain with forks, separating the kernels into one pile, while pitching
the chaff into another.

The men did not own the land they were working, but provided the labor
for the estate. Like many wealthy landlords, the Goshtasb family owned numerous villages and countless tracts of land, but spent most of the year in the comfort of the capital city, far from their great landholdings. They provided the
machinery, tools, water, and seed for the laborers to work the land and make it
productive. The peasants, in exchange for their hard work, would get to keep
only a small fraction of the income derived from the sale of the crops, and most
landlords profited hugely from the arrangement. It was not until 1967, many
years later, that land reform under Mohammad Reza Shah broke up the great
holdings of such prosperous, often absentee landlords and for the first time gave
peasants the deeds of ownership to the lands they worked. But at the time of
which I write the peasants were, for all practical purposes, feudal tenants.

Arriving at Vanak village, Parviz and I would wander through its dusty lanes
and knock on doors of homes to ask if the occupants had any eggs to sell. Narrow wooden doors opened to reveal one- or two-room mud hovels fronted by
miniature dirt courtyards, where a couple of scrawny chickens scratched for
food, clucking and pecking amidst a number of young children who had flies
swarming around their eyes. A large date sometimes hung from a string around
the neck of the youngest—a sort of pacifier or teething ring. Others wore
amulets with prayers imprinted on them to ward off the evil eye, that mystical
force often blamed for sickness, injury, and death. Some had *salak*s on their faces
or scalps—large sores that oozed a thick yellow discharge and attracted swarms
of black flies.

The women were unveiled, their hair covered by multicolored scarves knotted under the chin or looped around the neck and flung over one shoulder.
Their long-sleeved dresses, made of brightly colored prints, dropped to midcalf
over long, loose cotton trousers, invariably black. Some were happy to make a
little money and gladly shooed the chickens off their nests, reaching in to pull
out eggs that were still warm to the touch. Others were annoyed at our intrusion

and answered crossly that they did not have any eggs for sale. Most of the time, however, they greeted us with a courteous *"Befarmaeed,"* even though it was highly unusual for strangers to be knocking on their doors. Parviz and I, tutored by a mother who was not averse to doing unusual things, would continue from door to door until our basket was full—or until our money ran out. We would then carefully and triumphantly carry home our precious cargo.

Some years later my memories of Vanak helped inspire a village dance, stripped, of course, of the poverty and facial sores, but colored by the dignity, simplicity, and harmony of village life. Twenty years after Parviz and I went on our egg-buying excursions, however, there was not a trace of Vanak village left because Tehran expanded and spread northward, devouring open spaces and villages alike in an unprecedented building boom that created an expanse of concrete and steel out of a once-bucolic landscape.

Although neither Mummy nor Daddy knew how to swim, they made sure that all of us learned how. When I was seven or eight, they signed me up for swimming classes at one of the pools that had recently opened in Tehran. Situated in an expansive garden with majestic trees casting welcome shade on the outer rims of various playing fields, the Amjadieh sports complex was enormous. So were its twin pools. Tiled in blue and equipped with diving boards of various heights, one pool was reserved for swim team practice, and the other was open to the public.

I arrived for swimming lessons to find that I was the only girl in a class of six or seven boys. At first abashed, I quickly adapted to the situation and found that I could readily outswim any of them. The coach was solicitous and taught us well, but, following the norms of the society, he believed that the crawl was "just for boys" and that the only swim strokes girls should learn were the breaststroke and sidestroke, so those were the ones he taught me.

Once I knew how to swim, I would frequently go by myself, with Parviz, or with friends to slice through the magnificent lanes of the pool. Sometimes we would go *en famille* for a picnic, and we children swam, while Mummy and Daddy relaxed in the shade. Acquiring a tan was not something to which we aspired because we considered nothing more desirable than having fair skin, but, what with the scorching sun and cloudless skies of Tehran's summers as well as our skin's inclination to tan easily, it was a losing battle. I would envelop myself in large towels and tried bleaching my skin with yogurt, but neither approach did much good, and inevitably by summer's end I was several shades darker.

One summer a great swimming meet was held in the enormous Manzarieh pool situated high up in the mountains. A special grandstand at the top of the bleachers had been built for the Shah and Queen Fawzieh, from where they could watch the competitions. Fawzieh was the first of the Shah's three wives and the sister of King Faroukh of Egypt. She was a diminutive brunette of great but "cold" beauty, as Mummy used to say. Unhappy in the king's palace surrounded by court intrigue and far from home, she had built an impenetrable shield of reserve around herself. The marriage did not last long.

To be appearing in front of royalty was a great honor. Daddy made it clear he expected me to win the race. "We all know you are a good swimmer," he said. "Go out there and *win* this race." Fathers, of course, did not accompany their children to such events in those days; they had more important things to do. But he always expected a detailed report of my activities as well as of my school work, and I knew he would expect a report on the swimming race.

I had practiced and prepared for the event with the boys and was put out, on the day of the competition, at being separated from this familiar group and placed, instead, with a group of girls—all total strangers. The man in charge handed me a swimsuit that matched those of the other girls and instructed me to put it on and join them. I did so reluctantly.

We lined up at the edge of the pool on elevated platforms and waited for the pistol shot that would send us headfirst into the water and headlong into the race. I swam hard and fast, but after a few minutes, lifted my head and saw no one around me. I turned and saw the rest of the group trailing far behind. I realized I was going to win this race easily. I felt sorry for the other girls because they were *so far* behind me. I wanted to win the competition, but not by half a pool's length! So I slowed my pace to allow the others to catch up a little. I did not intend to let them overtake me, just to lessen the gap, but I miscalculated, and suddenly out of the corner of my eye I saw one of the girls almost abreast of me. Spurred by the threat of being overtaken, I started swimming fast and furiously, but I had lost too much time, and what should have been an easy win ended instead in a tie. All the way home I worried about what Daddy would say. To my relief he was delighted that I had done so well and gave me a big hug. I did not tell him that I had practically given the race away.

Another summer my parents rented a small house in Dezashoob, located right at the base of the Alborz Mountains. An aggregate of walled gardens and magnificent villas, many with private swimming pools, Dezashoob offered the wealthy an ideal place to spend their summers, with its high elevation, spectacular mountain views, bracing air, sunny days, and cool nights.

My parents, of course, were not wealthy, nor did they own an elegant villa, but they were able to rent an extremely modest two-room house with a minuscule yard where we would spend the summer. The house was within walking distance of the Tajrish bazaar, a miniature covered marketplace where we wandered through dusty alleys to buy bread, produce, and other necessities. Mashd Mahmad and Batool stayed behind in our Tehran house to look after it and to protect it from burglary, so we had no help, and Mummy did her own shopping, taking us children along.

Narrow and winding, the lanes of the Tajrish bazaar were lined with small stores. Far smaller and more modest than the Tehran bazaar, it had no piles of carpets or gold or silver or hand-tooled copper or leather goods. The shops met the everyday needs of a poorer clientele. At the entrance of one store sat a wizened old man on a stool, a felt cap on his head, fingering his prayer beads. At another, a young man, several days' stubble on his face, pulled out bolts of fabric for his customers, most of them heavily veiled women. Nearby, large open sacks of lentils, split peas, rice, and other staples almost blocked the doorway to the grocer's, and large glass jars of turmeric, saffron, cinnamon, and dried limes lined the shelves inside.

This bazaar was where housewives brought their copper pots to have them refurbished with a new layer of tin. A shriveled wisp of a man squatted near a large copper pot, turning it rapidly. Dipping a cloth into a small pan of what looked like melted silver, heated from below by a small gas flame, he daubed a thin layer of liquid tin over the pot as he turned it, smoothing it out evenly all over. A few doors farther down, another man was fitting a piece of china where it belonged in a broken bowl, piecing it together like a jigsaw puzzle, then gluing and clamping it.

Just inside a bend in the alley, a young boy sat surrounded by a growing pile of green walnut hulls, which he split open, deftly separating the outer green fuzz from the hard brown inner shell with a sharp knife. His hands were stained a dark brown. The walnuts would be dried for sale or sold as a snack while still fresh to the Thursday afternoon crowds that strolled on Pol-e Tajrish, the Tajrish Bridge, just outside the bazaar. The green hulls, too, would be used—along with pomegranate skins and cochineal bugs—to create the natural dyes that accounted for the lustrous colors of the famed Persian carpets before chemical dyes made their appearance.

Here in Dezashoob there were few itinerant vendors, and we purchased most of our food in the bazaar. The narrow lane suddenly opened onto a large central atrium, where fresh fruits and vegetables were piled high on carts and in stalls. Oranges, plums, and pink-flushed apricots competed with pears, peaches, and sour cherries for our attention. Green beans, purple eggplants, and red tomatoes vied with radishes, cucumbers, and row upon row of fragrant herbs tied in bunches. Mummy bargained hard for everything.

In the butcher shops just outside the atrium hung carcasses of lambs covered with flies. The butcher would reach up and lift a carcass off a large metal hook, slam it onto a large wooden board, and carve off a piece according to Mummy's specifications. Next door, ducks hung by their feet, their plucked necks looking long and lean, while live chickens cackled in a crowded pen nearby. Not far away a steaming cauldron of *seerabi* (sheep-entrail stew) permeated the air with its pungent aroma.

Nearby, an *imamzadeh* attracted the pious and the desperate, who brought their prayers and sometimes their sick or their handicapped, hoping for a miracle. Down the middle of the narrow lane a man with nothing but stumps for legs coasted along on a wooden board set on wheels. He navigated with his hands on the ground. He begged, and sometimes Mummy would give him two rials. By the time our shopping was done, each of us had a string bag, full and heavy. These bags would feel even heavier as we made our way home.

Sometimes if we had more than we could comfortably carry, Mummy would hire a porter. Attached to his back with wide straps, like a knapsack, was a wedge-shaped block covered with coarse carpeting. Atop this block sat a large basket in which he carried his customer's purchases. For just a few rials he would carry them all the way home for us.

The Tajrish bazaar changed little through the years and remained surprisingly unscathed by metropolitan expansion. Although eventually some of the stores acquired refrigeration for their dairy products and other innovations took root, it managed to maintain its soul and character intact. Eventually, however, it was struck by natural disaster. A terrible flood crashed down the mountainside, smashing and sweeping away everything in its path, engulfing part of the bazaar and its unfortunate occupants in a torrent of water. In a visit to the Tajrish bazaar many years later, however, I found it restored and still standing. Although a profusion of jewelry shops and the overhead flapping of prominently displayed blue jeans and T-shirts had slightly altered its character, it still retained much of its simplicity and authenticity.

One end of the market opened onto Pol-e Tajrish, which was not a bridge at all, but a great square built across a riverbed, where we often joined crowds of strollers milling around in the fresh cool of the evening. Here hundreds of families congregated after the sun went down. Behind the square, the mountains rose, jagged, harsh, and imperious. Huge boulders marked its ascent. A single road led up the mountainside at a sharp incline. A few venturesome souls would start making their way up its paved surface, but seldom got very far before they felt winded and turned back. Pol-e Tajrish was not for hiking or mountain climbing, but for passing a few leisurely hours. Hiking had its own time and place—but definitely not in the big square, where high heels and elegant fashion prevailed. Some years later my future husband and I sat holding hands on one of the big boulders of Pol-e Tajrish one evening, the lights of Tehran twinkling off in the distance, and made plans to get married and then go to the United States for further education. At the time it seemed like an impossible dream, but the beauty of Pol-e Tajrish was conducive to dreaming impossible dreams.

At that elevation there was always a fresh breeze blowing. All around the square vendors parked their carts, and as a tempting aroma of charcoal-broiled corn on the cob filled the air, they hawked their ware, calling out with a loud singsong, *"Ballal, ballal-e dagh daram."* Other vendors sat on a stool next to a gas-fueled lamp selling walnuts fresh out of the shell or fresh almonds, whose crunchy texture and marvelous flavor were enhanced by the brevity of the time they were in season. Still others would sell us dried chickpeas or mixed nuts and dried figs, which they would hand to us wrapped in small cones made out of old magazines or newspapers. Years later American-style popcorn was sold alongside these traditional snacks.

One of the things Parviz and I enjoyed doing on these outings on Pol-e Tajrish was looking through the peepholes of the *shahr-e farang,* a portable nickelodeon. For a few *shahi,* a paltry sum, the owner of the contraption turned a crank that set colorful pictures of Europe rotating slowly before our eyes. Sumptuously luxurious palaces, swans with graceful necks in shaded pools, verdant pastures, and brilliantly colorful flowers flitted before our eyes. Parviz and I had, of course, been to Europe and had access to books and magazines with beautiful illustrations, so it was not so much the pictures themselves that were the attraction, but the lure of peeping through the holes to see what we could see. Years later my own children were equally enchanted when their father made them a *shahr-e farang* out of an oblong shoe box and magazine pictures glued together into a long scroll wound around a wooden dowel. They squealed with delight as they took turns peeping through the holes while he turned the pictures, one after another.

Parviz and I had no idea, of course, that the cinema and modern theaters were even then supplanting the *shahr-e farang,* as they had already supplanted so many indigenous entertainments, such as the *khaymeh sayeh-gardoon,* a shadow play in which wooden or tin forms were silhouetted against a large cloth; the *khaymeh shab-bazi,* marionettes; or *rooband-bazi,* a theater of masks, in which animals or humans suffer conflict and misfortune, only to end up triumphing over adversity. Watching the slowly turning pictures of the *shahr-e farang,* we could not know that in just a few years it, too, would disappear.

At the other end of the bazaar stood another huge square lined with small rug and carpet shops, shoe shops, headquarters of bus lines, and a pharmacy. That summer in Dezashoob we had reason to be grateful for the presence of the pharmacy, for Parviz broke his wrist when a slender limb at the very top of a tree he was climbing snapped under him. He must have been eleven years old. With no transportation at hand other than Kaveh's stroller we somehow managed to wheel Parviz to the pharmacy in Tajrish square.

In those days the practice of setting bones was not limited exclusively to physicians, for many butchers and pharmacists were highly skilled in the art. The Tajrish pharmacist examined Parviz's wrist and set the bone with a quick jerk that made my brother scream. Then with two smooth pieces of wood and bandages the pharmacist created a splint and immobilized the wrist.

In retrospect it might have been best to leave well enough alone. At least Mummy seemed to think so. She had developed a healthy respect over the years for folk medicine and traditional cures, and was well versed in the use of medicinal herbs, concocting some at various times to treat everything from diarrhea to allergies. At least once a month she would give us enemas "to clean out" our insides, and whenever I had an attack of hives, she would give me some foul-tasting *sheer-khesht*. Happily, she was not given to using leeches, but once, when I had a bad bronchial cough, she brought in a local healer to "cup" my back over Daddy's objections. Throwing a match into a small glass cup, the healer rapidly placed it and then five others on my back, where the burning matches created a vacuum that drew my flesh up into the cups, with a soothing sensation of warmth. I was terrified that the lighted matches would burn me, but, of course, they did not, and the method seemed to work, for my cough cleared up.

Daddy, ironically, believed only in modern medicine, which sometimes had the unexpected consequence of being too much of a good thing. When I was about eight, I had a persistent light cough and sniffle caused by a postnasal drip. He took me to the best ear, nose, and throat doctor in town—a German physician who strapped a rubber bucket below my chin and proceeded to remove my adenoids—without benefit of anesthesia. Needless to say, I was crying as the blood gushed from my mouth and filled the bucket, at which point he picked up the offending adenoid he had just removed and said, "Why are you crying? Is this what you are crying for?" And he dangled the piece of raw meat before my eyes. After days of pain and suffering I continued to sniffle and cough. Much later we learned that my symptoms were all due to an allergy.

After the pharmacist set Parviz's broken wrist, Daddy insisted on taking Parviz to a medically trained physician. The doctor x-rayed the wrist, reset it, and put it in a cast. That night Parviz was moaning with pain. His hand was swollen and blue, for the cast was too tight and had to be removed. Slowly, laboriously, in the middle of the night, the doctor slit it open on one side with a razor blade while Parviz screamed. Weeks later the wrist emerged from a second cast decidedly crooked and had to be broken and reset for a third time. In the end Parviz's wrist remained permanently misshapen.

Such mishaps were a normal part of growing up in that part of the world. One mishap I had, however, was most unusual. I was just three years old, and Parviz was four. We had gone *en famille* to spend a hot summer's day with my parents' friends the Hariris, who owned an enormous garden in Shemran, a suburb at the foot of the mountains. It was a pleasantly shady place, full of fruit trees of various kinds. A water channel flowing under it provided an abundant supply of water for the trees.

The arid plains of Iran have been irrigated for centuries by an ingenious underground canal system made of *qanat*s that carry water from the mountains for miles to the cities and villages below. These subterranean channels tap underground aquifers at depths of fifty to three hundred feet. Dug into the alluvial fans that drop from the slopes of the mountains to the valleys, they range from one to eighteen miles in length and at regular intervals have openings, or "mouths" (*darkand*), where vertical shafts leading down from ground level to the conduit below provide access to its waters. Viewed from a plane flying overhead, the mouths of the shafts, regularly spaced and with a circular mounding of dirt around the edges, look like rows of anthills. The earliest written references to them date from the eighth century B.C.

Every mile or so an opening has steps leading down to the underground channel, enabling people along the route to tap into its life-giving waters. Villages often grow around such openings. Sometimes a large landholding contains one, as the Hariris' garden did, providing a constant and reliable supply of fresh water from the subterranean level, where it does not evaporate even in the hot, dry summer air. The vaulted roofs of the conduits measure approximately three feet across and five feet at the highest point, just high enough for a child to stand up in. *Qanat* and well cleaners known as *moqanni* keep the roofs of the channels repaired and the streams clear of silt and debris and other blockage. Building the *qanat*s and keeping them clean are laborious and expensive tasks, skills for which the Zoroastrians are particularly noted. Collapsing roofs are a great danger to a *moqanni,* who always says a prayer before entering a *qanat* and refuses to work on one if he thinks it is an unlucky day. Seen from the bottom of the access steps, the water channel looks like a covered stream, the bed paved with loose stones and rocks, and the vaulted ceiling made of either hard soil or well-packed coarse conglomerate, but occasionally of soft soil held in place with baked clay hoops. Back then the aggregate length of all the *qanat*s in Iran exceeded one hundred thousand miles, providing 75 percent of all the water used. Before its piped water system was installed in the 1950s, Tehran alone had thirty-six *qanat*s, all flowing from the foothills of the Alborz Mountains eight to sixteen miles away. These are now diverted to agricultural use. Nowadays numerous cities and villages have piped water and no longer rely on *qanat*s, but in rural areas these conduits still flow.

We had gone to the Hariris' for Friday lunch, Friday being the Muslim Sabbath. We and our hosts sat cross-legged around a *sofreh* on a carpet enjoying a sumptuous midday dinner. Diverse dishes of *khoresht* and *pollo* covered the table-cloth, along with the traditional flat breads, yogurt, and *sabzi,* all followed by mountains of luscious fruits in season—apricots, peaches, plums, and cherries. After we had eaten, the servants cleared the *sofreh* and set up a card table and chairs for the grown-ups to relax over a game of cards. Parviz and I wandered through the garden, where I plucked cherries from the trees and hung them over my ears, pretending they were earrings, while he climbed to the highest branches and bounced up and down while taunting me for not daring to climb that high.

As Mummy told it, she was deeply engrossed in the card game when Parviz came running up to her, laughing, "Ha ha ha, I pushed Nesta into the hole." Mummy did not pay much attention, thinking he was joking or just trying to get her attention. "Don't be silly," she said, "Now run along and play with Nesta, and keep an eye on her." But he kept pulling at Mummy's skirts and insisting with glee bordering on hysteria that he had pushed me into a hole. She put her cards down and looked around to see where I could be and suddenly realized that indeed I was nowhere to be found. Her sense of panic increasing every moment, she followed Parviz, who kept repeating that he had pushed me into the hole, while pointing toward the *qanat* opening. By now all the grown-ups were distraught and questioning him. He led them to the opening, climbed down the steps, and, peering up with a by now anxious smile on his face, pointed with his chubby hand to the swiftly flowing stream. "We came down here to splash in the water," he said, "And I just gave her a tiny push. She fell in."

Mummy and Daddy quickly sent for the *moqanni* to search for me in the *qanat*. Descending into the subterranean channel, he followed its course some distance downhill, but still could not find me, saying the current was particularly strong at that point and that I must have been washed downstream. With Mummy's and Daddy's anxiety increasing each passing minute, a search party rushed to the next *darkand,* a kilometer or two away, hoping against hope to catch me there. I can still hear the wonder and relief in Mummy's voice whenever she retold the tale. "We found you at the next *darkand*, all balled up, caught behind a large boulder," she said. "You were bruised and unconscious, and had swallowed a lot of water." Mercifully, I have absolutely no recollection of the event.

Caravan

O tentsman, haste, and strike the tent, I pray!
The caravan's already under way;
 The drummer sounds already the first drum;
 Their loads the drivers on the camels lay.
 —Ahmad Abul-najm Manuchehri,
  exordium to *Qasida*

MUMMY AND DADDY both suffered from aches and pains in the joints. They called it rheumatism and were firm believers in the effectiveness of hot mineral waters for curing such vague and uncertain maladies. Whenever they could, they arranged to go to Ab-e Garm, a remote village high in the mountains, where the warm sulphurous waters had a reputation for being both malodorous and restorative. The mineral-laden muds had long been known for their rejuvenating qualities and were used by women to recapture their youth and beauty.

Such trips required much preparation because we had to take everything we might possibly need for two to three months of camping. There was no motor road to Ab-e Garm then, only trails, and we traveled by mule and donkey caravan, our equipment piled onto the backs of the sturdy animals. We would be able to buy bread, meat, and fresh vegetables in the nearby village, but we had to take large tents, sleeping cots, bedding, linens, towels, camping stoves, cooking utensils, clothing, books, games, dry-food supplies such as rice and beans, and medicine. The trip took several days, and we needed ten mules and donkeys to carry our belongings.

Our first trip to Ab-e Garm was an extended family venture. Together with my cousin Pari's family we were going to spend the entire summer in the cool upper reaches of Mount Damavand. The day of our departure was a busy one for Mummy and Aunt Doris. They supervised the servants' packing of the equipment, making sure nothing vital was left behind, and saw to it that everything was strapped securely into place. The servants would stay behind to take care of the house, and my parents would hire villagers to help with the work once we arrived in Ab-e Garm.

Our equipment was loaded, and each family member was helped up onto a mule, where we all sat astride a bulging saddlebag. The muleteers gave a heave and a boost along with a *"Ya-Allah,"* guiding our feet into the stirrups. I felt peculiarly self-conscious sitting up on top of a mule. Not used to looking down at the world from such a great height, I felt exposed and slightly ridiculous. Actually, a little girl atop a loaded mule was not much of a novelty in that time and place, so nobody paid much attention, although for me it was a new experience. We proceeded along the edge of the major highway leading north of the city, where we met my Aunt Manijeh and her family.

Our combined caravan was an impressive one, totaling perhaps twenty animals. They ambled along single file, while the muleteers walked alongside and prodded the burdened creatures, urging them on with a poke to the haunch or a loud *cluck-cluck* followed by an abbreviated *"yallah."* Once north of the city, the traffic thinned, and we passed long expanses of low mud walls that hid from view all but a glimpse of the upper stories and tops of the trees of elegant villas and the beautiful gardens behind them.

We passed through stretches of foothills where we rode in the shade of tree-lined streams, whose rushing waters lulled us into a dreamy enjoyment of the majestic scenery unfolding before us. Several times our way was obstructed by flocks of fat-tailed sheep tended by lonely shepherds. Some of the sheep had splotches of bright orange on their fleece where their owner had dyed them with henna, demonstrating either an artistic touch or a belief in the protective powers of the herb. The shepherd herded them across the path, using a large stick to prod them in the right direction. As a practical matter, they had the right of way, for there was no hurrying them. Our caravan came to a stop, and we waited.

When the road finally cleared, we started the upward climb. The surroundings grew more barren, rocky, and rugged, and we passed the first of several waterfalls. A torrent coursed out of a narrow gorge to fall straight down from a dizzyingly high precipice. It crashed onto huge boulders hundreds of feet below, shooting magnificent spray into the air. Wild shrubs, fed by the water, clung tenaciously to the rock facade, seemingly defying gravity—testament to the skills of a master landscape architect. When the caravan stopped to let the animals drink and rest, we children headed straight for the pool of icy cold water foaming and swirling around the rocks. We caught our breath as we waded in; our feet tingled so much we could not bear to stand still, so we jumped around and screamed and laughed as we splashed and dunked each other.

As we continued our climb, the trail narrowed, and the sun bore down on us with increasing harshness. Mummy and all the other women wore broad-brimmed straw hats. The men were bareheaded, except for the muleteers, who wore black felt hats and walked alongside the animals, moving back and forth the length of the winding line, prodding here, poking there, and occasionally tugging at the harness of a recalcitrant mule. The men's feet, little protected by their cloth *geeveh,* were so hardened to the rough terrain that they leaped easily from one craggy rock to another. They ate little and rested even less. Their baggy shirts and cotton trousers flapped loosely against their frames. Exposure to the sun and wind had parched their faces into wrinkled leather. I felt sorry for them and guilty at riding while they walked, but I kept such foolish thoughts to myself, for it was well known that man's condition was ruled by the accident of one's birth and that there was nothing one could do to change one's *qesmat.*

As we climbed higher and higher, the trail grew ever more treacherous and steep. Hardly wide enough for a man to walk on, it hugged the side of the mountain from which it had been hand chipped many years ago. Below us spread a gaping chasm, and I fearfully clutched the saddle as I saw my mule's hooves send loose stones bouncing down the mountainside. As far as my eye could see, range after range of mountains thrust their massive peaks upward, as if ripping apart the sky. They seemed to mock our puny efforts to scale their heights. The brilliant blues and reds of the saddlebags added splotches of color to the brown landscape, complementing the bright blue beads draped on the harness and across the brow of each mule and donkey to protect them from the evil eye. The mules staggered under their heavy loads and occasionally resisted by slowing down or coming to a full stop and refusing to budge. Then the muleteers yanked on the reins and beat the mules over the head, all the while cursing

On the way to Ab-e Garm: spectacular mountains as far as the eye can see.

and swearing. "May God strike you dead, you son of a dog" was one of the milder imprecations hurled at the unheeding creatures.

The carpeting of the saddlebags chafed my legs as I sat astride the mule, but that was the least of my concerns. I was afraid that the beast would crush my leg against the cliff side or go hurtling down into the abyss, carrying me with it. I tried to avert my eyes from the steep incline below and to keep them fixed on the summit of Mount Damavand as Mummy had told me to do. It was covered with snow, even in the summer, and made a conveniently visible landmark. Every time my mule stumbled, I clung to the reins and repeated to myself, "Mules are sure-footed animals and never fall." I had heard Mummy say this, and I found it reassuring to repeat. I had trouble staying awake, for we did much of the traveling very early in the morning and late into the night so as to avoid the intense heat of the midday sun. A couple of times, I dozed off in my saddle and woke up with a jolt, clutching at the reins to keep myself from falling off. A full moon lit up the trail, casting an eerie light on mules and riders, now a row of dark silhouettes against a broad ribbon of silver—a spectral caravan like the one described by the poet Sa'di, who said: "O caravan of life, go slowly, slowly."

From time to time, we stopped at the teahouse of a small village perched in isolation on a stone ledge that jutted out from the mountains. Here, seemingly at the very summit of the world, we ordered hot tea—although these teahouses are known as *qahveh-khaneh* (coffeehouses), linguistic testament to days long gone when coffee was the national drink. We also had fresh bread, feta cheese, and dates, then rested our tired bodies on flea-infested bedding rolled out on the floor. The mules and donkeys drank from a nearby stream. Clustered together in the shade of some trees they ate hay, while the muleteers checked for loose horseshoes before attending to their own needs.

We were relieved when Ab-e Garm finally came into view. The villagers greeted us warmly. Our arrival was a happy event for them, for we were a large group and would provide income in return for their help with chores and securing provisions. Of course, they would also collect fees for our use of the mineral waters. Several men helped set up our tents on a gentle slope on the outskirts of the village. They helped unload the pack animals, set up the cots in rows, and fueled the kerosene lamps and camping stoves. We had six cots under one canvas roof for our family, each covered with a coarse brown wool blanket. My cousins, aunt, and uncle shared another huge tent.

On many evenings we children would play Snakes and Ladders or Monopoly or Pacheesi. We often played cards on Parviz's cot, and sometimes, when he realized he was losing the game, he would yank the blanket off, sending the cards flying in all directions and putting an end to our game. But what we enjoyed most of all was sitting around the campfire telling stories. We would take turns, and I would sometimes fall asleep with images of scorpions and tarantulas invading my dreams because these creatures were the favorite subjects of Parviz's tales. Every night before climbing into my cot, I would gingerly pull back the covers and check for scorpions.

Pythons, although not indigenous to Iran, also penetrated my slumbers, for my cousin Kitty would tell us fantastic stories of the snakes she had encountered when visiting Parsi relatives in Bombay. Some years earlier her mother, who was pregnant with my cousin Pari at the time, had woken up from an afternoon nap to find a python curled on her stomach. My aunt had lain frozen with fear, not daring to move or scream, until the python slithered away without harming her.

Kitty was a gifted story-teller, able to hold her audience in rapt attention. It was she who first introduced me to the epic myths of Ferdowsi, the great tenth-century poet, and I could hear the pride in her voice as she emphasized that his best-known work, the *Shahnameh,* is based largely on Zoroastrian mythology. My favorite tales were of heroic Rostam's victorious encounter with the evil *div* Akvan. But most of all I was moved by the account of Rostam's ill-starred battle with his own son, Sohrab, whom he slew tragically without knowing their relationship. I listened wide-eyed to the adventures of Khosrow Parviz and Shirin; the romance of Manijeh and Bijan; the tragic deaths of Siyavush and of the wise and benevolent king, Kay Khosrow. In every tale I encountered the names of my relatives, for my brothers, father, uncles, aunts, cousins, grandfather, and many other relations carried the names of their mythical ancestors.

Some evenings the grown-ups would take turns reciting poetry in a contest of memory known as *mosha'ereh*. Daddy would usually start the game, reciting two lines. Kitty or some other family member would take up where he left off, starting her recitation with lines that began with the last letter of the last word Daddy had recited, and so it went, each participant taking turns. I would listen with rapt attention, amazed at how well everyone knew their poetry, how easily they could come up with apt lines. Some evenings they would take auguries from a book of poems by Hafez, whose words were then interpreted as predicting the future—happiness or disaster or love or success. It took much coaxing and threatening to get us children to go to bed.

In the morning the sun rose early, waking us with its intensity. But no matter how early we awoke, the village girls were already outside our tents with baskets of freshly picked raspberries, thick fresh cream, and hot bread from the village bakery. Two of them would stay to help Mummy prepare the elaborate midday dinner. Cooking on camp stoves presented no difficulties for her because it was the same equipment she used in our kitchen at home, but preparing the meals was nevertheless a long and tedious task. Fortunately, the girls were young and strong and accustomed to working hard. They would carry water from a nearby stream in pails fashioned from discarded petrol tins. They believed that running water was always clean, but Mummy wasn't taking any chances, so she boiled the water we used for drinking. Neither of the girls could read or write. That they were not already married probably meant that they were under twelve years of age, although back in those days some village girls were married off as young as nine and ten. I sometimes watched them as they worked and tried a couple of times to make eye contact with them and smile, but they had been trained to accept their destiny, to mistrust strangers, and to keep their station in life. They avoided looking directly at me.

Mummy bought freshly slaughtered lamb and occasionally a chicken from the village butcher. We ate as well there, high in the peaks of Damavand, as we did at home: Mummy prepared fancy rice dishes, including my favorite—*istan-bolli pollo*—made with fresh tomatoes, braised lamb, and green beans, spiced with cinnamon and cumin. By village standards our cooking equipment was elaborate, our meals abundant. The villagers did their cooking in clay or copper pots over open fires. Their daily fare was *ab-goosht,* a thick soup of garbanzo beans, yellow split peas, a few potatoes, onions, and sometimes a lean bone added for flavor. They would eat this meal with flat bread, which they broke into the soup, adding bulk as well as flavor.

The houses of Ab-e Garm, less prosperous than those of Vanak village, had no enclosed courtyards, and family life spilled over into the scraggly lanes of the village. I could see women stirring *ab-goosht* over a fire, then turning to rock a swaddled baby to sleep in an improvised cradle that consisted of nothing more than a large cloth hung between two trees like a hammock. Toddlers played in the dust nearby. I felt a deep sadness come over me at seeing how impoverished they were. I pondered how some people were born to fortune and others to misfortune. I knew, of course, that there was nothing to be done about it, although I wished mightily that something *could* be done.

There were two *hamams* in Ab-e Garm—one for men and the other for women and children. They were easily recognizable by the large red cotton wraps drying on clotheslines strung outside in the sun and by the glass spheres on the roofs that allowed light into the interior. A matronly attendant sat in the entrance chamber of the women's bathhouse. Next to her was a table with a small copper tray for tips. It was her duty to collect fees and direct the work of the bath attendants who scrubbed down the clients with goat-hair mitts, tinted their hair with henna, or removed body and facial hair with *vajebi,* a white paste. Beyond the entrance chamber was a common room for undressing. Along one wall ran a raised tile platform on which people placed their clothes, all neatly wrapped in large cotton squares.

After undressing in the common room, we went through another door to enter the bathhouse proper. Through the clouds of steam I saw half a dozen women, some naked, others with cotton wraps around the waist, and several nude girls and very young boys. Some of the women were having their hair shampooed or dyed with henna. Others were scrubbing the children with a *keeseh* or soaping them. Some soaked in the *khazineh* for the final rinse. Because we had private stalls in Tehran, I was unaccustomed to group bathing, but no one paid the slightest attention to me, and I quickly got over my embarrassment.

The bath chamber was hexagonal, and along its entire perimeter spigots and basins provided hot water for the clientele. Mummy warned me not to set foot in the *khazineh,* for a pool in which everybody dipped was bound to be unhygienic, so we confined ourselves to using the spigots, filling a bowl with water and pouring it on ourselves or on each other as needed. In time Ab-e Garm's communal bathhouse was torn down, the *khazineh* destroyed, and a modern bathhouse like those of Tehran, with private stalls and showers, was built in its place. By then a road to the village had been built linking it to the capital.

Daddy had come to Ab-e Garm to be cured of his aches and pains—Mummy, too, but I suspect she had mostly come to be rejuvenated. Every day they would go up to the sulphur baths and soak in the healing waters. I did not go with them—the waters smelled like rotten eggs—but Mummy also went up the mountainside to the banks of a stream where the mud was famous for erasing crow's feet and skin splotches, and on those occasions I went with her.

I would pick wildflowers or splash my hands and feet in the stream or jump from boulder to boulder, crossing from one bank to another, while Mummy gathered the rich black muck and smeared it over her face and neck. She would leave it on for an hour or so and could neither smile nor talk while it dried, fixing her face in a mask intended to defy time. Finally, she would rinse the mud off, bending over the stream and cupping the water with her hands, happy in the certainty that the mud had restored her skin. I don't know whether it had or not; she was a youthful-looking woman anyway. Aunt Doris did not seem interested in rejuvenation. She was still young enough to laugh at the idea of crow's feet.

A warren of indistinguishable, flat-topped mud hovels fronted by weather-beaten wooden doors, Ab-e Garm was similar to thousands of other villages set sometimes precariously in the extraordinary heights of the Alborz Mountains. At a distance the huts seemed to be stacked one on top of the other, but a closer look revealed distinct levels connected by narrow dusty lanes that wound through the village in an intricate maze. The monotony of the earthen colors was relieved only by the green of carefully tended vegetable plots and of trees along the banks of the stream that coursed through the village.

Occasionally Aunt Doris and I would go together to the village bakery to buy bread. One day as we headed in that direction, we heard from a distance the rhythmic beat of a drum accompanied by a *dohol.* A cross between a horn and a recorder, the *dohol* has a distinctively deep, nasal sound. Drawn by the music, we hurried toward it and came upon a group of women crowding around a sloe-eyed bride barely past puberty. Her long-sleeved tunic of forest green fell below her knees over several layers of ankle-length skirts, the top layer glittering with gold thread. Gathered at the wrist with a band of gold, her tunic was partially covered by a festively red bolero that camouflaged her swelling breasts. The brilliance and glitter of her dress clashed incongruously with the simplicity of the plain black cotton trousers that showed beneath her skirts. Covering her head was a white shawl, richly decorated with small coins and pendants that glinted in the sun. As the women pressed around her, two musicians played the *dohol,* while the drummer beat with sticks on either side of a *naqareh,* a drum held upright in front of him with a cord that looped around the back of his neck. A little farther down the road were the groom and a number of men crowding around him. He was dressed in black cotton pants and a white tunic caught at the waist with a wide red cummerbund.

Just in front of the groom some of the men were snapping their fingers loudly while alternately raising one bent leg behind them in a typical peasant step. Then, as we watched, six or seven young men locked arms in a line and started stomping and leaping in time to the music. They raised clouds of dust as they circled and crouched, then jumped up and stamped as they landed. The women, gaily dressed in the colors of a Persian carpet—orange, green, blue, and red—clapped their hands to the music. Their faces were unveiled, as was the custom among tribal and village women. Their heads were covered with brightly patterned shawls held in place by a knotted length of contrasting fabric that looped around their heads, its ends hanging freely down their backs like long braids.

An older woman stepped forward and started dancing, her hands held high, her head at a proud tilt. There was a mischievous gleam in her eye, for such events were also occasions to pick prospective brides, and older women often served as matchmakers. She sometimes clicked her fingers and sometimes spun around, her skirts a swirl of color. A group of women formed a circle around her, some clapping, some raising their arms overhead, bending from side to side while bobbing with a lilting motion. The dancing woman coursed the circle and came to a sudden stop in front of another woman, inviting her to join in. Soon there were three women dancing in the circle. One waved a handkerchief over her head, then circled it around one wrist and tossed it upward into the air, reenacting an ancient courtship gesture. Two more women waving handkerchiefs joined in, and I watched, entranced, as they flipped their handkerchiefs, their wavelike rising and falling recalling the ancient *moj-pa* (wave step), largely displaced by the hip and pelvic movements introduced by Arab conquerors in the seventh century. Leaning to the left, the women circled to the right five or six times, then stopped abruptly, the kerchief waving coquettishly. Years later I would perform with Mrs. Cook's troupe a dance inspired by the *raqs-e dastmal,* the handkerchief dance I saw here in Ab-e Garm.

The villagers smilingly invited us to join the festivities and dance with them. As usual Aunt Doris created a sensation with her fair skin and blond hair. She laughingly resisted the villagers' insistence that she join in the dancing, saying she did not know how. After watching a while, we politely declined their gracious invitations for us to join them for the wedding feast and went excitedly back to the family to relate our adventure.

Talk of a wedding elicited a rash of salacious comments, and although I was sent out to play when such things were discussed, my cousin Kitty took it upon herself to pass on the forbidden knowledge. There had evidently been much laughing and smirking when Daddy had said that certain powerful landowners sometimes exercised rights of ownership over the tender young brides of their villages, claiming the exclusive right to enjoy their virginity. Someone else had reported that when the brash young sons of the great landholding families went hunting on their lands or came to the village to collect revenues, the villagers would hide their most beautiful virgins for fear that their youthful beauty might catch the eye of one of these arrogant lordlings. Of course, such tales were spun in the distant city of Tehran, where precious few knew what was really going on in remote mountain villages. Perhaps these stories were just the figment of lascivious imaginations; perhaps such things really did happen. I do not know.

One night a commotion outside our tent woke me. I found out there had been an accident in the village and that Mummy was being summoned to help. It was not that she had any medical training, but she was a foreigner, which meant she must be well educated, at least by the villagers' standards. In any event the villagers did not have access to medical doctors; women were the ones who delivered babies, exorcised bad spirits, wove spells and charms, and tended the sick, for they were the ones who had special knowledge of herbs and magic formulas, prayers and talismans.

I saw Mummy wrap herself in a warm dressing gown and depart with several villagers, who spoke to her in hushed but urgent tones. They lit the way with a lantern, and I watched the light dance toward the village, then dwindle and shrink until it was just a dot. A moment later it was gone. I lay in the dark wondering what was going on. Then I heard screaming—piercing and shrill. I felt chilled under my blankets, and my hands felt cold. I held my breath. Curiosity and wonder gave way to fear and anxiety, spreading icicles down my legs.

Perhaps it was just a few minutes, but it seemed like hours before the screaming stopped, before a tiny dot of light in the distance announced Mummy's return, before the dot grew into a round bright ball approaching our tent, before I could vaguely make out Mummy's silhouette, before "What happened?" and "Hush, now, go to sleep."

The next morning I woke to find Mummy gone to check on her patient. I was forced to restrain my curiosity. Not until she finally returned in midmorning did I get the full story of what had happened. She told me the villagers had called her to tend to a little girl who had accidentally fallen into an open fire and been badly burned over half her body. Mummy applied vodka to the burns so they would not get infected. "It is a good thing they don't know I was using alcohol," she said. "They would have been outraged." She did not need to explain to me that the villagers would have considered the substance *najess*—unclean— because drinking alcohol is forbidden to Muslims. The next day Mummy applied iodine to the wounds, prompting more screams.

My heart ached for the little girl and the pain she was enduring. Only much later did I realize how difficult it must have been for Mummy, too, how much courage it must have taken for her to treat the child, with no medical training and only the most rudimentary bandages and iodine in her first-aid kit. Yet she had unhesitatingly done so, knowing that she was the only "doctor" within hundreds of miles of the village and the only hope for the child's survival. Mummy did what she could. We will never know whether that little girl in Ab-e Garm recovered. If she did, she was probably scarred for life. If she did, she owed her life to Mummy's ministrations.

Some years later we returned to Ab-e Garm. This time we rode in a bus on top of which our belongings had been loaded. Careening around the sharp bends at incongruously high speed, the bus driver leaned on his horn each time he approached a blind curve. The road was too narrow for two vehicles to pass each other, and encountering another truck or car meant slamming on the brakes, coming to a screeching stop, then maneuvering to make the other driver back up his vehicle, squeeze it closer to the edge of the abyss, and give way sufficiently for our bus to scrape by. Sometimes our driver would win the battle, sometimes his adversary would. At no time were the lives of the passengers of the slightest concern—or so it seemed. Mummy and I clung to the arms of our seats for dear life and swallowed hard every time we encountered another motor vehicle. Fortunately, traffic was sparse.

This time we did not need a tent because Ab-e Garm now had small mud rooms to let, and this time Mummy and I traveled alone.

Life and Death

Two days there are whereon to flee from Death thou has no need.
The day when thou art not to die, the day when death's decreed;
For on the day assigned by Fate thy striving naught avails,
And if the day bears not thy doom, from fear of death be freed!
—Isma'il Kamal ed-Din

IT WAS AUNT DORIS who first taught me how to do the clog step. Standing opposite each other in our Persian garden, we would hold hands, dance a Germanic step, and sing, "I'm a lassie from Lancashire, just a lassie from Lancashire. There's no one who's fairer or rarer than Sara, my lassie from Lancashire." None of it ever struck either of us as odd or incongruous.

But Aunt Doris's presence in our home created problems—serious problems. At the time large numbers of British, Russian, and American troops were stationed in Tehran. Although Iran had declared its neutrality at the outbreak of World War II, its ties with Germany were particularly strong. German experts of all kinds had started coming to Iran in the 1930s to help lay the first north-south railroad across and through the Alborz Mountains. They founded an industrial school, Madreseh-ye San'ati, to help train Iranian engineers and technicians. For its part, Iran imported machinery, construction materials, and manufactured items from Germany to implement its industrial program. Germany extended special barter and easy repayment arrangements, making it Iran's premier trading partner. Daddy, who was involved in the import-export business, made frequent trips to Germany, and both he and Mummy spoke German fluently. They had close German friends who had lived in Iran for many years.

But after Germany declared war on Soviet Russia in 1941, every German in

Iran became suspect in the eyes of the Allies, who demanded that Iran expel all German foreign agents in order to uphold its neutrality. Reza Shah proceeded to expel all German nationals, foreign agents or not, including my parents' close friends. I remember their tearful parting. These Germans were leaving behind many friends and also a part of the world where they had lived happily for many years and that they had come to love.

The Allies were not satisfied with the expulsions and used the issue of foreign agents as a pretext to invade Iran. While Russian forces entered from the northwest, the British attacked from the south, landing at the head of the Persian Gulf and sinking every one of Iran's naval vessels, with a considerable loss of life. After three days of token resistance Reza Shah abdicated the throne. Sent into exile by the British, he eventually died in South Africa in 1944. His son, Mohammad Reza Shah, succeeded his father to the throne, and in January 1942 Iran signed the Tripartite Treaty permitting Great Britain and the Soviet Union to station forces on Iranian soil until the end of the war. That same year forty thousand American troops, officially known as the Persian Gulf Command, were allowed to enter the country. The Allied powers now used the roads and railroads Reza Shah had built with German assistance to transfer war materials to Russia to prosecute the war against Germany.

So it was that thousands of British, Russian, and American soldiers could be seen in Tehran. Long convoys of trucks full of armed troops became a common sight, both in the capital and in outlying areas. Smart-looking young men in uniform swarmed over Tehran's cafés, restaurants, movie theaters, and—it was whispered—red-light district. Street urchins picked up snatches of English and learned to follow GIs with an insistent, "Hello, Johnny. Shoe shine, Johnny?" Because the American GIs were not part of an occupying force, they were embraced more readily than were the British and the Russians. Besides, they had money to spare and seemed liberal with their largesse, which made them the favorite targets of beggars, pickpockets, and street scamps. The modest amounts the GIs gave away seemed like small fortunes to the ragtag kids who pestered them.

The British opened their Green Room and the Americans their Culture House, outreach centers where young Iranians could study English, read books, put on plays, and in other ways get a whiff of British or American culture. The principal propaganda arm of the Russians was a hospital, but they also had a movie theater in town, where they showed Russian-language movies. I cannot remember ever going to see one. In any case I believe their theater had a difficult time competing with the Hollywood movies that flooded the city, making Rita Hayworth, Spencer Tracy, Loretta Young, Betty Grable, and Fred Astaire household names.

To my mother and my aunt, two English expatriates, it seemed only natural to volunteer at the British canteen, where servicemen went for recreation, a drink, and a good meal, hoping at the same time to meet an attractive young woman who spoke English. When Daddy objected, the sisters insisted it was their patriotic duty. In the cultural milieu into which my mother had married such consorting with men was highly offensive behavior, so she and my father had many an ugly confrontation over her time spent at the canteen. The family gossip and outrage were relentless, feeding Daddy's sensitivities over the matter, and Mummy finally gave in and stopped her volunteer work.

Not long afterward she had a request from Radio Tehran to become their English-language newscaster. With her excellent diction and clear enunciation she was perfect for the part, and she seemed pleased by the opportunity. Several times Parviz and I managed to stay up late to listen to her deliver the news in her clipped British accent as though she had been doing it all her life. "This is Radio Tehran," she would begin. "Today German forces entered Paris . . ." I was too young to understand the import of the news she was delivering, but thrilled at hearing her voice coming over the radio. Her blossoming career was short-lived, however. Because she did not drive, someone from the radio station had to fetch her to take her all the way to the station and then return her every evening. Daddy objected to her working and did not offer to take her himself. Reluctantly, she gave up radio announcing after a few short weeks.

Daddy also disapproved of Aunt Doris's volunteer work, for she started meeting eligible young men at the canteen. Many a British lieutenant or colonel fell in love with her, but every time a beau would come to call or take her out or ask Daddy for her hand in marriage, there would be a scene. Daddy was intensely jealous and acted as though he owned her body and soul. He would drink heavily on such occasions and then pick a quarrel with the offending beau and order him out of the house. Afterward there would be angry words and tears. Mummy despaired of her sister's ever getting married.

One evening Daddy became very drunk and was in an ugly mood, for a young officer of high rank had come to ask for Aunt Doris's hand in marriage.

My brothers and I had gone to bed but were not yet asleep. When we heard yelling and scuffling down below on the terrace, Parviz and I crept out of our beds and onto the veranda that overlooked the terrace and pool. We saw a veritable tug-of-war going on: our father on one side, grappling with the British officer, with our very pregnant mother clutching at Daddy's clothes trying to restrain him, and the officer on the other side, defending himself as best he could with Aunt Doris tugging at *his* clothes and trying to pull him away from the altercation. "Stop it, you fool. Let him go," Mummy was screaming, while Daddy yelled, "I'll kill him! I'll kill him!" The upshot of the brawl was that the officer fell in the pool. Water splashed all over the flagstone terrace, drenching Daddy, who stood angrily looking down at the unfortunate beau from the edge of the water. There was not much danger of the officer's drowning, but his dignity was sorely damaged. He emerged dripping from the water and bowed out of the scene as soon as he could collect himself. We never saw him again.

Some weeks later that summer there was a phone call for Daddy, who was still asleep. Glancing at the clock, I saw that it was past ten and thought I had better call him. He was sleeping in one of the guest rooms at the end of the hall, for Mummy was by now in the last few weeks of her pregnancy, and she and Daddy had moved into separate bedrooms. I tiptoed upstairs so as not to awaken the rest of the household and knocked lightly on his door. There was no answer. I turned the knob and quietly pushed it open and stood rooted to the spot, as if hit by a bolt of lightning.

There lay Daddy and Aunt Doris asleep on the bed, naked, with their arms wrapped around each other. Catching my breath and clapping my hand to my mouth, I stepped back and started to close the door, but it was too late. Daddy had awakened. Averting my eyes from his nakedness, I matter-of-factly told him that there was a telephone call for him, and he—just as matter-of-factly—reached for his bathrobe, put it on, and went downstairs to take the call.

Neither of us ever mentioned the incident. Perhaps he thought I was too young to comprehend what I had seen. After all, I was not yet eight years old. Although I did not fully know the facts of life, I was old enough to realize I had stumbled on a dark secret. I knew that Mummies and Daddies did "funny things" after they were married and that they were supposed to do those things only with each other. Exactly what they did, I was not sure. I knew instinctively, though, that Mummy would be greatly upset if she ever found out that her own sister had been doing such things with Daddy, so I never breathed a word of it to her—or to anyone else. Mummy must have found out anyway, for not long afterward Aunt Doris packed her bags and returned to England. My questions as to when she would be coming back were met by a rather stony "I don't know." We never saw or heard from Aunt Doris again. To this day I do not know what became of her.

Soon after Aunt Doris's departure my baby brother, Kaveh, was born. Mummy had always had a soft spot for infants, and whenever we passed one on the street, she struggled to resist admiring it, for everyone knew that open admiration of a child might cast the evil eye on it. The least compliment paid to a child had to be followed by *"mashallah,"* "praise be to God," to combat the power of the evil eye. Mummy knew, however, that if she praised the beauty of a baby, even if she clearly said *"mashallah"* afterward, its mother would surely blame her if the baby became sick.

My mother was familiar by now with all the local superstitions. If someone sneezed once as she was getting ready to leave the house, she would either delay her departure or change her plans and stay home because that sneeze was a signal to wait, and disregarding the signal might bring some calamity down on our heads. Or if someone sneezed twice, she would go ahead with her plans, secure in the knowledge that all would be well. In the end, though, her adherence to all the proper rituals meant to ward off misfortune did not help her much.

Her own baby, her last, was exceptionally good-natured as well as beautiful. He became the center of the family's attention, and we all doted on him, especially my father. Plump and good-natured, with large black eyes and full, round cheeks, Kaveh had an infectious chuckle. It made us laugh to see him stand in front of the radio, bouncing up and down, up and down, sometimes toppling over in his enthusiasm. Daddy would clap his hands when Kaveh danced or keep time with a loud *beshkan,* a cracking noise made by joining the hands and rubbing the index fingers together. "Son of a king," Daddy would repeat again and again, and "golden penis," he would sing, keeping time with Kaveh's dancing. He would cradle the little fellow in his arms and carry him around the house, cooing and talking baby talk to him. I had never seen my father happier. Parviz would sometimes joke that when Kaveh grew up, he would become my dancing partner. We all watched Kaveh proudly as he smiled his first smile, took his first steps, spoke his first words, in Persian, in English.

Not long after his birth we moved into a new house that presented a re-markable contrast to our old one. It was very modern, one of the first of its kind to be built in Tehran, with large glass windows that made me feel extraordinar-ily exposed—to burglars and to the prying eyes of neighbors. Instead of looking inward, it looked outward onto the neighbors, onto their houses and gardens, and onto the world outside. Instead of having clear *andaroon* (interior) and *biroon* (exterior) spaces, it combined the two. Its most startling statement of modernity, however, was its low garden walls. It took a while for us to get used to them be-cause we were still accustomed to tall protective barriers to the outside world. Although our previous house had also had large glass doors and windows, all of them had opened onto our own garden, which was enclosed by tall walls. It was a strange feeling, therefore, to go out to the yard to play and to realize that the neighbors could see me from behind their shuttered windows if they so chose. My first few times in the yard I was painfully self-conscious. As I bounced a ball on the flagstone, I moved without spontaneity, for I was sure someone was watching me. As I bent over to smell the flowers in the border beds, I took care not to let my skirt hike up, and when I reclined on a lawn chair with a book, I was careful to keep my legs crossed so as to not let my underwear show.

Mummy, as usual, was totally lacking in self-consciousness and—to the con-sternation of her family and the delectation of the neighbors—would spread a towel in the sunniest spot in the yard and sunbathe, her scantily covered body exposed to full view. "You should be ashamed of yourself," Daddy blurted out one day when he saw her stretched out "virtually naked" in the sun. "It is the nosey neighbors who should be ashamed of themselves," she retorted, adding that they should have better things to do than watch her sunbathing. She refused to be browbeaten into conforming to such "narrow-minded" attitudes. "I am sunning in the privacy of my own backyard, and if the neighbors don't like it, they should not spy on me," she said angrily and went right on basking in the sun. Daddy sulked, embarrassed but helpless. Slowly the rest of us adapted and learned to accept, if not to be at ease with, our—and Mummy's—exposure.

The yard in our new house was minuscule in comparison with that of our previous home, and the pool was exceptionally small. The location of the house, however, more than made up for such deficiencies. Near the British and Russ-ian embassies, it was in the best part of Tehran, much closer to my school and to dance classes. It was just off Pars Street, close to Shah and Ferdowsi Avenues, but on a small side street, a *koocheh,* that shielded us from traffic noises yet did not prevent our hearing vendors who hawked their wares, bringing fresh produce right to our doorstep. Early every morning they would trot their donkeys down our *koocheh,* their singsong calls announcing their arrival, their saddlebags laden with fresh milk or mounds of tiny cucumbers freshly picked or bright red tomatoes so ripe they had to be sold that very day or they would rot and have to be thrown away. From a distance Naneh would hear the milkman calling his wares and stop whatever she was doing to find a large *koozeh.* She would hurry to the door with it, and the milkman would ladle milk into the clay jug until it was filled, sloshing large white drops on the ground as he did so. Our other servants, Mashd Mahmad and Batool, had left us, and only Naneh remained to help with the housework. The proximity to central shopping areas for other necessities, therefore, was crucial. Nearby, the enticing aroma of a traditional bakery announced the availability of local flat breads—*sangak* and *taftoon* and *lavash*—and not far away, directly opposite the imposing gates of the British embassy, was a bakery where European breads were sold—French and Italian white bread, German pumpernickel, and Russian whole wheat.

The war in Europe was still raging, and its effects continued to spill over into Iran in many ways. Large numbers of Polish refugees, fleeing the horrors perpetrated by the Nazis, flooded into Iran, bringing with them a scourge that was new to our country—typhus. A lethal disease, it was transmitted by lice, which, in the primitive conditions of public hygiene in an underdeveloped country such as Iran at the time, spread the disease like wildfire. Radio bulletins went out describing measures we could take to protect ourselves from infestation. Among these bulletins were warnings not to ride buses and to avoid going to movie theaters, bathhouses, schools, and other public places that were difficult, at best, to avoid. The school authorities distributed lumps of camphor to students with instructions to pierce it with a needle, thread it with a string, and wear it around the neck to ward off any contaminated lice—a measure as unlikely to succeed as wearing garlic to ward off ticks in the Virginia woods in the summer.

I was ten years old at the time of the typhus epidemic. I took as many precautions as I could and avoided going to the movie theaters or riding buses, but they did no good. I came down with red spots on my stomach and a high fever that lasted for weeks while the doctors and my mother tried desperately to save my life. Every evening, as my fever started the inevitable climb above the 104-

degree mark, Mummy would have Naneh bring into my room a large bucket half-filled with tepid water. The two of them would help me to sit up, dangle my legs over the edge of the bed, and put my feet in the bucket. They kept me propped up for ten minutes or so while the tepid water cooled my body and started to bring my fever down, but it would inevitably climb back up again. Several times they did not think I would survive.

The illness and the convalescence took three months, during which time I was completely bedridden. For weeks on end I had only liquids to drink, and every day a nurse would stop by to give me an injection, an ordeal I dreaded. The needle she used was thick, and the injections were painful. My hair started to fall out, and the doctors advised Mummy to have my head shaved to "strengthen" the hair so I would not go bald. She did not have the heart to do that, but one day came in with a pair of scissors and with great sadness cut off my long black locks, one by one. As for me, I was just relieved that she had not shaved my head.

One day while my mother was placing cold compresses on my forehead and I was drifting in and out of consciousness, I heard screams in the yard. Mummy left abruptly and did not return for a long time. I wondered what was going on, but was too sick and weak to leave my bed and go onto the veranda overlooking the yard to see what had happened. Later in the day, when Mummy came in to feed me my liquid diet and take my temperature, I asked her what all the screaming had been about. She told me Kaveh had fallen into the pool and almost drowned. "But don't worry," she said, "he's all right." For days afterward, whenever Mummy came into my room, I would ask her how Kaveh was and wondered why I did not hear him crying. "He must be growing up," I said. "Is that why I don't hear him crying anymore?" "That's right," Mummy replied without any change of expression, while hot knives of grief must have been jabbing at her heart. "He's growing up. He doesn't cry any more."

As my fever dissipated and I started to feel better, I kept begging her to bring Kaveh into my room so I could see him. She fended me off by saying it would not be right to expose a little two-year-old child to my germs. Weeks later, as I grew stronger and more insistent in my demands to see my baby brother, she came into my room one day and sat on the side of my bed. Her face was white and drawn. She held my hand and said, "Now that you are better, I am going to have to tell you something very sad. You will have to be very brave about it." I still remember the controlled tone of her voice, her lack of tears. I still feel the agony of an irretrievable loss, of a mother's unbearable pain. A tender young two-year-old child who was his father's delight, the light of his mother's life, a joy, a promise, a gift from the heavens, had been rudely snatched away.

Kaveh had fallen into our small garden pool. He was gulping water when they fished him out, but was still alive. If anyone around had known how to give artificial respiration, he might have been saved. Instead, while someone telephoned frantically for a doctor, Mummy had held him upside down and slapped him on the back to expel the water from his lungs, but it had not worked. By the time the doctor arrived, it was too late.

I never saw my mother cry. Deep sighs often escaped her and troubled looks, but never tears. Whatever hurt and pain and sorrow she suffered were buried deep inside her and never shared with anyone. English to the core, she despised public displays of grief. It was almost as though she had a patience stone, *sang-e saboor,* as the Persian saying goes, and to it alone confided her anguish. To this day it pains me to think how my innocent questions must have tortured her, and I am filled with awe that she could endure such sorrow and not show it.

On the thirtieth day after Kaveh's death relatives came to commemorate the sad event and offer their condolences at the ceremony known as "the Month." They were weeping and wailing and beating their chests. Mummy was not. Their display of grief filled her with a cold fury. Her expression betrayed not only the depths of her sorrow, but her contempt for the open grief Daddy's relatives displayed. "The bastards," she seemed to be saying, her lips tightly compressed. "All these people who have criticized me and gossiped about me behind my back—here they are now pretending to be so sympathetic. And anyway, why can they not grieve in silence?"

My aunts were wearing black and seemed shocked that Mummy was not. They wore no makeup. My uncles had black armbands on one sleeve of their suits. As they entered, each one took Mummy's hands, then Daddy's, kissed each one on both cheeks, and offered their condolences, often with tears streaming down their faces. They then greeted other relatives in turn, but somberly, as was appropriate for the occasion. They took their places in a large circle in our living room in straight-backed chairs that had been set up for the occasion. Daddy wept uncontrollably. One of my aunts sobbed audibly. As for me, I felt my grief welling up afresh. I was inconsolable and cried till my eyes were swollen and my throat choked up. Aunt Farangis put her arms around me and comforted me. I found myself wishing that I could be helping to serve the tea and cookies that would normally be passed around when we had visitors, but according to custom nothing was to be served, not even the *lork,* the *seerok,* and the *halvah,* in three colors (white, brown, and yellow), that were set out on a table along with flowers, a picture of Kaveh, and some sticks of burning *ood,* incense that filled our living room with a spicy fragrance. The *seerok* and *halvah* would not be served until after dinner later that evening, and the *lork* would be offered to departing mourners to take home with them. So there was no bustle of activity to camouflage the somberness of the occasion. While my father wept, my mother walked through the necessary ceremonies with a stony expression, her pain showing only in her eyes. In this respect she totally failed to adapt to her husband's culture.

Ave Maria

Ave Maria gratia plena
dominus tecum
benedicta tu nin mulieribus
et benedictus fructus ventris tui, Iesus.
—Ave Maria (Hail Mary)

KAVEH MUST HAVE BEEN the glue that held my parents' marriage together because after he died, things started to fall apart. Daddy began drinking vodka for breakfast, arrak for lunch, and vodka again for dinner. In between he drank whatever he could get his hands on—all on an empty stomach. His eyes were glazed much of the time. He was invariably in a foul mood and snapped and snarled at the servants, at my brothers, and particularly at Mummy. We children avoided him as much as possible, using great ingenuity to make sure we did not run into him. When I did inadvertently see him, he was always gently affectionate, and I felt guilty at how his hugs and kisses repulsed me. I would smile weakly in response and then escape from his embrace to my room, to school, or to dance class, where I could lose myself in a fantasy and put him out of my mind.

Between him and Mummy there were frequent, violent explosions as well as much silence. Mummy tried hard to curb his access to liquor. She removed all alcoholic beverages from the liquor cabinet and got rid of them. She would try to coax Daddy into eating something—anything—in the hope that food in his stomach might mitigate the wretched effects alcohol had on him, but it was useless. He had no appetite, and time and again I saw her draw an empty bottle from its hiding place—under the sofa, behind a settee cushion, or from the back of a bureau drawer where Daddy had, like a child, tucked it under a jumble of socks

123

and underwear. Mummy would retrieve the incriminating evidence with a sigh and confront Daddy, who always protested his innocence. An ugly row would follow, accompanied by accusations, anger, and frustration on Mummy's part and by vehement denials, pouting, and sulking on Daddy's. There were times when the shouting matches would deteriorate into fistfights, when Daddy would strike out insanely at Mummy, calling her a whore and a bitch. At such times my oldest brother, Iraj, felt compelled to intervene to protect her. Many of these scenes mercifully occurred when I was out or asleep, but I could sense the tension in the air when a battle had just occurred, and I saw and heard enough to know what was going on.

One day when I returned home from school, I was startled to see Daddy lurking in the shadows of the hallway. He put his finger to his lips and gestured to me to come to him, but quietly. "Sh-sh-sh," he whispered. "Those damned German spies next door are at it again! Such strange things going on over there. Look. Mrs. Kunemann is hanging from a rope from the upstairs balcony, and she is spinning around and around. Come and see, but hush; she mustn't know we are watching." Alarmed, I followed him up the stairs on tiptoe and crouched down next to him where he had flattened himself against the wall and was peeking cautiously out the window of the upstairs landing. What did he mean? What was he talking about? He gestured to me to stay low so as not to be seen. I looked out at our neighbors' balcony railing and saw a broken clothesline flapping in the wind. As I watched, a strong gust caught it and flung it upward where it turned and jostled against the brick wall before dropping down again into a gentle swing, back and forth, back and forth. The German spies were all a hallucination.

So it had come to this—so much alcohol, so much numbing of the senses and stupefaction that Daddy's normally intelligent mind had been gripped by delirium tremens. Of course, he refused to see a doctor. I do not remember how he pulled out of it, whether he was hospitalized or Mummy called the doctor in to see him against his wishes, but a few weeks later he was his normal self again, only occasionally drunk.

Unlike Islam, Zoroastrianism does not forbid drinking, and Zoroastrians are well known for their skills in cultivating vineyards and producing wine, but the tenets of their religion have always advocated self-discipline and an eternal vigilance against polluting or abusing any of Ahura Mazda's creations, including one's own body—a tenet Daddy chose to ignore. His excessive drinking was not only polluting his body but also striking lethal blows at the cohesion of our family.

Many nights the voices downstairs became so loud I would put my hands over my ears as I cowered in bed. One morning, following just such a night, I tiptoed quietly downstairs through a deceptively serene house and into the living room. I loved this room. Mummy had beautifully and tastefully decorated it with an understated elegance. It was a space where I had spent many happy hours quietly reading, dancing, and playing the gramophone. I opened the door to go in and stood riveted to the spot, my hand frozen on the doorknob. I caught my breath as, for a moment, my heart seemed to drop to my feet. Our beautiful salon looked as though a tornado had crashed through it. All the lamps were ripped from the walls, hurled off the tables, dashed to the floor. Flattened shades, twisted stands, and fragmented pieces of glass were scattered everywhere. Several delicate gilt side chairs lay overturned on the floor. The glass top of the coffee table had a series of perfectly aligned spokes radiating from its shattered center. I gasped. "How could he do this?" Even as I asked the question, I knew the answer. Daddy must have drunk too much and become violent. He would probably remember little or nothing of the fury he had vented on the living room, on Mummy, and on his family. I picked up the side chairs, sat down in one of them, and stared at the havoc. It was too much. Overwhelmed by a sense of helplessness, I just sat and looked blankly at the mess. There was no way I could put it all back together again.

When Mummy found me sitting there, she took me by the hand and led me out, closing the door behind us. We did not discuss what had happened. By the time I came home from school that day, the debris had been cleaned up, the room returned to some measure of normalcy. Soon after that, though, I found myself on my knees in that very same living room, pleading with Daddy not to separate me from my mother. The idea of leaving her and going to live with him was more than I could bear. "Please, please, Daddy," I wept, "Don't take me away from Mummy. Let me stay with her." My parents had been talking about separation and divorce, even though it was against the tenets of the Zoroastrian religion, and Daddy had threatened to take me away when they split up.

The atmosphere in the house was tense and strained. Mummy and Daddy were not oblivious to the effect this atmosphere must be having on me and my brothers, perhaps which was why they decided to send Iraj to the United States. He had just graduated from high school. He kept getting caught between my parents in their confrontations, and they realized they needed to send him away. They somehow managed to scrape together the money for his airfare and sent him off to America to live with our uncle Shahbahman, who lived in California with his Austrian wife. It was understood, of course, that this uncle would take in Iraj, but many years later I learned that, in fact, Iraj had lived with our uncle's family for only a short time and that he had been for all practical purposes on his own, working his way through college, occasionally sleeping in his car to save on rent, and selling his blood to a local blood bank to pay for his books.

The strain at home started to show in my schoolwork. The situation was more than an eleven-year-old girl could bear. I became inattentive at school. I stopped doing my homework and my grades dropped. I quarreled with friends. I could not bring myself to share my pain with anyone, but word got out. My classmate Claire put her arms around me and tried to broach the subject, but I bristled and denied that my parents were considering a divorce. It was so embarrassing; I did not know anyone else whose parents were divorced. Claire persisted, and I finally broke down and cried, unburdening myself on her shoulder. It was a relief to be able to talk about the situation.

When school let out for the summer, I no longer had a refuge from the storm engulfing us. Worried about the effect the incessant tension and quarreling were having on me, Mummy enrolled me in an Italian boarding school run by Benedictine nuns who had a summer garden near Shemran, a suburb in the cool foothills of the Alborz Mountains. A charitable school filled largely with orphan girls whom the nuns had taken under their wings, it charged very low tuition and was eager to accept young girls whose tender age made them ripe for conversion. Under the circumstances I welcomed the idea of boarding there, for Mummy had lost touch with her sisters and could not send me to stay with any of them, and she did not want me staying with Daddy's family, who had gotten caught up in the embitterment and taken sides—against Mummy, of course.

Mummy and I got off the bus in front of the massive gates of the walled school compound and walked together up a path lined with cypress trees. Water chan-

With Iraj *(left)*, Parviz *(right)*,
and Mummy shortly
before Iraj's departure for
the United States.

nels on either side lent a pastoral freshness to the air; the tumbling waters gurgled and murmured pleasantly. Nearby were groves of fruit trees—peaches, pears, and apricots. Neither Mummy nor I spoke. We passed several large tents set among the trees. Finally, a modest building came into view, and we headed toward it.

On the way we passed a picnic table under a large oak tree, where we saw three young girls scribbling in notebooks. All identically dressed in long-sleeved black uniforms with white collars, they looked up as they heard our footsteps, started to giggle, and whispered to each other behind cupped hands. One of them called out, "Look at the European doll coming up the pathway. Oh, it's Shirley Temple—look at her hair all done up in curls." Although I knew instinctively she must be taunting me, I chose to take the remark as a compliment and looked straight at her and smiled. Although I did not realize it until later, my nonbelligerent response won me a friend.

We met the mother superior with her black flowing skirts and long full sleeves, her face framed by white linen and a black veil that fell gracefully down her back. Around her neck, a wooden cross dangled from a chain, and a heavy mass of keys and rosary beads hung from her belt. She spoke only Italian, so another nun who could speak Persian helped enroll me in the school for the summer. I was informed that like the other girls I was to wear the standard uniform. Its black severity was only slightly softened by the white collar at the neck. When I came back the next day, I would need to bring only towels, shoes, and changes of underwear. Several of the girls in the school milled around us, looking me up and down, whispering to each other, and occasionally giggling. Mummy's obvious foreignness seemed to make an impression and perhaps explained my Shirley Temple likeness.

The next day Mummy and I returned, lugging a suitcase made heavy by the large number of books I had packed between the towels and underwear. *The Iliad, The Odyssey, The Three Musketeers, A Tale of Two Cities, The Scarlet Letter, The Adventures of Huckleberry Finn,* and *Uncle Tom's Cabin* weighted it down. Mummy and I hugged each other, and she left me with a sigh. We shed no tears, for we both knew it was a sensible resolution to a difficult situation. The novelty and strangeness of the place did not intimidate me, and I felt some relief at being away from the interminable quarreling at home.

A nun showed me to one of the tents set up in the garden. Lifting the tent flap, I saw a row of six cots, one of which she indicated was mine. There were no wardrobes, and I was to keep my personal belongings in my suitcase under my cot, but first they had to be inspected and approved by the mother superior.

I opened my suitcase for inspection and was appalled when I was told that no one was allowed to bring fiction, *roman,* into the camp. I protested, pointing out that the books were not romances (in the sense in which *they* were using the term), that they were all literary classics, and that I should be allowed to keep them. A close inspection of my books and a conference between the nuns and the mother superior followed, and I was eventually told that an exception would be made in my case and that I could keep my books. I could not, however, keep my mirror. Mirrors only led to vanity and would not be tolerated here. Also, I would not be needing the bathing suit I had brought because if we did ever go swimming, we would swim in our regular uniforms, long sleeves and all. I stared in disbelief as I listened to the enumeration of regulations. I was to attend mass every morning at six o'clock sharp. At mealtimes I was to eat all the food placed before me. There were to be no second helpings and no food left on my plate. Two girls were never to sit alone together because "the devil might come between them." We must always be in a group of at least three, preferably more. Used as I was to the freedom allowed us in Community School, I chafed at these restrictions, which struck me as ludicrous.

I would have to adjust to other peculiarities as well. The Presbyterian missionaries who taught in Community School dressed in regular street clothes, were married, and had families. And although at Community School I had daily

Bible studies, they were part of a rigorous academic program that included the sciences, mathematics, French, Latin, history, and geography. In the Benedictine school, on the other hand, the emphasis was on prayer and catechism. The nuns wore severe black habits and greeted each other with "Veni sanctus spiritus," to which each replied, "Veni numen cordia." Their principal goal was not educating the girls entrusted to their care, but indoctrinating them in a special brand of Catholicism, saving their souls, and assuring their ultimate entry into heaven.

At first I found fault with everything. These people were so narrow-minded! "Don't do this," and "Don't do that." They all prayed at the drop of a hat—before meals, after meals, first thing in the morning, last thing at night. Their food was atrocious. Every day we had bread and lentils for lunch. For the first two weeks I had a continuous stomachache.

Most of the girls were orphans. A very few had parents who, for various reasons, were boarding them here. It was all very strange and new, but I knew it was better than being at home right now. Then one day I discovered the piano. A nondescript upright that was badly out of tune, it nevertheless entranced me. One of the girls taught me some simple tunes, and I became inseparable from the dilapidated instrument, spending every spare minute I had playing on its grungy keys.

Sister Savina was the resident music teacher, and she responded to my enthusiasm. She had a soprano voice that was warm and clear, and I fell in love with her lyrical rendition of "Deus Angeli." Moreover, she was pretty and had a sweet expression that I found irresistible. When she stroked the keys on the piano, she touched my heartstrings. She started teaching me to read music and play—first some Clementi, then Bach, Haydn, and Mozart. I became infatuated—with her, with the piano, with the magical sounds emanating from the keyboard.

I stopped criticizing the school and fell into the routine, greeting everyone with "Veni sanctus spiritus," looking forward to eating bread and lentils, and enjoying the prayers with their rhythmic repetition and their mystical overtones. I started responding to the early morning masses with wonder and rapture, entranced by the repeated chanting of the "Kyrie Eleison, Christe Eleison," by the rich harmonies of the baroque chorales, by the soaring crescendos of the organ. I gazed lovingly at the jewel-like windows, at Christ twisting in agony on the altar cross. The solemn ringing of the bell during mass moved me, as did the

In the Italian Benedictine school, 1946. Sister Savina is at center. I am on the right.

hushed reverence of those receiving the host. The mystery and ceremony and beauty intoxicated me. Before the summer was over, my resistance to Catholicism had started to soften.

I had daily catechism studies. Unlike the Bible classes of the Presbyterian Community School, where Dr. Elder encouraged us to contemplate the complexity of moral truths, to weigh the dilemma of conflicting values, and to address profound ethical issues, here I was expected to memorize. In Community School we discussed these issues: Was there a justification for telling a lie if it meant saving someone else's life? Was stealing ever admissible? Would it be justified if it were done in order to feed one's starving family?

By contrast, at the convent I found myself memorizing by rote and receiving only curt, evasive answers when I asked questions. "What is the Immaculate Conception?" I asked Sister Elvira. She scowled and answered, "Just memorize what is in the book." "What is a virgin birth?" I asked Sister Madeleine. "Just learn your lesson by heart," she answered crossly. I was expected neither to question nor to understand what I was memorizing. Faith was the sole requisite, obedience the only acceptable behavior, memorizing and believing the only goals. I started to acquiesce. I memorized and was congratulated and applauded. I stopped asking questions and was praised and singled out for special treatment. Sister Elvira took me in hand and started instructing me in the tenets of her faith. The Catholic religion was the only true religion, she said, the only path to heaven. Only by converting to it could I save my soul.

Subtly but surely I began to feel guilty for any and every "sin" I had committed in my few short years—every lie I had told, every "bad" feeling I had ever had, every temptation the devil had ever tripped me up with, every twinge of lust to which I had succumbed. I had been going, after all, to an American school. Mindless of the mores of the country in which I lived, I had grown up flirting with boys, dancing with them—often quite closely—sometimes holding hands, sweaty palms notwithstanding, and playing spin the bottle, which gave boys and girls a pretext to kiss each other at parties. The few times I had played this game my heart had throbbed wildly, the blood had rushed to my temples, and I had felt a delicious tugging sensation below my navel. All these feelings I now recognized as sinful lust.

Just a few months earlier I had in total ignorance attained puberty. I had been astonished one day to find blood in my panties. I had kept changing my underwear, hoping the bleeding would stop, but it had not. Filled with anxiety, I had finally told Mummy what was happening. To my relief she had explained that I was now a "woman" and would from now on bleed in this way for several days each month. She had given me a supply of cotton padding and safety pins and had calmed my fears by telling me I was now a "grown-up."

My breasts were already full and round, and elicited many salacious comments when I walked down the street. They made me the target of much unwanted attention and some molestation. There was the pharmacist who leaned over the counter one day and handed me my package with one hand and deftly fondled one breast with the other before I pulled back, enraged. There was the uninvited hand that emerged from the tightly packed crowd at the cinema and darted up my dress for one split second, then disappeared before I could strike out at it, leaving me fuming. And there was the neighbor, an older man, who made me blush by talking about my "pomegranates" whenever he saw me.

Then there was the time I was traveling by train with Daddy and an "uncle," a distant relative, who found himself alone with me when Daddy stepped out of the cabin to smoke near an open window in the throughway. My "uncle" came up behind me, slipped his hands under my arms, grabbed my breasts, and squeezed them hard. "What are these called?" he taunted. "Tell me. I won't let go until you tell me." It hurt, and I fought him off and went to Daddy in tears, complaining about what had happened, certain he would chastise the young man, but to my astonishment Daddy simply laughed softly, put one arm around me, and gave me a comforting hug. He said nothing to my uncle, but took pains from then on never to leave the two of us alone. All these incidents now filled me with an uneasy feeling of guilt.

Looking back, I can see that I probably encountered more than my share of sexual harassment. For one thing, Mummy allowed me to use makeup at an early age. Many of my friends at school similarly used lipstick and powder—it made us feel grown-up and glamorous, and my mother knew that I would not be overly obsessed with makeup if I were allowed to use it freely and were taught how to use it with restraint. But we were living in a country where most girls were allowed to use makeup for the first time only on their wedding night. Makeup on my face was enough to make strangers view me with suspicion, for lipstick marked a woman as either being married or indecent.

For another thing, it was most unusual for a young girl of the newly emerging middle class to ride a bicycle to school or to walk alone on the streets of Tehran. A relative or a servant usually accompanied unmarried girls wherever they went, or a chauffeur drove them. Mummy, however, would have none of that. Our family could not afford a chauffeur, nor would any of us think of imposing on Daddy to transport us, nor could Mummy spare a servant from the many daily chores required in running our household. Above all she simply did not believe in coddling me.

I remember well that when I was just six years old and starting the first grade, she had Mashd Mahmad accompany me to school, but only for the first week. From then on, she warned me, I would be on my own. I was to pay attention and learn the way. We lived then at Darvazeh Dowlat, a good forty-five minute walk from school. Although there was little traffic on the streets, there were lots of twists and turns on the way, but these difficulties did not deter Mummy. At the end of the week she told me I would have to get to school by myself. I protested that I did not know the way, shedding tears and pleading, but it was no use. "You will find the way," Mummy firmly insisted, pushing me out the door. She did not linger there to see whether I would head out in the right direction. She knew, of course, that I would. To my surprise I found my way without difficulty and from then on went by myself wherever I needed to go, whether on foot, bicycle, or public transportation—even after dark because most of my dance classes were in the evening.

In addition to my being regularly out on my own, my attendance at the American school probably increased the frequency and intensity of the gauntlet I ran daily. A coeducational school was so unusual and such an affront to accepted norms that it evoked much gossip about what went on behind its walls. Persian public schools were strictly segregated by sex. After all, the education of girls was a fairly new development, and girls' schools had only in recent decades overcome the intense hostility and suspicion that had earlier labeled them as hotbeds of promiscuity. Although by my time they were fairly common, they remained strictly segregated. Mixed classes existed only at the university level.

When Reza Shah dragged Iran into the modern age, he not only roused the nation from its torpor, but shook it to its very foundations. Before his reign an elaborate system of veiling, incarceration, and subordination of women had for centuries ensured that no woman would be seen by a man who was not her father, brother, or husband. Veils had built an impenetrable wall around women, rendering them invisible lest sight of them excite men to uncontrollable passion. Women's voices had been silenced by a code that idealized self-effacement, passivity, and compliance. Houses had been surrounded by high walls and sectioned into men's quarters and women's quarters. Early marriage and arranged marriage had been the norm.

Under the new order women were suddenly finding the protective covering of the chador snatched from their heads, leaving them exposed to the gazes of nonrelated men. Modern transportation, housing, and recreation were also throwing them into greater contact with such men. Attendance at school required girls to walk unveiled in city streets. Shopping was no longer a simple transaction at the greengrocer's on the corner or at the traditional bazaar. All over the city new stores had proliferated, requiring women to transact their purchases, including underwear, from men dressed in coats and ties but of questionable origins. Cities sprawled, compelling extensive travel on public buses where a woman might have to take a seat next to a total stranger. Luring young and old to their elaborately draped halls, movie theaters necessitated the seating of men and women side by side in closely spaced seats. Their lit screens portrayed societies where men and women mixed freely and where women sang with bare faces, danced with bare legs, fell in love, and voiced their opinions. Through

movies, books, radio, and an ever-increasing number of foreigners, Western influences and strange new ideas further penetrated the country. Now there were
not only large numbers of Russians, Britons, French, and Germans in Iran, all
bent on pursuing their particular diplomatic, military, business, educational, or
missionary goals, but also Americans, Iraqis, Indians, and Italians—making
money, establishing schools, spreading their faith, or implementing military and
diplomatic strategies.

What is more, large numbers of common people started traveling abroad and
imitating Western ways, often superficially and blindly. Women of the wealthy
classes spared no cost or effort to acquire the silkiest stockings, the brightest lipstick, the deepest décolletage. Wearing elegant clothes suitable for cocktail parties, they paraded the latest fashions on the main streets of Tehran during late
afternoon strolls or shopping expeditions. Beauty salons and outdoor cafés
sprang up everywhere, public swimming pools exposed men's and women's
bodies to an unprecedented degree, and skiing became the rage.

All these changes tore at the sanctity of tradition, assaulting the conviction
that the natural order of the universe designated certain spaces for women and
others for men. With old truths and certainties under attack exterior social controls broke down before inner ones had been built to take their place. Men had
relied on veils to suppress the supposedly uncontrollable urges that welled up inside them at the sight of a woman. They had kept women locked up, hidden
from sight, camouflaged behind tentlike drapery. Now suddenly women were
everywhere, many barefaced, beautified, provocative—and dangerous. They
shocked traditional sensibilities. Decades later Iranian revolutionaries would try
to restore the old verities, to re-cover women's faces, to keep them out of the
public eye, but by then the veil itself would have undergone a subtle change in
meaning, becoming an instrument of nationalism and ironically at times a tool
for the empowerment of women. The education of women would work profound changes in Iranian society, and women would become a significant force
to be reckoned with, in spite of their reveiling.

During my time, however, most of the changes had been dictated by fiat and
had been preceded by little preparation. Much of the population was still illiterate, still uneducated, still deeply traditional. Although modern cities had sprung
up, ancient villages continued to scratch out an existence; taxis had arrived on
the scene, but *doroshkeh*s competed with them for passengers; cars and trucks

clogged the wide avenues of Tehran, but laden donkeys still plied the narrow alleys. An educated elite and emergent middle class led a relatively modern life in a sea of traditional attitudes and beliefs that had changed little, if at all, from centuries past. This coexistence created an enormous disjunction, and I often found myself caught in the middle.

Although beach resorts beckoned to the Westernized to swim and bask in the sun wearing sometimes skimpy bathing suits, they also attracted more traditional women, who dipped into the Caspian Sea clutching their chadors beneath their chins. Predictably, these veils would spread out on the surface of the water, leaving the women with their wet underwear clinging to their bodies in a manner that revealed their womanhood far more than a bathing suit would have done. Still, their chadors marked them as traditional women, and they were not subjected to the same harassment as those of us who wore bathing suits.

Sitting on the beach, I often suffered the indignity of seeing young men draw close with the sole objective of looking down the front of my swimsuit. Out of the corner of my eye I would see a group of young men looking at me and laughing among themselves. Then one would start strolling toward me, getting closer and closer as I became more and more uncomfortable. I knew better than to say anything, for any reaction on my part would have called forth a stream of invective laden with sexual innuendo. Before walking on, the young man would take a good look at what little he could see of my bosom. It was infuriating.

The continued hold of tradition on the populace led the emerging middle class to take great care to uphold at least the appearance of propriety. The unprecedented mobility and visibility of women led to a renewed emphasis on a code of conduct designed to maintain the mores of a bygone age, so along with other westernized young women I learned to lower my eyes, to cultivate a shy demeanor and quiet voice, and to keep my legs tightly closed and my skirts well pulled down, for these gestures had become the hallmarks of modesty. A seemly demureness was my armor, my chador. Yet for some it was not enough. Many still considered it an evident truth that decent women did not show their faces in public and that sending young girls and boys together to school was asking for trouble. Foreigners might send their innocent young girls to school with boys, but foreigners were well known for being overly permissive and lax, especially about such things as virginity.

Traditional Persian mores required a girl not only to be a virgin before marriage but to have had absolutely no contact with the opposite sex. To have so much as held hands with a boy before marriage was enough to brand a girl as *kharab* or spoiled goods. What is more, females must be faithful wives, no matter what the circumstances. Even the *appearance* of any form of intimacy was enough to compromise their reputation.

Even Aisha, the Prophet Mohammad's favorite wife, was not above reproach for having been careless of her reputation when, having accompanied the Prophet on a war expedition, she had allowed a young man to guide her back to Mohammad's caravan after finding herself accidentally left behind. The Prophet's faith in his wife had been badly shaken until God informed him that Aisha was innocent of any wrongdoing. If even a woman of Aisha's stature could incur gossip, what could other women expect? They would do well to avoid any appearance of misbehavior that might damage their reputations and compromise their families' honor.

Example, precept, and custom encouraged reticence and shyness in matters of the heart. Although Persian literature, especially Ferdowsi's *Shahnameh,* did contain examples of bold and assertive women, such as Tahmina, a legendary princess who passionately offered herself to the great hero Rostam, confessing that she was "rent in twain with longing" for him, she was hardly the ideal held up to young girls. Rather, the ideal woman was repeatedly characterized as de-mure lover, devoted mother, and faithful wife. Modesty and chastity were the at-tributes young girls were to cultivate. Even the legendary Tahmina, for all her bold independence, was a virgin before marriage and remained faithful to Ros-tam for the rest of her life, in spite of her separation from him.

So great was the concern over the virginity of young girls that the first gen-erations of Iranian girls to attend public schools were discouraged from compet-ing in sports for fear that their hymens might tear. Not until Reza Shah's days did girls engage in such activities on a large scale. By my time girls' gymnastics and other sports were a part of most school curricula and were fairly common-place. Premarital contact between boys and girls, however, was not. Most mar-riages were still arranged, although new ideas of love, romance, and personal choice were slowly starting to make inroads.

As some of the older systems of sexual segregation started to crumble, new mechanisms sprang up to ensure that boys and girls were never given the chance to be alone. Self-control was an idea that was rejected as unreasonable, inadequate, and unnatural. Because the modern lifestyle was so fraught with dangers for the chastity of young girls, outside controls continued as the principal mechanism to ensure no contact with the opposite sex. It was not thought possible, therefore, that girls could go to school with boys and *not* be promiscuous. Always an anachronism in Iran, such coeducational foreign schools were eventually swept away four decades later by the fury of the 1979 Islamic Revolution. They were closed down, their students dispersed, and their personnel sent packing.

Cotton and Fire

Man I found fore-doomed to sorrow, made to suffer: wretched man!
Each in varying proportion bears his burden of distress;
Unto none they grant exemption from the universal ban.
—Abul Faraj of Sistan, fragment of poem

THE DANCING AND HAND HOLDING that went on in the Community
School parties during my adolescence were admittedly unacceptable behavior
by Persian standards, even though most of the dances were school sponsored and
carefully chaperoned. One did not foolishly expose cotton to fire, as the expression went, for the outcome of such exposure was predictable. By American standards these coeducational activities were just a normal part of growing up, but
they fueled gossip and wild fantasies in the imaginations of a populace used to
rigidly policing female chastity.

One rumor held that the boys and girls in our school fondled or petted each
other in the bathrooms. Not only were such allegations untrue, they were ludicrous. Dalliance there might have been, but certainly not in the bathrooms. The
facilities were separate for girls and boys. They were located outdoors and stood
back to back, with an unscalable, high dividing wall that effectively would have
made it impossible to access the bathroom of the opposite sex. Open pits with a
stench that made one desperate to get out as quickly as possible, our toilets were
unheated in the winter, dank and foul in warm weather, with doors that did not
close properly—hardly conducive to romantic sentiments. Besides, even American mores of the day did not condone premarital sex, and the most fraterniza-
tion I ever saw included some hand holding, an occasional stolen kiss, and much
dancing cheek to cheek.

Within the context of Persian mores, however, the whole idea of male-female nonromantic friendship was rejected as being against nature, impossible, fraught with grave danger. I was flying in the face of deeply held convictions, therefore, when I walked home from school every day with Igor, a boy of Slavic origins who lived just a few blocks up the street and who had been a classmate ever since the first grade. Neither of us had the slightest romantic interest in the other. We were simply good friends, and our paths home happened to coincide. But seeing us walking together day after day, most Tehranis would have found that impossible to believe.

As I look back, it is really not surprising to me that all the attacks on my innocence came not from the boys at Community School, where the flirtation, the dances, and the joshing and joking were allowable, but from outside the school—from men who had lost the restraint of tradition but had not yet learned to use inner controls to handle the more visible, proximate presence of women in public spaces. They knew that making passes at me constituted a flagrant violation of accepted norms, but considered me fair game because I was a "modern" girl. It was as though men could not be expected to resist the allure of a pubescent girl when the outlines of her breasts bulged beneath her garments. It was her fault for exposing herself so shamelessly and for going out in public unchaperoned. As I advanced into my early teens, I encountered more frequent, varied, and insistent unwanted sexual advances as the breakup of my parents' marriage inadvertently exposed me to an array of predators.

As the tensions kept mounting at home, Daddy started spending more and more time with the Goshtasb family, where the six sisters, including the beautiful Parvin, fawned over him and made him feel wanted. Now that his sister, Aunt Homa, was married to their brother Fereydoon, the Goshtasb girls were his sisters-in-law, and he could associate with them freely. He took full advantage of the liberty. In the same way that the Italian Benedictine school provided a safe haven for me, the Goshtasb home provided a refuge for my father—a place where he felt welcome and could temporarily set aside his family conflicts and concerns. It was also a place where he could enjoy complete cultural harmony, for the Goshtasbs not only spoke his language, communicating in Dari, but also, unlike Mummy, shared his culture.

Aunt Homa and Uncle Fereydoon had returned from Germany and now had a little boy, a toddler under two years of age. The young couple had decided to break with tradition and live in a separate house, for they had become used to their independence during their year abroad. Daddy was helping them move into a house they had rented in a suburb at the foot of the mountains. None of them could foresee that the move would be accompanied by tragedy.

Daddy came home one evening with his face contorted with grief. He was so choked up he could hardly speak, but finally managed to sob out the dreadful news—Fereydoon had had a terrible accident on the road to Shemran. His motorcycle had struck a tree; its handlebar had rammed into his stomach and crushed his liver. The doctors did not hold out much hope for his survival. For the next two days Fereydoon's closest relatives hovered around his hospital bed, hoping, praying, and imploring the doctors to save him. All their hopes for the future were invested in this only son, brother, husband. He was barely twenty-five when he died of his injuries. The family was devastated—his wife, mother, and sisters almost prostrate with grief. The next day, as Mummy, Daddy, and I stepped into the huge salon where the Goshtasbs were receiving condolences, I heard Fereydoon's mother wailing with a tremulous voice, "Oh ill fortune, oh ill fate! Alas! Alas! Dear God, why did you not take me instead of him? Even now, take me, take me. Why could you not spare him—the light of my eyes, the solace of my old age? Too young! Too young! He was too young!" As she wailed, she struck her forehead and tore at her hair, while her daughters stood on either side trying to restrain her, their eyes red, their cheeks wet with tears, their occasional sobbing involuntary.

When Daddy came in, Homa threw her arms around his neck and cried out loud, "He's gone, gone. My husband, the love of my life, my dearest one is gone forever. How can I live without him? Why has he abandoned me, abandoned his little son? His dear, dear son who will never again make him smile and laugh. Alas! Woe is me. I am the most unfortunate of women." Daddy stroked Homa's hair and cried with her, until she finally quieted down.

But soon Parvin resumed the lament. "Oh, brother dear—so rare a gem, so precious, brave, and strong, so young, so young. Why did God snatch away our only brother? It would have been better not to have had a brother than to have him taken from us so cruelly, so cruelly." In rhythmic counterpoint the women vented their sorrow, one picking up where the other left off, with brief interludes of calm. They rocked back and forth in agony, beating their chests, unburdening their grief in a chorus of lamentation the likes of which I had never heard before, for I had been too young to attend Grandfather's funeral and had been sick in bed for Kaveh's, as well as for the third—and tenth-day observances that were held. The only grieving I had seen was at the thirtieth-day commemoration of Kaveh's death, and that was nothing compared to this. The men, too, wept without inhibition while reciting the attributes of the deceased, each outdoing the other in lauding his virtues.

Through it all Mummy sat quietly, her face drawn, her eyes sad but dry. Daddy's tears trickled down his face as he comforted various members of the family, moving from one to another, sharing their grief with the common language of free-flowing, vocal lamentation.

As for me, I was unable to resist the waves of sorrow resonating through the house. I sobbed and cried as one person after another expressed unbearable anguish, each responding to the other's lament like chimes sounding in the wind. Later there was a long funeral procession to the *aramgah,* where a priest recited prayers from the Avesta. Then the lament recommenced in an ever-growing crescendo as the coffin was lowered into the pit, the male members of the family threw fistfuls of dirt on the coffin, and the women tossed red roses, carnations, and cyclamen into the grave, where they were quickly buried under clods of brown earth. Everyone sobbed uncontrollably—everyone, that is, except Mummy.

Not long after Fereydoon's death rumors started circulating that he had been deliberately hit by an English jeep and that his death was the result of British attempts to prevent German-educated engineers from establishing factories in Iran. Fereydoon had been planning on setting up a tire factory with the help of the Germans. It might be tempting to scoff at such conspiracy theories except that there were several circumstances that fueled suspicions: Fereydoon's body was found many yards away from the main road, and within a short span of time several other Iranians who were setting up factories or establishing important trade with the Germans were killed.

Had Fereydoon lived, he would have inherited a great fortune, much land, and a number of villages. His death left Homa a widow at the age of twenty-one. After the funeral Daddy spent even more time with the Goshtasb family. Mummy smarted over the way he was taking advantage of their grief to "weasel his way into their good graces," as she put it. "He can be so charming when he wants," she said. We saw less and less of him until he finally moved in with his brother, Uncle Aflatoon, thus giving himself free rein to spend as much time as he wanted with the Goshtasbs. He had not insisted on taking legal custody of me when he left, even though under the law he was entitled to do so. I was grateful, for I knew that legally mothers could have custody of daughters only till the age of seven and of sons up to the age of two. Perhaps Daddy was not vindictive after all, or perhaps he did not want the responsibility. In any case, after the early threats and power games, the matter was dropped and not mentioned again. One consequence of Daddy's departure was an enormous sense of relief. Another was a great sense of insecurity, although Mummy tried her best to hide her financial anxieties from us. Once Daddy left, he contributed no more financial support, either for Mummy or for her children.

Shortly before moving out of the house, Daddy arranged for Parviz to live with Aunt Pari and her husband, Firooz. He then presented me with a peculiar choice. Before washing his hands entirely of financial responsibility for me, he offered either to put me through nursing school, in which I had no interest, or to buy me a piano. I chose the latter, but I might as well have chosen the moon, for he never followed through on his offer.

Mummy was faced with having to pay the monthly rent and provide our food and other necessities. She had no savings, no work experience, no relatives she could call on for help, and no bank account, so she resorted to subletting the upper two floors of the house.

All the elegant rooms of our home were now off limits to us—the dining room, the living room, the charming little "brocade room," with its paisley-printed furniture that Mummy herself had upholstered, all three upper floor bedrooms and bathrooms, and the two verandas. My mother and I were relegated to the basement, with its damp walls, its one and a half rooms, kitchen, maid's room, and bathroom. Fortunately, it had a separate entrance, and Mummy ingeniously draped cheerful hand-blocked fabric on the walls, set up two sofas that could double as beds at night, and converted the adjoining storage space into a small study.

Although it was a tolerable enough living space so far as I was concerned, from then on I never brought friends home, for they all lived in spacious homes where they entertained their friends. Having friends over to visit would, under my new circumstances, have been painfully embarrassing.

Mummy relied on old friends for sympathy and companionship and started seeing more of Rose Hariri. "Aunt Rose," as I called her, had suffered experiences in life that made her particularly sympathetic to Mummy. She and her husband had long been my parents friends, and it was in their country garden in Shemran that I had almost drowned in a *qanat*. Aunt Rose was a loyal wife, a fabulous cook, and an impeccable housekeeper, but she was plain and—most unfortunately for her—unable to conceive. One day her husband had simply brought home a new wife. Aunt Rose for all practical purposes became a mere housekeeper in her own house, robbed of status, security, and love. With no family to turn to and no independent income to fall back on, she had little alternative but to put up with a bad situation. She had turned to Mummy for comfort and support to help her through her misfortunes. Now it was Mummy who turned to Aunt Rose.

Daddy's departure was meant to be a separation, and Parviz's stay with Aunt Pari temporary. The separation was meant to give my parents breathing space in which they would either work out their differences or make the rift permanent. But one day an ominously official-looking envelope arrived in the mail. Mummy looked at it with some misgiving and set it aside "until later." That afternoon she went over to Aunt Rose's house and took the envelope with her, for although she spoke Persian fluently, she could not read it. When she came home that evening, Mummy's face was ashen, her mouth tightly drawn. I looked questioningly at her, not daring to ask what the matter was. I did not need to, for she broached the matter herself, telling me that the envelope contained her official divorce papers. "Just like that," she said, "after twenty years of marriage." Daddy, the scion of a prestigious Zoroastrian family, whose religion decried and forbade divorce, had quietly and simply gone to a Muslim *mahzar,* a registration office, unilaterally declared three times that he was divorcing his wife, and received his total and unequivocal freedom. Mummy had had absolutely no say in the matter.

In spite of all the differences and difficulties I do not believe Mummy had expected Daddy to move out permanently. There had been no final agreement or settlement between them. She had not hired a lawyer and had not realized that Daddy could divorce her without her consent. Clearly, in spite of the many years she had lived in Iran, she was still an outsider. Yet going back to England was not an option, for the great distance between her and her sisters had gradually eroded her ties with her own family and with her homeland, where on rare visits she had found herself a stranger. The one sister with whom she still communicated, Aunt Stella, was now living with her family in Mysore, India. As a divorced woman, Mummy was alone and unprotected. Although Islamic law decrees that a man must pay his wife alimony for three months, Daddy never came through even with that amount. Perhaps he reasoned that not being a Muslim, he did not have to do so. Through everything I never saw my mother shed a tear.

Little did we imagine that matters would get even worse. A few months later Mummy was shocked to hear that Daddy had eloped with the beautiful Parvin. They had flown to America. Mummy was stunned. She had not expected this turn of events. She would not have been surprised to learn that Daddy was having an affair—but marriage with a woman twenty years younger? She sat down with me one afternoon and over a cup of tea calmly told me what had happened. She even managed a laugh of derision over Parvin's having been disowned and disinherited by her father as a consequence of having eloped. "He won't be getting his hands on her money," she said. It was one of the few derogatory remarks I ever heard her make about my father. And still she did not cry.

By now Mummy was single-handedly supporting us. At least she had been spared the expense and stress of also caring for Parviz. But one consequence of subletting the upstairs rooms was that we had a series of total strangers in our house, most of them transient, single males—English officers, American servicemen, an Iraqi businessman, an Indian diplomat. They were usually in Tehran only briefly, without their families. Most of them came and went with total indifference to the landlady and her daughter, and we saw little enough of them. Some of them occasionally brought home lovers. Late at night I could hear women's voices and muffled laughter outside the front door. Then the key in the lock, the door opening and closing, footsteps going up to the top floor, and then silence. By now I was in my early teens and knew something about the facts of life. What I heard made me extremely uncomfortable. Daddy's relatives started to gossip and complain that Mummy was running a brothel and dragging the family name into the mud. They could not, of course, admit that renting out the house was Mummy's only means of survival and a direct consequence of Daddy's having abandoned us. She was in no position to monitor the friends her tenants brought to the house and could hardly stand watch at the front door in the early hours of the morning.

I was physically mature for my age and poised in social situations. By the age of thirteen or fourteen I could easily have passed for seventeen or eighteen, and during the next few years some of the tenants took an interest in meeting me. There was the American serviceman Danny, who wanted to marry me, but I was thirteen and not in the least attracted to him. The Pakistani friend of one of the tenants proposed marriage. By then I was fourteen and quite repelled by him. Then there was the American serviceman who tried to put his hands into the pockets of my slacks, the American embassy employee who brushed his hand over one of my nipples as his friend photographed us, and the tenant who said he could give me "an injection" that I would enjoy.

We also housed an Iraqi businessman whose hobby seemed to be seducing young women and who did not hesitate to try his skills on me, knowing full well how young I was. He took every opportunity to waylay me, entice me into a corner, and fondle me. I fought him off ferociously, scratching, and even biting to get free of his grasp. I had seen him bringing home an array of young women and taking them upstairs. I had no intention of joining their ranks. His forcible molestation of a fourteen-year-old girl would have been regarded as a criminal act in any society, let alone in Iran, yet I had no one to turn to for help because Mummy and I had never discussed sex in any shape or form. I had to confront this degenerate Don Juan on my own. And from the depths of my being I somehow found the moral strength to resist his blandishments until, providentially, he became interested in his best friend's wife, succeeded in seducing her, and finally married her and moved away. I never saw him again, but I suffered tremendously from feelings of guilt. I was too young and inexperienced to realize that I had done surprisingly well to fend him off and that *he* was the one at fault for molesting me.

I latched onto Catholicism as a path to salvation, a way to be forgiven for my transgressions—to keep me from going to hell for that insistent pull in my crotch. The only obstacle to my conversion was that I had to have Mummy's permission to become a Catholic. She was steadfast in her refusal to give me permission. She put it to me in practical terms that I could understand, speaking of postponement rather than denial. "What if you become a Catholic and then fall in love with a man who is not Catholic? Then you won't be able to marry him. Why don't you wait a few years? You can always do it later," she said. I asked Sister Elvira what I could do to save my soul now that my mother would not allow me to convert. "If you pray hard and genuinely feel sorry for having sinned, then perhaps God will forgive you," she replied. I prayed fervently, with many an ardent "mea culpa," and repeated my "Ave Maria" again and again.

By the end of my second summer at the Benedictine boarding school near Shemran my ties with the convent were secure, woven as they were of strands of religious fervor, aesthetic sensibility, and budding puberty. Although I continued to go to Community School during the regular school year, I returned almost every evening to the Catholic school for Sister Savina's free piano lessons and to practice because I did not have a piano at home.

The beauty of the large cathedral in central Tehran encouraged me to continue going to mass on Sundays. Its stained-glass windows, its glittering altar, its writhing Christ on the cross, and its soaring gothic arches transported me into a state of ecstasy. I loved the rites and the rituals, the kneeling and rising, the signing of the cross, the burning of incense, and the reciting of the Latin Liturgy, which I knew by heart even though I had little idea what it meant. It all gave me a feeling of spiritual uplift that I took to be a religious experience.

Although my love of music and my guilt feelings were equally responsible for the enormous pull of the Catholic Church, I probably took to its teachings so readily because I found much of it surprisingly familiar, both from my Bible studies and from Zoroastrian precepts. Christian teachings about God and Satan recalled the Zoroastrian beliefs in the forces of good and evil, life after death, a day of judgment, and the coming of a savior. That familiarity, combined with turbulence at home and my tempestuous encounter with early adolescence, served to heighten the church's appeal. For a while I was utterly captivated.

Gradually, however, I found my feelings cooling toward the Benedictine nuns and their religion. When eventually I joined Mrs. Cook's ballet company and the nuns saw on cinema marquees the photographs of Aida, Wilma, and me dressed in flimsy skirts, our midriffs bare, our legs showing, they clucked and shook their heads about it, the mother superior herself confronting me with the "sinfulness" of my behavior. I had trouble reconciling the shame they suggested I should be feeling with the pride I took in our performances. Their reaction upset and annoyed me. Like so many others in my environment, they believed my dancing was endangering my soul. Why could they not see that it was beautiful art and spiritually uplifting? They were as irritating to me as those good-for-nothings in the audience who whistled and "meowed" whenever we performed the *Dance of Love*.

Mrs. Cook had taken her inspiration for this dance of romance from early Persian history, casting me as a Sassanian princess. I was to be bold and chaste at the same time. Another of the students, Daneshvar—with features so classical that he might have stepped straight off the bas-reliefs of Persepolis—played the role of my lover. In spite of his arched eyebrows that met at the center and his dark eyes that smoldered with passion, vanity, and sometimes rage, I had little fondness for him and found him too formal, too "Persian," because I was used to the company of American and European boys, but we must have put on a persuasive performance. Judging by the hoots and howls our dance sometimes elicited, our audiences must have concluded it was a dance about the physical consummation of love. Perhaps it was. All I know is that with arched backs, interlaced arms, swayings back and forth, and intimate gestures we conveyed a story of courtship and love. The whooping came whenever Daneshvar held my hands as he bent over me with a sinuous arabesque, while I arched away from him in a deep backbend. I was so mortified by the audience's reaction that I tried to persuade Mrs. Cook to change the choreography, but she was outraged at the idea. Like Mummy, she hated prudery and was certainly not going to allow a few "dirty-minded" members of the audience to alter her creation. In any case she knew she stood on solid ground, historically and artistically. As for the Catholic nuns who disapproved of our endeavors without even having seen our performances, they succeeded only in hurting my feelings.

Years later in a museum somewhere I was fascinated to see vases, vessels, goblets, fragments of mosaics, and frescoes from the Sassanian period in which Persian dancers and musicians tinkled finger cymbals, rattled tambourines, strummed lutes, or waved scarves, much as the girls in our troupe did. What most amazed me was the striking resemblance between the Sassanian dancers' head gear, hairstyle, and costume and the corresponding items I wore for the *Dance of Love*. Like them, I wore a brocade jacket with long, wide sleeves, its hem grazing my knees. Beneath it I had on transparent long pants caught at the ankle with elastic and ankle bells. On my head was an imitation gold crown, with tufts of my hair elaborately curled against its surface and pinned there above the forehead, with the rest of my hair falling to my shoulders. I was startled at how accurately our dance captured history and legend. It was one of the highlights of our repertory and always brought down the house, applause drowning out the occasional ribald hoot. When the nuns looked at the photographs of my performances, however, they saw neither history nor art—only sins of the flesh.

There were other reasons why my infatuation with Catholicism started to wane. I began to see more clearly that Zoroastrians, Muslims, Jews, and Christians *all* believed their faith was the one true faith. What right did the Catholics have to assume that all non-Catholics would suffer in purgatory or go to hell forever? In school history classes I began to learn more about Protestantism, the Renaissance, the Reformation. I read Voltaire and Rousseau, and was exposed to the ideas of the Enlightenment. Gradually I started questioning my acceptance of Benedictine Catholicism.

My disillusionment grew when the nuns took us swimming and insisted that we wear our long-sleeved encumbering uniforms even though we were all girls, surrounded by high walls, with not a man anywhere in sight. That was exactly the kind of prudery Mummy had fought against all her life, only now it came not from Iranians, but from Italian nuns.

I became even more skeptical when I encountered at a party one of the young girls I had known at the convent, a novice who had been preparing to enter the sisterhood and had always worn a habit and wimple. Relatives who were opposed to her becoming a nun had abruptly pulled her out of the convent at the age of seventeen. I was shocked to see her in street clothes. Her lips were bright with vivid, scarlet lipstick; her dress was excessively clinging, seductive, and revealing. She smoked, drank, laughed loudly, revealed as much leg as possible, and apparently interpreted her new role as beautiful temptress. Although she was indeed beautiful, she came across as coarse, vulgar, and ignorant. Rather than giving her an educational foundation and preparing her for the outside world, her upbringing in the convent had left her totally unequipped to participate in mixed company or to deal with the realities of life outside the convent walls. Like a domesticated cub released into the wild to fend for itself with no preparation, she was ill-equipped to deal with her newly found freedom.

Seeing her, I felt grateful for the freedom Mummy had always allowed me and deeply convinced that it was better to give young people freedom, while arming them with a standard of ethics that would enable them to distinguish right from wrong and to rein in their appetites. Some years later, when I was seventeen, I had a remarkably different experience with Catholicism when, after graduating from the American high school, I attended the Ecole Jeanne d'Arc.

Not only did the French nuns who ran the school dress differently, with wide-brimmed wimples and blue tunics, and speak differently—French instead of Italian—but their mission was also different. Their primary interest was in promoting the French language and culture. Here, too, we memorized, but what we learned by rote was French literature, history, and geography, as well as mathematics based on the metric system. Here we were encouraged to read and to borrow books from the school's small library. Enjoying the school's competitive and stimulating environment, I realized that there were many forms of Catholicism, just as there were many forms of Islam or Protestantism or Judaism, and that my experience with the Benedictine nuns had been a singular one in a unique time and place.

Although I was not in the end converted to Catholicism, my contact with the Italian nuns had a lasting impact on me. Occurring at a crucial time in my life, it prompted me to think more deeply about spirituality, sexuality, and the arts. Was it possible to be concerned with spiritual matters and also to dance? Was it really sinful to perform on the stage? Did I really have to be a Catholic for my soul to be saved?

Gradually and perhaps not quite consciously I started to sort through my ideas. Slowly, imperceptibly, I turned away from the Catholic Church and began to rely less on forces outside myself for moral guidance. At the same time I moved more toward expressing my thoughts and feelings through music, dance, and literature, finding intellectual stimulation and spiritual release in the rhythm and harmony inherent in graceful melody, movement, and poetry. I was starting to find my wings.

Picking Up the Pieces

If lovers were not addicted to music and dancing
why would I sing all day and night
like a wailing flute?
—Jalal ad-Din Rumi, "Inner Sunrise"

THE PRECARIOUS FINANCIAL SITUATION in which Mummy now found herself left her little time to dwell on her psychic wounds. She busied herself keeping the house attractive, tidy, and rentable. She repaired furniture, placed ads in the newspaper, collected rents, paid bills, and attended to the various needs of our ever-changing tenants, more and more of whom were now members of the Allied armed forces.

Naneh, who had been our live-in maid for as long as I could remember, had finally grown too old and rheumatic to continue working and had gone home to her village to live with her sister. I was desolated when she left. In her place Mummy hired a young village woman named Sakineh. Strong-willed and stubborn, she drove Mummy crazy with her insistence on doing things her own way. Sweeping was done with short-handled brooms in those days, and Sakineh raised clouds of fine dust whenever she swept. Mummy kept trying to get her to hold the broom closer to the floor so as not to raise so much dust, but it was no use. "Like this," Mummy would repeat with some irritation, holding the broom just a few inches from the floor, but Sakineh was incorrigible. She seemed to think that the amount of dust she could raise was a testament to her skills.

A pretty woman, Sakineh had sparkling black eyes and an impish defiance in the toss of her head. Although she always covered her hair with a scarf, the buttons on the bodice of her cotton flowered dress were often undone. When she first started working for us, she would wear her chador when cleaning the tenants' rooms, but after a while she dropped the pretense and swept and made beds upstairs with her unbuttoned bodice proudly revealing the creamy tops of her ample breasts. Her favorite chore was shopping, which gave her an opportunity to haggle with the neighborhood shopkeepers and to display her pretty face and bosom along with her bargaining skills. Her chador was little hindrance to flirtation, for she would drape it over her head, wrap it tightly around her waist and tuck it in so as to leave her face and chest exposed and her hands free to carry the shopping baskets, thus meeting the requirements of both tradition and her own fanciful whims.

The tenants made constant demands on Mummy and Sakineh. One wanted warm milk every evening before going to bed; another needed a button replaced on his shirt; still another insisted on having a warm bath in the upstairs bathroom, even though there was a public *hamam* just half a block up the street and getting the hot-water system going required several hours of work for Mummy and Sakineh. Sometimes Sakineh would go upstairs and stay there an inexplicably long time, and I suspect some of the tenants made other kinds of demands on her. I am sure Mummy suspected it, too, but she said nothing.

I am embarrassed to admit that I, too, made petty and often unnecessary demands on Sakineh, calling for her to bring me a glass of water when I was studying or telling her to iron a skirt or blouse for me when I knew perfectly well she was busy plucking a chicken or scaling a fish. Domestic help was cheap in those days, and room and board were considered part of the payment for services. Salaries were meager at best. Often illiterate and largely unskilled, servants usually lived in and remained on duty morning, noon, and night, their well-being and leisure depending entirely on the benevolence of the employer. Sakineh had spunk, though. She defied me, and when I complained, Mummy calmly let me understand that I was being unreasonable and that Sakineh's time should be spent on more important matters than waiting on me hand and foot.

Mummy had other problems to worry about. On top of everything else, she occasionally received reports on Parviz's scrapes and misadventures. We heard that he had been filching money from Aunt Pari, sometimes skipping school, and getting into other trouble about which I heard only dark muttering, for Mummy tried to keep much of my brother's behavior from me. Finally matters came to a head, and Parviz was expelled from Community School for putting bullet cartridges containing small amounts of gunpowder into the coal stove in his classroom. The ensuing explosion was sensational, terrifying some of his classmates and delighting others. As he explained it later, shrugging his shoulders, "They weren't really dangerous," but they did make a big bang. His teacher and principal were not amused, so he was expelled from school and told he could never come back. Parviz would now have to go to a Persian school.

It was a wrenching adjustment for him, for although he spoke Persian well enough, he could read and write it only at a fourth-grade level, and he was now in junior high school. The public schools were well known for the harsh methods they used to control and discipline students. Parviz's new teachers insisted that he learn to write with his right hand, although he was left-handed. In those days students were routinely caned on the hand with a fine willow branch for even minor offenses—for being tardy, not paying attention, giving the wrong answer, talking, or passing notes to other students. As Parviz related it, "One of the boys wet his pants at the blackboard for fear of scribbling the wrong answer and being caned for it. He got a caning for wetting his pants." Learning was largely by rote memorization, and Parviz was not used to this method.

When Daddy and Parvin returned to Tehran—with a newborn infant—Parviz went to live with them. From time to time he would come to our home for a visit and report with great glee how he had dribbled cold water on the baby's face or pinched him and made him cry. But even though the infant was Parvin's, Mummy reprimanded my brother for mistreating a baby.

I saw little of Parviz now. Whenever I did, he would complain about his back, which caused him so much pain that when he went fishing or hiking in the mountains, he would have to lie flat on the bare ground every so often to ease the pain before he could continue. Daddy took him from one doctor to another, and each doctor gave a different diagnosis, ranging from curvature of the spine to "he masturbates too much." In desperation Daddy arranged to send my brother to the United States for treatment, so now it was Parviz's turn to fly to California and move in with Uncle Shahbahman. Medical examinations revealed that far from being caused by masturbation, the pain was a result of tuberculosis of the spine that had progressed so far as to require a bone graft. Skillful surgery saved Parviz's life, although full recovery was a slow and painful process. Uncle Shahbahman and his wife not only took Parviz in, but took care of him during his convalescence and even managed to find part-time work for

With my brother Parviz
shortly before he left to go
to the United States for
treatment for his back.

him in my uncle's lab. Their help enabled him to make a good recovery and eventually go on to college and become a chemical engineer. He and our brother Iraj became fast friends.

Mummy and I settled into a quiet, peaceful routine after Parviz went to the United States. Although our living circumstances were greatly reduced in terms of elegance, space, and comfort, they were vastly improved in terms of serenity and freedom from friction. Uncertain and insecure though Mummy was, she no longer had to cope with Daddy's alcoholism and Parviz's truancy. Besides, she had her freedom, even though she had neither deliberately nor actively sought it.

I saw little of my paternal cousins anymore and developed closer friendships at school, especially with Toori, a new classmate who was half German. I also threw myself into the role of Miss Hardcastle in *She Stoops to Conquer* and then quickly thereafter into the character of Topsy in a stage production of *Uncle Tom's Cabin,* a role I drew not so much for my acting abilities as for my frizzy hair, which Mummy braided into a myriad thin plaits, with ribbons at the ends. I joined the choir and placed first in a schoolwide poetry-reading contest. I also won several spelling bees—effortless successes, I will admit, because I was a naturally good speller and never studied for any of the contests—and occasionally choreographed and performed short ballets during talent shows at school.

Sister Savina continued to give me free music lessons, and I played the piano almost every day. I had much leisure to read and developed a passion for Shakespeare, Dostoevsky, Wordsworth, Coleridge, and Hawthorne. At thirteen I was at an age when a single sexual scene in a book was enough to recommend it for reading, so my classmates and I would sometimes circulate such books among ourselves with much whispering and giggling. Pornography was unknown to us, and our idea of a titillating book was Pearl Buck's *The Good Earth.*

I often listened to the American Armed Forces radio station and knew all the lyrics of the most popular songs of the day. "I Walk Alone," "Don't Fence Me In," and "I'll Be Seeing You" formed part of my singing repertory and helped shape my perception of the war and of the world. I also knew all the latest dance steps, and my classmates and I danced many a night away to the music of Benny Goodman or Harry James, taking turns winding up the gramophone, teaching each other how to samba, rhumba, or jitterbug, happy to be dancing—girls dancing with other girls if boy partners were lacking.

At Mme. Cornelli's ballet school we had for the first time two young men to dance with in our performances. They were as different as day from night. Shuric was a short and stocky Russian with tightly curled blond hair and blue eyes. Kotic was an exceptionally tall Armenian Russian with black hair and dark eyes. They had both grown up in Iran and spoke Russian and Persian fluently, and English passably well; Kotic also spoke Armenian.

Although these boys had no ballet training, they had grown up learning Armenian and Russian folk dances and were able to learn quickly whatever Mme. Cornelli required of them. Years later I learned that the internationally renowned dancer Nureyev had similarly had his early training in Russian folk dancing rather than in ballet. Shuric and Kotic were agile, young, and strong, and made perfect dance partners for our end-of-the-year recitals. Until they appeared on the scene, girls dressed as men, sometimes with mustache and sideburns pencilled on their faces to enhance the illusion of masculinity, had danced our male roles. Now for the first time we had real male partners. Now we could leap into a jeté and, propelled by a pair of strong arms, soar high into the air before being set down ever so softly. Now supportive hands could twirl us around at dizzying speeds, adding momentum and bravura to our spins. A friendship quickly developed between the two boys and three girls of the group; we often saw each other outside of dance classes, going to the movies or to parties together. I gradually developed a crush on Kotic, but he did not seem to return the sentiment.

Mummy gradually expanded her circle of friends and acquaintances, and sometimes she would have English or American friends over for drinks, assigning me the task of passing the hors d'oeuvres among the guests. Sometimes she and her friends would dance late into the evening while I changed records and wound up the gramophone. Although Mummy drank only moderately, her guests consumed a good bit of liquor. I never drank at these parties. Although some of my friends were experimenting with social drinking and smoking cigarettes just to seem grown-up, I was a confirmed teetotaler. As for smoking, one time Parviz and I had tried burning a twig and puffing on it in the back yard. Needless to say, it was an unpleasant experience and cured us both of wanting to smoke.

Out in the city liquor flowed abundantly, as numerous bars sprang up to cater to the foreign troops stationed there. Although some of these bars had opened after the British and Russian invasion of Iran in 1941, many more appeared after the Lend-Lease Act of 1942 brought American engineering and transport troops to the country. Conspicuous both for their general friendliness and openhandedness, the American men in uniform also had the reputation of being the primary and best-paying foreign customers of the bars and of the red-light district. The British soldiers had less money to spend and were more subdued and reticent. The Russians had even less money and, of all the Allied forces, seemed most to shrink from contact with the local populace.

Foreign troops and their military vehicles were a constant reminder of the war that continued to ravage Europe. Massive convoys of army trucks regularly rumbled along roads and highways, the benches in their open beds packed with uniformed men with upright rifles aligned like vertical posts in a fence. I often stopped and watched them as they passed, sensing the aura of power they projected. The American intervention in the war had brought to Iran thousands of U.S. troops and technical advisors whose extraordinary energy and know-how had increased the capacity of the Trans-Iranian Railway fivefold and had enabled the United States to deliver to the Red army 4 million tons of equipment and goods, 150,000 vehicles, and 3,500 aircraft.

We were kept informed of the events in Europe by BBC news broadcasts as well as by the American Armed Forces radio station. Over the years the names Sevastopol, Stalingrad, Dunkirk, and Tobruk became part of our vocabulary. Movietone newsreels, which preceded featured films in the movie theaters, stamped on our minds images of bombed-out shells of buildings; piles of rubble; cannons roaring; rifles flashing; planes swooping, diving, and bombing; men, women, and children screaming, fighting, falling, dying. Prime Minister Churchill and General Montgomery, or "Monty," as Mummy referred to him, were clearly the heroes of the day. Mummy obviously took pride in them, and we joined her in cheering them on. Hitler, Mussolini, Goebbels, and Göring were the unmistakable villains. We hated them and wondered how men could be so evil. Not everyone felt as we did, however. Although Iran had sided with the Allies, there were still pro-German elements in the country among those who had had close business ties with Germany or who had studied in Germany or were enamored of German culture. My friend Toori's father was ardently pro-German, and I would smoulder with anger whenever he let loose a pro-fascist, anti-Allies diatribe.

Some pro-German sympathizers were simply ardent nationalists who believed it was in Iran's best interests to side with Germany rather than with the Allies. Many kept their opinions to themselves, but others were outspoken in their pro-Axis sentiments. One notably vocal sympathizer was Uncle Shahbahram, Daddy's younger brother, father of my cousin Shirin. Uncle Shahbahram had spent many years in Germany, and his wife was German. During the early years of the war, when my parents were still together, we would huddle around our shortwave radio and listen to him, broadcasting Persian-language news and propaganda from Berlin. It made Daddy furious, for although he had conducted much business with Germany, spoke German fluently, and had visited Germany many times, his sympathies in the war were with the Allies.

Uncle Shahbahram was an eloquent and persuasive speaker. His opponents condemned him for his broadcasts and branded him a traitor and a spy, but it was not clear for whom he was supposed to be spying. Some alleged for Germany; others claimed for England. In the byzantine tangle that characterized Iran's relations with the great powers of the day, misinformation and disinformation were commonplace. Given Iran's past unfortunate experiences with Great Britain and the Soviet Union, it did not seem all that far-fetched for people to allege simultaneously that Uncle Shahbahram was spying for the Allies and for Germany. Considering that he had at one time worked for the Anglo-Iranian Oil Company, some thought that his pro-Axis leanings were more apparent than real and that he was actually a double agent, a British spy posing as a pro-Axis sympathizer. The arguments of those who made these allegations were bolstered by the fact that after the war he became a Persian-language newscaster for the BBC's foreign news service.

Before the Allies invaded Iran on August 25, 1941, forcibly removing Reza Shah from power, Iran's leanings had been toward the Axis powers. Many nationalists of the day believed that Germany could be profitably used as a countervailing force against Great Britain and Russia, both of whom had played fast and loose with Iran's early attempts at establishing a constitutional monarchy and had at one time carved Iran up into spheres of influence, agreeing to share the country between them. I am inclined to think that Uncle Shahbahram might have been one of those nationalists who believed that in order to rid Iran of the interference of Great Britain and Russia in his country's internal affairs, it was in the nation's best interests to side with Germany.

I had an unusual opportunity to observe his patriotism when he came to see the first public performance of Mrs. Cook's dance troupe in a Tehran theater. Some family members had criticized Mummy for allowing me to dance in public. Our family name was, after all, held in high esteem, and it would not do to have it dragged through the mud. Uncle Shahbahram attended the opening to see for himself just how much damage was being done to the family reputation, but to his surprise he found our performance deeply moving and serious of purpose, tapping as it did into the audience's sense of pride in Iran's past glories, its history, its literature, its music, and, yes, its dance. He came backstage to congratulate us, and tears welled up in his eyes as he embraced me and told me he wished that it could have been his voice reciting lines from the great poets as the orchestra played and we dancers glided, dipped, and leaped, celebrating Iran's great past in a whirl of exuberant motion. His tears, to my mind, were convincing evidence that he was a true nationalist.

In the early years of the war before my parents broke up, when the news from the BBC announced Axis advances on many fronts, Mummy and Daddy would discuss the events in anxious tones, but quietly, so as not to alarm us. Later, during the bombing of London, it became more difficult for them to conceal their concern, and I would try to imagine what it must be like to take refuge in an air-raid shelter every time the sirens sounded. In school we rolled bandages as part of the war effort. I felt guilty when Mummy admonished me for my wastefulness when I picked at my food or left too much on my plate.

"There are children starving in Europe," she would say with some vexation. Although I felt sorry for the starving children in Europe, I could not see how cleaning my plate was going to help them, so I only pouted and spread the food around with my fork.

Even during the Anglo-Russian invasion of Iran in 1941 we did not entirely brush up against the reality of war. Although Iranians fought and died resisting the Allied invasion, the activity was far from the capital, in the extreme north and south of the country, and the encounter was mercifully brief—a matter of four days. In Tehran we followed the news on the radio with some agitation and fear, and when Allied planes flew overhead, we briefly panicked and ran down to the cellar, expecting them to bomb and strafe the defenseless city. Instead, they dropped propaganda leaflets denouncing Reza Shah for his pro-Axis bias and advocating on behalf of the Allied powers.

Similarly, the bloodletting of the war in Europe was at a comfortable distance. Once in a while an eruption would occur that forcefully brought home to us how closely Iran's destiny was tied to those far-off events in Europe. Three years into the war, in 1942, we started to see long queues of shivering people waiting in line to purchase bread, a staple rapidly becoming increasingly scarce and of poorer quality. The texture and taste of the normally delicious native flat breads had deteriorated markedly. Parts of the country were suffering from famine; wheat was in short supply, and the indigestible bread that we almost choked on was being adulterated with barley, millet, bran, and poppy seed. Sometimes we would find pieces of string in it. It was so inedible that Mother started substituting rice for the usual bread we ate for breakfast. The wealthy were able to buy wheat on the black market and have it privately baked for a high fee, but in some provinces riots broke out because bread was an important staple for a largely poor population. Without it people went hungry.

Many pro-Axis newspapers in Iran blamed the shortage on the occupying powers, claiming that they were buying up all available supplies of wheat in order to feed their armies on other fronts. The Allies dismissed these charges, claiming not only that they had not taken any wheat out of Iran, but that they had actually brought seventy-five thousand tons into the country and that only hoarding and price gouging by Iranian government officials could account for the scarcity of wheat.

Whatever the cause, matters became so bad that rioting broke out in Tehran.

Barely ten, I was playing pin the tail on the donkey at a birthday party being given for David Elder, one of my classmates, when the disturbances occurred. I had just had my first taste of peanut butter and was enjoying a rare treat of cake and ice cream when David's father burst into the room and broke up the party. "You must all get home as fast as you can," he told us, his voice revealing his anxiety: rioting and looting had broken out in various parts of the city in protest over the unavailability of bread.

I headed home on my bicycle as fast as I could, taking my usual shortcut down a narrow alley when suddenly I heard loud and angry shouting behind me. Turning my head, I saw a band of workers, carrying shovels and picks, chasing me with raised fists. Terrified, I pumped the pedals fast and furiously, putting distance between my pursuers and me, until they were finally lost from sight. I was badly shaken, but arrived home safely, although I was at a loss to explain why the mob's rage and anger should have been directed against me. Perhaps they had taken me for a foreigner or for a "wealthy" and "modern" girl. I do not know. Aware of the mindless rage that could unexpectedly turn a crowd into a destructive force, I felt grateful for having escaped harm. For the next few days we all stayed close to home, from where we could hear the roar of huge groups of demonstrators agitatedly shouting slogans in front of the Russian and British embassies, those symbols of power and intervention.

About a year later, in late November 1943, an armed British soldier stopped me as I took my usual route past the Russian embassy on my way to school. "You cannot go down this street," he said, barring my way with his rifle. He seemed astonished when I asked him in perfect English what was going on. He laconically replied that he had orders to prevent anyone from going that way, so I took a long roundabout route to school. Later that day I learned that Churchill, Roosevelt, and Stalin were all meeting in Tehran at the Russian embassy. Their various arrivals in Iran had been kept secret from the public for security reasons, and the cordon of empty streets maintained around the British and Russian embassies for several days was also a matter of security. This historic meeting came to be known as the Tehran Conference.

There were other ways in which our lives were touched by the foreign troops stationed in Iran—both the British and, increasingly, the American. After her divorce, Mummy started going to dances put on by the American armed forces in their Amirabad barracks. There was much gossip about what went on at these events, and very few young women from "good families" went to them. Those who did were usually Armenian or of other foreign extract, or they were Iranians hoping to find an American husband who would take them to the United States. It was difficult to keep secret one's attendance at these dances because the women had to wait at bus stops to be picked up by conspicuously American army buses for transport to the barracks. As the women stood at designated bus stops in small groups, passersby would often hurl insults at them, the more common ones being "whore," "cunt giver," and "traitor." The women would not answer, but would avert their eyes, turn their backs, or keep on talking with a friend.

Although going to an army dance might be innocent enough behavior in some societies, the young women knew that in this particular society it was considered not only inappropriate, lewd, and licentious, but also traitorous because the army was that of an occupying force. They realized that by going to the dances they were running the risk of ruining their reputations even though the army, showing uncharacteristic sensitivity to local mores, made sure the dances were carefully chaperoned and regulated. Among other regulations, no one was allowed to leave the dance hall during the event, and when the band had packed away their instruments, the young women were returned by bus to the spot where they had boarded. Still, the dances were meeting places for young men and women, and often a chance encounter would lead to a later rendezvous.

Mummy took me with her to a dance once. No one under eighteen was allowed, but no one questioned my presence. I was twelve years old at the time, but looked eighteen, and no one dreamed how young I was. Mummy and I waited at the bus stop, boarded a bus, and rode to the barracks. We were driven first to a large open-air amphitheater where the USO was putting on entertainment for the American troops. Bright lights played on an enormous stage where a row of long-legged young women in black lace stockings kicked their legs high and rapped a smart rhythm against the floor. A barbershop quartet sang a medley of songs, followed by a comedian who told jokes I could not understand. The play of colors on the stage enchanted me, and I was amazed at the dancers' long legs and awed at the roar of the crowd when it broke out in laughter.

At the dance after the show we found ourselves in a spacious, softly lit hall, where an orchestra was playing "Good-night, Sweetheart" and dozens of men in uniform were shuffling across the floor, each one clasping a partner in his arms.

Many of them were dancing very close. Later, when the music changed, they started jitterbugging, the men frenziedly spinning their partners around or lifting them up into the air and bringing them down first on one hip, then on the other. The women's skirts swooshed and twirled prettily, revealing legs, garter belts, and silk stockings. Mummy and I stood with a group of young women who were giggling and joking with each other, waiting to be asked to dance. Nearby stood a group of young men, eyeing the women, laughing among themselves, elbowing or nudging each other from time to time. No one looking at the two of us would have guessed that we were mother and daughter. Besides being a beautiful woman, Mummy was diminutive, perky, and slim, all of which made her look much younger than she was. Before long a young man in uniform asked her to dance, while another came up to me and was soon swooping me across the floor. A few minutes into the dance, a hand tapped my partner on the shoulder, and I found myself dancing with someone else. I jitterbugged, foxtrotted, waltzed, and tangoed with one partner after another until midnight.

While leading me across the floor, one young man from Mississippi expressed outrage that several black soldiers had had the "gall" to cut in and dance with me. "Back home they would not dare do that," he said, barely keeping his anger in check. That was my introduction to race relations in the United States. Although I knew enough U.S. history to know of the enslavement of blacks and of their eventual emancipation, I had no idea how deep-seated American racial prejudices were. I would not again hear blatant racism so openly expressed until some years later in the 1950s, when I was shocked to see the sign "Whites Only" at restaurants, rest stops, and theaters in the southern United States and when a welcoming administrator at the University of Georgia took pains to explain to me that "colored people" were "inferior" to whites and that I should treat them accordingly. At the USO dance in Tehran, however, I puzzled briefly over what the Mississippian had told me, then dismissed it. I was too busy spinning across the floor.

Another young man, a redhead from Arkansas who told me his nickname was Red, was a superb dancer and led me smoothly through a complex series of steps. During one slow number he pulled me close and pressed his cheek against mine. I had never danced cheek to cheek before and could feel the blood rush to my head. My heart started pounding, and my palms got sweaty, much to my consternation. "I must be falling in love," I thought. At the end of the evening I left with my head spinning. For several days I sighed and mooned over Red, humming "Good-night sweetheart, till we meet tomorrow" and longing to go to another USO dance, where I just might meet him again. However, there was to be no "tomorrow" because someone must have seen Mummy boarding the Amirabad bus with me, and a few days later Daddy came over in a rage and up-braided Mummy for having taken me to an army dance. "How could you even think of taking her with you?" he shouted. "You will ruin her reputation." Much to my regret, Mummy never took me with her again.

Daddy and I saw little of each other at this point. Once in a while I would go over to see him at his office to avoid visiting him at his home, for I resented his new family and was angry over the way he had treated my mother. I did not look forward to these visits. Often strained, they were frequently prompted by Mummy's need for a little extra cash. Although she did not talk about it, I could sense her frustration over her inability to get Daddy to contribute anything to-ward my expenses.

On one occasion she bought a length of silk, made me a beautiful dress, then sent me to Daddy's office to show it to him, instructing me to tell him it had been made by Madame Marie, a professional dressmaker, and to ask him for the money to cover its cost. I did so reluctantly. After chatting with him for what I considered a decent length of time, I drew the dress out of a shopping bag and showed it to him. Squirming inside, I told him it had been made by Madame Marie. Daddy was not fooled for a minute. He examined the buttonholes care-fully, checked the seams and the hem. Unlike Mummy, he had some experience with tailors and knew what fine details to look for. He knew Mummy had put me up to lying and could clearly see that doing so made me uncomfortable. Mercifully, he did not make an issue of it, but gave me just enough cash to cover the cost of the fabric. After all, he was an expert in textile technology. Mummy was glad, however, to have extracted any amount of money from her former husband, no matter how little. As the Persian saying goes, plucking even one hair from a bear is providential.

Although my visits to Daddy's office were often awkward and strained, I could not help being struck by how much he had changed. He seemed more content, less morose, more like the father who had romped with Kaveh, shown me how to draw faces, and laughed out loud when I told him I had *almost* won a swimming race. Amazingly, Daddy had stopped drinking!

Was it possible, then, that Mummy actually *had* "driven him to drink," as he often claimed? Were his and my mother's differences so irreconcilable that rupture was the only remedy, the only hope for a renewed life free of the debilitating effects of alcohol? Was she partially responsible for his addiction? I do not know.

What I do know is that Daddy had stopped drinking altogether. When I finally made my peace with Parvin some years later, I was struck by how accommodating she was, how affectionate and loving toward him, how compatible they seemed. I decided then that Parvin was really better suited to Daddy than Mummy had been, and I was envious of my half-brothers for having enjoyed Daddy's best attributes instead of his worst. But perhaps it was all an act and his abstinence only temporary. Perhaps he ultimately took up drinking again. All I know is that for some reason Parvin, after being a seemingly devoted wife to Daddy and model mother to their three sons for many years, unexpectedly turned like a wounded creature and divorced him. Much later I learned that, in fact, their marriage had been exceedingly contentious and tumultuous.

The Joy of Dancing

O body swayed to music, O brightening glance,
How can we know the dancer from the dance?
—W. B. Yeats, "Among School Children"

IT WAS 1946. I was fourteen and in my third summer at the Italian school when Mrs. Cook's dream of forming an Iranian ballet company started to take shape like a germinating seed. Although my home was peaceful now, I was still drawn to the convent—for its spiritual dimension, its exquisite little church, and its run-down, out-of-tune piano. The end of the school year and the onset of summer found me boarding once again in the garden compound of the nuns. When Aida came to the convent to persuade me to join Mrs. Cook's enterprise and to participate in the command performance in honor of the American ambassador, she also told me that we had been invited to attend a ball at the palace the next week and that Mummy was invited, too. At that, any reservations I had melted away. When I excitedly told Mummy about it, her reaction was more restrained than mine, but she raised no objections, for she realized how much it would mean to me. We accepted the invitation.

I soon found myself caught up in an intense schedule of rehearsals that kept me out of the convent school for many hours at a time. Mummy had talked to the mother superior, and I was granted more or less unrestricted freedom to come and go as I pleased, creating resentment among some of the other girls because the nuns were clearly making an exception in my case. But their resentment amounted to no more than grumbling. The mother superior had granted me free passage in and out of the boarding school, and that was that.

First we would be going to the palace ball—in less than a week's time. It was to be a black-tie affair. A ball at the palace? What on earth would we wear? Mummy was hardly in a financial position to have a ball gown made for me or for herself. I panicked at the thought of appearing in a less-than-appropriate gown, but as usual Mummy's resourcefulness came to the rescue, and we spent some time in the big bazaar in southern Tehran where we had often shopped together for shoes, artifacts, or piece goods. Only this time we went to the "American bazaar," a section of the old bazaar that took its name from the piles and piles of used clothing that lined its passageways. Thrown together in an indistinguishable jumble of assorted sizes, shapes, and colors, huge quantities of secondhand clothing collected in the United States to help war refugees had somehow ended up in the old bazaar, where they were sold very cheaply. Mummy had discovered that if she went carefully through the mountains of clothes, she could find some beautiful dresses that, with a little alteration, would clothe the two of us quite elegantly at very minimal expense, although, at that age, I would have preferred to die rather than admit to anyone where my dress came from.

With no ready-to-wear clothing in Tehran back then, men and women alike would buy fabric, take it to a dressmaker or tailor, then return several times for fittings. Some women did their own sewing at home, as Mummy had always done, but altering secondhand clothing turned out to be much simpler and cheaper than buying new fabric and spending hours cutting and sewing it. We both maintained a discreet silence about the origin of our wardrobes. For the upcoming ball Mummy had found herself a full-length lace dress in beige that skimmed her figure and flared out from just below the knees into a wide swirl. It would twirl out nicely on the dance floor. For me, she had found a fuschia chiffon gown, off the shoulder, with ruffles around the neckline. It was most flattering and made me look very grown-up. We bought some white lace gloves for a finishing touch.

The day of the ball, a limousine provided by the royal family stopped in front of our house. As we came out, the chauffeur touched his white-gloved hand smartly to his hat brim, bowed slightly, and opened the limousine door for us. Mrs. Cook was already seated inside. After we picked up Aida, Wilma, and their mothers, the limousine made its way up the steep incline of the road to Shemran.

At the imposing gates that fronted the palace a guard checked our names off the guest list and beckoned us through. A stately tree-lined driveway led to the main entrance. A uniformed attendant opened the car doors and ushered us through halls and into the ballroom, where a number of huge crystal chandeliers sparkled over our heads like clusters of diamonds suspended in midair. Enormous bouquets of flowers adorned a number of elegant Louis XIV side tables spaced at regular intervals. I was flattered at being in such sumptuous surroundings and such distinguished company. It was terribly exciting.

Several elegantly dressed couples were spinning gracefully across the spacious parquet floor to a sedate waltz played by a live orchestra. Other guests stood around the room, chatting, watching the dancing, sizing up the gowns, and evaluating the beauty of one young woman or another. We three girls, our respective mothers, and Mrs. Cook clustered together, watching. We knew no one in that crowd. An official in charge of protocol had greeted us with a few welcoming words and then left us to our own devices.

The Shah was at that time between his first and second marriages. His first wife, Fawzieh, had returned to her native Egypt, and he had not yet met Soraya, the woman who would become his second wife. It was well known that he had numerous beautiful mistresses and quite an eye for the ladies. That evening, dressed formally in uniform, he was dancing with a young girl who seemed not much older than myself. Blond and exceptionally beautiful, she wore a dark green taffeta dress that billowed out from her waist before dropping to her ankles. Someone whispered to me that she was the daughter of the French ambassador. When the music stopped, the Shah bowed graciously to her and escorted her back to where her family was standing, her father stuffily ambassadorial, her mother charmingly gracious. He exchanged a few words with them. Then, with a slow and stiff gait, he started walking around the room, greeting some, disdaining others, and all the while surveying the women.

While the orchestra played a sedate fox-trot, the Shah paced the room, scanning the guests for someone to invite onto the dance floor. As he approached us, he slowed down, spoke a few words to Mrs. Cook, nodded toward us, and then slowly headed in my direction. I could feel my heart pounding. Was he going to ask me to dance? He was getting closer. I must feign indifference. I looked fixedly across the room, while out of the corner of my eye I could see his polished shoes getting nearer. The shoes seemed to pause in front of me for one split second, but then moved on, to my enormous disappointment and relief. I would dearly have loved to be able to boast about having danced with the Shah, but at the same time I felt relieved at not having to deal with such an overwhelming prospect. Besides, I told myself, in view of the Shah's well-known penchant for the ladies, it would probably have been bad for my reputation to have danced with him. In a moment the orchestra was playing again, and he had a new partner. The rest of the evening was uneventful, and neither Mummy nor I was invited to dance, although, to my chagrin, Wilma was—just once. I must admit that I was a bit nonplussed at being a wallflower, a role to which I was not accustomed. It was almost a relief to head home.

The big day was preceded by several weeks of frenetic preparations. We went over and over our dances, rehearsing to the point of exhaustion, often late into the night. Our costume designer had outdone herself, creating dresses of extraordinary beauty that fit each of us to perfection. Miles of tulle, chiffon, lamé, and brocade had gone into their making, as well as much creativity, imagination, and ideas borrowed from polychrome Persian miniature paintings. I tried on my various costumes, spinning around in front of the mirror to see how the skirts flared out. They could not have been more exquisite, but they were also sleeveless. We would be dancing bare-armed and bare-legged, and as we looked at our reflections in the mirror, Aida and I realized that some painful hair plucking was in order.

The next day we sat cross-legged on a ragged *gelim* and took turns being depilated with nothing more than basting thread and the *band-andaz*'s skill. It was a painful process. Running the thread adroitly across my leg, the *band-andaz* caught the hair where the two threads intersected, plucking it out in fine rows. It felt as though she was running an electrically charged filament across my leg. I gritted my teeth while she labored in silence, her body swaying forward and back. She often prepared young brides for their wedding nights, plucking hair from the client's arms, legs, eyebrows, and, if necessary, upper lip and forehead. As she worked on my legs, I was reminded of one of my classmates who, that same year, had prepared for her wedding night by having her pubic hair plucked instead of removed with *vajebi*. I could not help thinking how painful it must have been and swore to myself I would never endure such excruciating torture. Mummy and Aunt Doris, I knew, shaved their genitals, for in this part of the world pubic hair on women was considered distasteful and unalluring. So prevalent was that attitude that I accepted it unquestioningly until much later I discovered, to my astonishment, that in the West women did not remove their pubic hair.

Her job finished, the *band-andaz* patted some talcum powder over my legs. I ran my hand over my limbs and was thrilled at the silky softness of my now stubble-free skin, delighting in the smooth and elegant look of my legs. It was worth enduring the pain, I thought, but I was glad it was over. It was now Aida's turn. Later she and I were exceptionally quiet as we made our way home, walking together for a block or two before going our separate ways.

Aida's mother, Mrs. Akhundzadeh, had agreed to serve as chaperon for our royal performance. In the palace we were shown to a guest room where we changed into our costumes and applied our makeup. The musicians came in a separate car and set up their music stands and their music. First the guests were to be served their dinner, and we would have to wait until they finished their dessert. It turned out to be an unexpectedly long wait, for it was nearly ten o'clock before they even started serving the food. We, of course, would not be able to eat until after the performance. As it grew later and later, Aida's mother became more and more furious.

Finally the signal was given that it was time for us to perform. By now tired, hungry, and dispirited, we entered the dining room, where the guests sat at elegant round tables in groups of six or eight, drinking their coffee. The small space that had been cleared for our performance inhibited our movements. The lack of a stage that would separate and distance us from the audience made me, for one, feel uncomfortably restrained. Aida and her partner started out with a rendition of *Majnun and the Tulip,* a dance that Aida herself had choreographed. Next I did a solo peasant dance, feeling wooden and stilted throughout, for I lacked space to move freely. We ended with an abbreviated version of *Caravan.*

The guests applauded politely, then continued their interrupted conversations, while we were shepherded to the kitchen for our dinner. Mrs. Akhundzadeh was livid. She had expected us to be treated like guests and at least to have been seated in the dining hall at a separate table, if not with the VIPs. "We are being treated like servants. Eating in the kitchen, indeed! What do they think? That you three are *motreb?*" And she lit into Mrs. Cook for having allowed such an indignity, for having permitted us—three girls from good families—to be treated like hired entertainers or worse.

The events of that evening threatened to abort all of Mrs. Cook's plans for launching a new dance company. Aida's mother told her in no uncertain terms that none of us was to be subjected to such humiliation again. Aida would not continue to dance with the company, although, as Mrs. Cook and everyone else knew, she was the backbone of the enterprise. Without her there would be no troupe. Wilma's parents, too, withdrew their daughter from the fledgling company, and I, of course, was not going to stay if my peers were not, although I was a little mystified as to what all the fuss was about. I had not particularly minded eating in the kitchen.

A few months later Mrs. Cook effected a reconciliation with Aida's mother, who extracted promises and assurances that we would all be treated with appropriate respect from then on. The fiasco at the palace had provided the germ of a new idea—a performance on the grounds of the American embassy, with an outdoor stage, colored spotlights, and plenty of time to plan the performance.

Mrs. Cook gave free rein to her fertile imagination and conceived a stage in the shape of the famous Khaju Bridge built by Shah Abbas in the sixteenth century to span the Zayandeh-Rood River in the fabled city of Isfahan. Carpenters swarmed over the grassy grounds of the American embassy, sawing, banging, hammering, measuring, raising, and lowering huge panels of plywood. They called out directions to each other to bring this, take that, move out of the way, or give someone a hand, cursing and swearing when something went wrong. Through it all Mrs. Cook supervised every detail, standing with her feet planted firmly under her massive frame or perched atop a stool, her flesh spilling over the edges, her poodle over her arm. She cajoled, screamed, shouted, begged, threatened, pleaded, cried, and once even fainted. Ever so slowly and in spite of a thousand impediments her idea took shape, and lumber, nails, and dreams were forged under her direction into a magnificent raised replica of the Khaju Bridge.

A noted scholar of Iranian architecture has characterized that bridge as "the culminating monument of Persian bridge architecture." A two-storied succession of twenty-three arches of brick stand on massive stone piers, creating a roadway that runs between high walls arcaded on the outer sides. Brilliantly colored tiles ornament a rectangle above each tapered arch as well as the surfaces of the pavilions in the center and at either end. Sluice gates enable the bridge to double as a dam, and, downstream, great flights of stone steps lead away from it down to the water, where over the centuries untold numbers of Isfahanis have picnicked and done their washing.

Our replica had a mere five arches instead of twenty-three and was arcaded only on the rear side so as to create a stage facing the audience, with the arches as a backdrop. But the play of colored lights on these five arches managed to simulate the magnificence of the original. Through dances that re-created the activities that swarm over and around the bridge, we managed to capture its spirit. Girls doing their washing, lovers meeting in the pavilion, a caravan moving slowly across its roadway—all were brought to life with an added magical touch. With imaginative lighting, graceful movement, and a dash of poetry, romance, and drama, we managed to highlight both the beauty and functionality of this historical monument.

Combining old and new dances, Mrs. Cook created a full-length ballet called *The Bridge of Isfahan.* She incorporated into it the *Dance of Love,* which I was to perform with Daneshvar on the Khaju Bridge. With an eye to historical detail she sent me to the beauty shop to have my hair done in the manner of a Sassanian princess. Such hairstyles can be seen in fresco fragments from the ancient palace of Ney-Shahpour and on terra-cotta ossuaries dating from Sassanian times (A.D. 224–642). One of these frescoes depicts a procession in which musicians play the lute, cymbals, and drums while acrobats, tumblers, and dancers leap, twirl, and pulse to the music. Each performer is wearing a crown-like headdress, with short curls adorning her forehead and long ones framing her face. I found the style most unflattering, and so, more concerned with vanity than with historical accuracy, I washed out the offending hairdo. Mrs. Cook was furious with me but was faced with a fait accompli and could do nothing about it. I doubt the audience would have known the difference.

There were probably no more than a hundred spectators at our performance that night. Rows of folding chairs had been set up in front of the stage. The American ambassador, George Allen, and his wife sat in the front row. The audience consisted largely of embassy personnel and members of the diplomatic corps. They were enthusiastic, greeting our presentation with rounds of applause and even a standing ovation. There were no catcalls here during the *Dance of Love.* A number of people came up after the performance and congratulated us warmly for having presented a beautiful and moving spectacle. Mrs. Cook was euphoric over our success. Smiling, she introduced Aida, Wilma, and me to a number of the invited guests and was at her best—gracious and charming. We girls were pleased at how well the event had gone and found it difficult to take off the costumes and greasepaint and to return to the humdrum reality of being mere schoolgirls. When I entered my school the next morning, it seemed more drab than usual after the excitement of the previous evening.

Life was not to stay dull for long, however, for Mrs. Cook, spurred to greater endeavors by the success of the embassy performance, made grand plans for a two-week run at a local theater. The boldness and brashness of the idea of having us perform for the general public, where *anyone* could buy a ticket and watch us, even now astounds me. Such a thing was unheard of in Tehran. Until that moment every audience for whom we had ever performed had been carefully selected, controlled, and circumscribed. Now the common people would be able to see us—with our faces, legs, arms, and midriffs exposed. Men—total strangers—would be able to leer at us, fantasize over us, scrutinize our bodies.

Aida's and Wilma's parents expressed their concern, as did Daddy. "It is scandalous," he said. "It will damage their reputations." "Any riffraff off the streets will be able to walk in and watch the girls perform," Aida's mother protested. But Mrs. Cook had anticipated the objections. She knew that having the patronage of the royal family lifted the endeavor to a high plateau in the eyes of the common people. These were the days when the royal family still enjoyed prestige, if not popularity, when it was still unimaginable that they would someday be overthrown, driven from the country, and maligned as forces of evil and corruption.

Our intrepid American director also knew that, unlike the members of any Western dance company, we girls must preserve our status as *amateurs* and make it clear that our dancing was not a means of earning a livelihood. She showed our uneasy parents her advertisements that emphasized the purely artistic aspects of our performances, and liquid silver coated her tongue as she sought to persuade them. Furthermore, she was certain that the lyrical magic of our creations would touch the patriotic sensibilities of even the most common man—that the thematic material of the performances, the sedateness of our dances, and the poetry accompanying them would deflect any expectations of lascivious entertainment. She had been horrified, upon first arriving in Iran, to find that native theater was practically nonexistent except for the religious passion plays. Theatrical productions were often Molière plays translated into Persian. In her work as chief censor of theater and cinema she had done everything in her power to encourage the production of indigenous plays. Now she intended to restore lyrical theater to its rightful place on the stages of Iran. She knew that once people saw how rooted in history and tradition our performances were, they would realize that our dancing was to be respected, not maligned. Our audiences would be familiar with the legends we were portraying and the poetry we were acting out. All these elements would touch their hearts and souls. In the end Mrs. Cook's arguments managed to overcome our parents' anxieties.

From the beginning it was understood that a mother would be present at every rehearsal, a visible chaperon—not needed so much to police us as to demonstrate to anyone and everyone that we were dancing with the approval of our families. Usually Aida's mother filled the role, but once in a while Mummy would take a turn.

Our parents, however, were not the only ones to raise questions. Photographs of us, dressed in full regalia, were posted on the exhibition cases below the marquee at the entrance to the theater. Word quickly got around that our pictures were pasted "all over town." The next time I went to the Italian convent for a piano lesson, Sister Savina took it upon herself to warn me it was a sin to allow the public to see my midriff. I felt humiliated and annoyed, but was convinced that the sin lay in the eye of the beholder, not in me. Needless to say, her words did nothing to deter me, but instead reinforced my disillusionment with the nuns and their "narrow-mindedness," one of Mummy's favorite terms.

Even others besides family and the nuns raised objections. One day during a Latin class at the Community School, when I could not give the correct response to a question, my Latin teacher turned on me with barely concealed fury and upbraided me for spending so much time on dancing and rehearsing and so little time on studying Latin. She was right, of course. I *had* been neglecting my Latin. With her face flushed red and the veins in her neck standing out she vented her anger in a voice that trembled, almost choking on her words. What she did not realize was that I *was* studying something—dance and, indirectly, Persian history and poetry. I had never much liked either her or the subject she taught, but now I absolutely hated her and disliked Latin more than ever.

For our first public performance Mrs. Cook choreographed a dance called the *Prayer of Darius.* It was accompanied by the recitation of verses of heroic epic poetry from Ferdowsi's *Shahnameh.* In this work the tenth-century poet composed in verse form a vast canvas across which Persia's mythical heroes hunt lions, fight the enemy, conquer adversaries, make love to beautiful damsels, strive, suffer, live, and die. Derived from ancient Zoroastrian legends, his epic heroes help to bridge the gap between Muslims and Zoroastrians, uniting them in their common literary heritage. Mrs. Cook found in them an endless store of dramatic material on which to base her choreography.

It is said that in antiquity temple attendants performed ritual dances in Zoroastrian places of worship, reflecting Hindu and Hellenic influences. On a terra-cotta ossuary dating from some time between the first and the fifth century A.D. appear female dancing figures, interpreted by some archaeologists as being Mazdian temple attendants performing ritual dances. In the Tehran museum a collection of small cymbals are labeled as instruments used by "Achaemenid dancers in ritual dances," dating from some time between 675 and 323 B.C.

Although the idea of ritual temple dances might offend certain religious sensibilities, it proved irresistible to Mrs. Cook, steeped as she was in Hindu and Greek as well as Persian lore. The *Prayer of Darius* immediately set the tone for the entire performance, conveying to the audience our seriousness of purpose.

Aida had the lead role. She was the golden statue of the daughter of Cyrus, whom Darius loved. She wore a long dress of gold satin, with large flaps in the back, the tips of which were attached with tiny rings to her pinkies, so that when she spread her arms, the flaps formed wings. The edges of her sleeves and skirt were trimmed with continuous rows of sequins that refracted the light and glinted as she moved. As the curtains rose, Aida stood on a raised dais, her wings spread. Her elbows slightly bent, she held her arms out in a formal, stylized manner in imitation of the five-thousand-year-old figurines of ancient Luristan goddesses. As the daughter of Cyrus started to move in a slow and stately manner, a voice recited: "This land of ours is a beautiful angel, whose locks are the forests on the shores of the Caspian Sea. The pearls of the Persian Gulf are the confetti showered on this bride."

As she descended from the dais with slow and regal steps, two temple fires—three-dimensional reproductions of the friezes of Persepolis—were spotlighted, one on either side of the stage. They were attended by two magi, whose movements around the sacred fires were grand and dignified. Each priest held up a large cymbal, and Aida flitted across the stage and struck one cymbal from below with a soft-headed drumstick. As the gonglike sound resonated through the hall, she twirled, her wings swirling softly, her long black tresses flowing around her in liquid circles, her golden dress shimmering as it caught and reflected the light. She flitted to the other side of the stage and struck the second cymbal. This moment of great drama and intensity was repeated again and again like a litany, with hypnotic effect, similar to that achieved by the repetition of rituals or prayers. As the curtains closed, a thunderous applause broke out, while many in the audience rose to their feet, crying "bravo, bravo."

Our show was an instant success. Far from being labeled "dancing girls," we were hailed as heroines. The critics were unstinting in their praise. By infusing ancient Zoroastrian rituals and legends with the magic and vitality of movement, Mrs. Cook had tapped into the Persians' pride in their ancient roots and unique cultural heritage. In the process she had also helped me to become more familiar with my paternal roots. Grandfather would have appreciated the irony, I am sure, that an American woman, a foreigner, non-Zoroastrian and non-Iranian, had helped to spark my interest in the Persian side of my cultural heritage.

Greasepaint and Black Gold

The king loved Esther more than all the women, and she found
grace and favor in his sight more than all the virgins, so that he
set the royal crown on her head and made her queen instead of
Vashti.

—Esther 2:17

THE SUCCESS of our first two-week theater performance left me exhausted
but exhilarated. Greasepaint had gotten under my skin, applause into my blood.
Returning reluctantly to the routine of the classroom, I found algebra, history,
and French sadly lacking in glamour compared to those passionate leaps across a
lighted stage.

What is more, I sorely missed my normal schedule of ballet classes, for Mme.
Cornelli had barred Aida, Wilma, and me from her studio. She was enraged at
what was, in her eyes, our defection. In a vitriolic outburst she told Aida's
mother that none of us was ever to darken the door of her studio again. Just
when she needed us most, we had abandoned her. Now, with the end of the war,
she was finally able to order toe shoes and train students properly. Now, finally,
she had Shuric and Kotic to partner us in our duets, and her ballet school
seemed on the verge of a dramatic takeoff. Just when we were starting to be
good dancers, we had betrayed her. "After all the years of training, they go off
and perform for someone else!" she exploded. "I don't ever want to see any of
them again!"

As for Mrs. Cook, she did not run a regular ballet school, but rented
makeshift space for our rehearsals wherever she could find it and when she

needed it. Ever since her latest undertaking had ended, we three budding dancers had found ourselves without a place in which to train. I felt the lack intensely.

But we did not languish long. Mrs. Cook's ever-fertile imagination dreamed up a new adventure for our troupe—this time in Abadan, a city in southern Iran, located on the delta of the Shatt-al-Arab (the confluence of the Tigris and Euphrates Rivers) at the northernmost point of the Persian Gulf, well known for its large oilfields. Once again I threw myself into rehearsals and felt challenged to exceed. Meanwhile we prepared for the long trip to the south.

Mrs. Cook now had a handsome young assistant, Nejad, who was always at her side. He was her right-hand man, her left-hand man, and, when necessary, her voice as well. A young man in his early twenties with little formal education, Nejad was intelligent, shrewd, calculating, and brash. He cut expertly through the byzantine tangle of bureaucracy, vested interests, and kickback schemes that Mrs. Cook had to deal with to get her project off the ground. Nejad knew how to bully and threaten or to drip honey and molasses when needed. He was also athletic and willing to learn to dance so that he soon became one of our principal dancers.

Chaperons, of course, were imperative to our trip. Eager for a change of scene, Mummy agreed to accompany me. As we set off, we were segregated into two buses—the male dancers, orchestra players, and their instruments in one, and we three girls, our mothers, Mrs. Cook, and Nejad in another. The only men on board our bus were the driver and Nejad. Of course, bus drivers were necessarily men, and naturally a group of traveling women needed a male escort to protect them from any dangers they might encounter along the way. Transport was uncertain and unreliable, the roads rough and risky, and from time to time travelers in remote parts of the country were known to have been kidnapped by brigands. Nejad filled the role of escort, protector, and guide, yelling at the bus driver to slow down, bargaining for our meals along the way, and miraculously securing help when the bus broke down in the middle of a flat and barren plain with no inn or gas station or human being in sight.

In the back of our bus were stacked several huge trunks full of costumes. Nejad sat up front with Mrs. Cook, while we girls sat in a cluster, chatting and talking excitedly, our mothers conversing in low tones. The landscape we were driving through was monotonous and drab. Then in the barren expanses unexpectedly loomed some baked-mud towers. Round and squat, they were topped with a turret. We wondered what they were, and Mrs. Cook explained that they were pigeon towers, that farmers spread pigeon manure out to dry on top of them to use for fertilizer.

Nejad would sometimes saunter to the back of the bus, stand in the aisle, and chat with us, teasing, flirting; sometimes he would tell us about the landscape through which we were passing, which he seemed to know well. To my embarrassment Mummy would occasionally put a handkerchief over her eyes, lie back in her seat, and take a nap. A nap was not out of the ordinary, but the handkerchief . . .

Our convoy traveled for what seemed like hours through empty desert and vast wilderness, sometimes stopping at oases where we could eat, refresh ourselves, and use the primitive facilities. But these oases were few and far between, so from time to time the two buses would stop so that the men could get off, move a short distance away, turn their backs, and relieve themselves. We girls and women stayed on the bus, averting our eyes and restraining ourselves until we could get to an inn or teahouse.

Gradually the terrain changed. The road grew steeper and more winding as we started up the craggy sides of the Zagros Mountains, where the higher reaches were covered with scrub and in April still had patches of snow on the ground. After we crested the mountains, the slopes grew gentler; they were flecked with bright green and dotted with spring flowers—tulips, anemones, and wild daffodils. We were now in Khuzistan Province, a triangle wedged between Iraq's border to the west, the Zagros Mountains to the northeast, and the Persian Gulf to the south. The terrain gradually became flat and stark. It was unbearably hot as we passed through an unrelieved stretch of arid desert. It did not seem possible that three great rivers ran through this province: the Karkheh, which flows down from the mountains of Luristan; the roaring Diz, along whose gorges the route for the Trans-Iranian Railway was laid; and the majestic Karun, which, with the Diz, eventually joins the Shatt-al-Arab on the Iran frontier. For hours all we saw was an endless expanse of desiccated earth relieved in its monotony only by rocks and the swirls etched into its surface by the wind.

Abruptly, small shrubs started signaling signs of life, and then occasionally the bleached terrain gave way to greenery as we passed through a fertile and populated oasis. As we passed through the tree-lined streets of one of these oases, we drove by an old building topped with a dome—Jondi-Shahpur, one of the oldest centers of learning in the world. In the Sassanian period, before the Arab conquest, Jondi–Shahpur was already well known for its medical studies. It still functions as a university. We slowed down to peer at it through the bus windows but did not stop.

Some time later, on a steep sandy rise, we spied a massive fortress, complete with crenelated ramparts. Mrs. Cook excitedly announced that we had arrived at the prehistoric city of Shush, known in English as Susa. The fortress, which loomed ever larger and more imposing as we moved closer, was clearly not prehistoric, so I turned to Mrs. Cook with a puzzled look. She laughed at my confusion and explained that French archaeologists had built the fortress in the nineteenth century to protect themselves and their archaeological findings against marauding Arab tribes. It had become the most visible landmark in Susa, indicating to travelers that they had arrived at this ancient city. Unlike the fortress, the city's oldest treasures were not readily visible from the road.

Mummy and I were relieved to be able to get off the bus and stretch our legs. She told me that she and Daddy had traveled with me to Susa when I was a little girl, but I looked at her blankly, for I had no recollection of the event. Mummy tried to get me interested in the historic significance of the ruins. Here were excavations of mud village settlements dating from the eighth millennium before the Christian era and a large artificial terrace that predated the pyramids of Egypt by one thousand years. Four enormous mounds held the foundations of fourteen or more layers of civilization superimposed on each other. Nebuchadnezzar reigned here, as well as Assurbanipal; and Darius surrounded the town with a wall and a moat, built a palace for himself, and in 521 B.C. made Susa the center of his empire. Long before that, this spot was where Queen Esther saved her people, the Jews, from destruction.

To my untrained eyes, however, Susa looked like little more than a maze of crumbling foundation walls situated in a barren and dusty plain. Although it was springtime, it was uncomfortably hot under the unfiltered sun that beat down on us, scorching our heads and parching our throats. Not a blade of grass or any kind of tree was anywhere in sight, and I found myself more preoccupied with my thirst than with the ruins. Mrs. Cook, on the other hand, visibly moved by the history and antiquity of the excavations, found a large boulder some short distance away, turned her back to us, and sat there alone, contemplating the remains of the ancient civilization spread at her feet. To her exasperation Aida and

I kept giggling over some trivial absurdity we found disproportionately amusing. Mummy, more tolerant of teenage foibles but aware of the inappropriateness of our behavior, tried to quiet our chatter. "Stop being silly," she scolded. "Let's go see the excavations."

We walked to the edge of the exposed foundations. They held little meaning for me until Mummy pointed out that somewhere here was the site of the palace of King Ahasuerus and Queen Esther. Suddenly, the dun-colored rectangular lines in the ground took on meaning. All at once the grand palace of King Ahasuerus rose up out of the dust and decay of centuries. This was the place where the king gave a banquet that lasted 180 days and where Esther's beauty captured the king's heart, ensuring that he would make her his queen. This was the spot where the queen, plotting against her enemy Hamman, prepared the banquets to which she invited only him and the king. I saw her in my mind's eye, a dark-eyed young girl not much older than I, who risked her life for the sake of her people by going unsummoned to see the king. Here she saved them from annihilation, and here, too, stood the fifty-cubits-high gallows on which Hamman was hanged, following which the Jews took vengeance on their enemies, slaying seventy-five thousand of them.

Seeing she had gotten my attention, Mummy went on to tell how Cyrus, Cambyses, Darius, and Xerxes traveled across these vast spaces with their royal retinues, for the Achaemenian kings had three capitals and constantly moved between them. They would come three hundred miles south to Susa for the winter, travel five hundred miles southeast to Persepolis in the spring, then eight hundred miles to the higher elevations of Hamadan, formerly Ecbatana, for the summer, and from there south to Susa again for the winter.

Having just covered by bus some of the terrain over which the Achaemenian kings and their imperial retinues used to travel, I was daunted at the thought of their covering such distances on horseback. To administer their vast empire efficiently the Achaemenians built hundreds of miles of highway, including the Royal Road, which ran from Susa up through Mesopotamia in Asia Minor to the city of Sardis, fifteen hundred miles away. Complete with posting stations, where fresh riders and horses replaced fatigued ones, these highways ran over some of the most difficult terrain in the world, including jagged mountains, rocky valleys, and inhospitable deserts.

I marveled at the hundreds of years of history lying buried in the dust of this landscape. My mind filled with images of galloping horses, a beautiful young queen, myrrh, spices, ointments, intrigues, plots, elaborate banquets, death, and destruction. Echoes of the distant past filtered through me as I stared out over the void and noticed for the first time how the light played on the barren soil, streaking it with purple and ocher. Breezes rippling over the surface of the nearby hill seemed to whisper and sing. I shivered in spite of the heat and turned only slowly and contemplatively when I heard Nejad urging me to board the bus. It was time to leave.

As we continued our journey, the landscape gradually became marshy and green, for many small streams eventually find their way into the Tigris River and into the Karun and its tributaries, all of which empty into the head of the Persian Gulf. We passed fields of sugarcane, and Mrs. Cook started pointing out various interesting sites. "These plains used to be the breadbasket of the Achaemenian Empire," she said. "And the Sassanians built enormous irrigation works along the rivers here, including many stone dams along smaller tributaries." A green vista was now unfolding before us. Palm trees proliferated, with their tall, bare trunks topped by umbrella-like fronds splayed outward. All the dried dates that the country consumed and exported came from this area. Of even greater significance to the development of the country, the first oil well, the Masjed-i-Suleiman, was dug in 1908 in the southwest part of this province.

Villages were closer together here, and the fields and groves were dotted with people. We saw young girls dressed entirely in black, their faces unveiled, their eyes heavily lined with kohl, a number of baskets or pots stacked on their heads. No dancers could have walked more gracefully or with a prouder carriage. Other young girls from a different tribe or subtribe were dressed in bright colors—fuschia, emerald green, purple, and blue. Tight-legged cotton pants descended to their ankles, flowered dresses stopped just below the knees, and large black scarves draped their heads, shoulders, and chests. The upper part of their faces were covered with striking, bright red masks that contrasted sharply with the black of their scarves. Richly embroidered, with slits for the eyes and a bill-like protrusion to allow for the nose, the masks made these girls look like exotic birds.

Whenever our bus made a stop, young vendors crowded around, thrusting their wares into our faces—glass bangles, slender copper bracelets, gossamer scarves, and heavy, dangling earrings. But I could not understand a word they were saying as they clamored for attention in Arabic, for Khuzistan had long been peopled by Arab tribes, whose language has remained Arabic, one of Iran's three major linguistic groups. I might as well have been in a foreign country and had to keep reminding myself that we were still in Iran. It was here that I started to grasp the rich diversity of this land's population.

The smell of oil hung like a pall over Abadan, assaulting our senses and overwhelming us even before we reached the outskirts of the city. Known as the City of Black Gold, it was and still is one of the most important petroleum-refining and petroleum-shipping centers in the world. "Phew," we exclaimed, "What a stink!" as we held handkerchiefs over our noses. However, within a couple of days we no longer noticed the odor but instead reveled in the mild warmth of early spring. We would be gone by the time the temperatures reached the summer high of 120 degrees.

Touring the city, we gawked at the houses the Anglo-Iranian Oil Company had built for its employees. Neat rows of identical homes set in straight lines, they did not even have low fences separating them—an astonishing novelty in this country. We had never before seen houses not surrounded by walls of some kind. We were told that all the houses had not only electricity, but also hot running water—still a rare amenity in those days.

Prosperous, tidy, and clean, Abadan exuded confidence. If anyone had told us then that some day a conflagration in this oil town would help spark an Islamic revolution, we would have been incredulous. Yet a little more than three decades later, on August 19, 1978, a fire would break out in a movie theater with locked exits. Hurling charges and countercharges, supporters and opponents of the Shah would accuse each other of setting the fire. Whatever the truth, 377 people would die in the blaze, resulting in an outpouring of rage, anger, and rioting that would spread to other cities throughout the country and across the world in an uncontrollable chain reaction. From Tehran to Tabriz and from the Hague to Los Angeles—wherever Iranian anti-Shah activists were to be found—riots would break out. The Abadan fire would signal the beginning of the end of the Shah's reign.

Long before that event, however, the "black gold" that had provided a seemingly endless source of funds for development would come to be seen as a "black blight" because of the meddling by foreign powers that it invited. When Reza Khan (later Reza Shah) seized military power in 1921 and set about to unify the country, Khuzistan Province was, for all practical purposes, a semiautonomous region ruled by Sheikh Khazal of Mohammara. The sheikh, with British backing and the help of Bakhtiari and Qashqai tribal chiefs, had been scheming with Iraq on the annexation of Khuzistan. Only two years after coming to power Reza Khan personally led a military campaign against the sheikh and crushed the rebellion.

In 1947, however, Abadan was exemplary in its peace and tranquillity, its past wounds stanched, its future conflagration unanticipated. With giant pipelines, huge drums, and elaborate machinery steadily pumping a thick liquid stream up from deep below the surface of the soil, its oil held out the illusory promise of prosperity and progress.

Wearing hard hats, we toured the oil facilities and saw spectacular gas flares light up the sky like blazing infernos as residual gas was burned off. Not until the 1970s would the wasteful burning finally end, when the building of facilities would enable the government to cap, liquefy, and transport gas via pipeline across thousands of miles to the Soviet Union and beyond.

On a boat ride on the Shatt-al-Arab River, part of which forms the boundary between Iraq and Iran, we drifted slowly past palm trees and picturesque scenes of women washing their clothes. The tranquility of the river was deceptive, however, for the two hostile neighbors had never been able to agree on the exact boundary between them, and Iraq harbored designs on this oil-rich province peopled by Arabs.

Some decades later, in 1980, the squabbling would erupt into a bloody war lasting eight years. The river had already witnessed a long history of wars and battles. As far back as 539 B.C., more than twenty-five hundred years earlier, Cyrus the Great had captured ancient Babylon by the stratagem of diverting this very river, following which he had freed the Jews in exile there.

Our audiences in Abadan consisted largely of employees of the oil company. Either British or Iranians educated abroad and somewhat Westernized, they responded warmly to our performances. Touring companies from other countries had preceded us in this modern company town, which made the audience's "bravos" all the more welcome as an indication that we measured up well to the competition. Mrs. Cook was elated—as were we. It was a heady experience, and

Aida, Wilma, and I laughed as we excitedly reviewed the near mishaps, the improvisations, and the triumphs that are part and parcel of any live performance.

As a finale to our weeks in Abadan Mrs. Cook arranged for a crew to film our dances. So we gathered, in costumes, on a lawn—itself a rarity back then—and while the orchestra played, we performed on the grass for the cameras. Copies of the film were to be sent to us in Tehran, but they never were, or at least I never saw them and to this day still wonder what became of them.

As we started the long journey home, I mulled over the thought that at the age of seven or eight I had traveled through much of this part of the country with Mummy and Daddy years before, when they still traveled often. But most of that early trip blurred together in my mind, reduced to memories of long, tiring hours of riding through barren wasteland and of being carsick. As we set out from Abadan, I recalled that Daddy had once taken us to Gachsaran, which is just a few hours drive northeast of Abadan. The name had stuck in my mind, although our destination I remembered only vaguely, nor could I remember where we were coming from. A few incidents of that trip, however, stood out with great clarity. It was during the season of the spring migrations of the tribes, and we had caught a glimpse of the great Bakhtiari tribe on its annual trek to the mountains. Each spring they made the arduous journey to the upper reaches of the Zagros Mountains, where they pitched their tents and grazed their sheep until the change of seasons and the coming of cooler weather sent them down into the warmer plains again.

We had caught our first sight of small bands of these rugged nomads in the early morning. I remembered as if in a dream the men riding horseback, herding flocks of sheep and goats, and stopping to let the animals graze before urging them onward. Dressed in the blue-and-white-striped goat-hair coats peculiar to their tribe, they sat with stonelike stillness in their saddles or galloped around the flocks in circles, keeping a wary eye out for an occasional stray. The women sat astride mules and donkeys, the bright reds, greens, and blues of their multilayered skirts spilling in bright bursts of color over the equally colorful saddlebags bulging with pots and pans, bundles of sticks for fuel, and other meager possessions. Many of the women held a child seated before them. Older children of four and five sat two together atop a bundle of bedding piled on a small donkey; I remember that they waved at us as our car drove by.

As I now recalled, Daddy had told us much about the Bakhtiaris, how hardy they were, what steep and difficult terrain they had to cover during their migrations, how they sometimes swam across raging rivers or floated across on inflated goatskin rafts. "It could take several days for a large group of them to cross a river," he had said. To traverse the mountains, they had to climb to an altitude of ten thousand feet, sometimes trudging through deep snow before descending to their summer pastures on the upper banks of the Zayandeh-Rood River.

He had told us also how the men, after pitching their tents, would go hunting for ibex and after eating might do a tribal stick dance. Sometimes they would practice riding at full speed across a meadow and, turning in their saddles, fire behind them—an extraordinary feat known as the Parthian shot. The Bakhtiari were such fine marksmen, he had said, that the Shah's soldiers were terrified by their skill and once refused to confront them, particularly after having seen the tribesmen kill every one of a band of government soldiers with a clean shot right through the middle of the forehead. That story had made a deep impression on me.

We had seen women cooking meals over an open fire, with only the most basic implements and ingredients, so I had thought that they were poor, but I was mistaken. Many of them, according to Daddy, were in fact quite wealthy. Some of the hereditary leaders of the tribes, the khans, had studied abroad and owned houses in Tehran, yet chose to return to the tribal tents and lands of their own people for at least part of the year. They had looked bedraggled to me, but Daddy had told us they had once been a major political and military force, for they were heavily armed, rugged, and independent.

At one time, he had explained, Bakhtiari and Arab tribal chiefs controlled this province and negotiated agreements with the British oil company in total disregard of the central government. But, as I mentioned, Reza Khan had set out to suppress the separatist movements emerging all over the country and in 1923 had crushed the rebellion here in Khuzistan, even though Sheikh Khazal enjoyed the protection of the British. I later learned that when Reza Shah had become king, he had transferred large numbers of tribal groups to remote, unfamiliar areas and had tried to disarm them in order to preempt future rebellions. Subsequently, his son, Mohammad Reza Shah, had forced large numbers of them to settle in villages. Used to a lean and rigorous life of herding, of hunting, of outdoor living, of leaving refuse behind when they moved on, and of living in harmony with the cycles of nature, they had had difficulty adapting to settled life. Enclosed in small huts with inadequate ventilation and poor light, great numbers of them had fallen ill and died. Stripped of their rifles, they could no longer hunt. Deprived of their flocks, they could no longer feed and clothe themselves. However, over the long term none of the Shah's efforts to break the power of the tribes had worked, and the nomads had kept resuming their old way of life.

The seasonal migrations, I have since learned, covered distances of two hundred miles or more and sometimes took weeks because the flocks of sheep and goats dictated the pace. Each evening the Bakhtiaris would pitch their black goat hair tents, propping up their distinctive side walls and sloping tops with poles. Rugs woven by the women would cover the floors. Wool blankets and thick felt mats would provide bedding, and copper utensils, earthenware jugs, and goatskin containers would suffice for cooking and storage. The Bakhtiaris would tend to stay in remote areas, as did all the nomadic tribes, and could usually be seen by outsiders only when the tribe was migrating.

On that trip with my parents, however, we had been able not only to see some of the Bakhtiaris, but also to visit with them. I remember a family had stopped by the roadside to eat, and we could see the men seated cross-legged near a smoking fire made of branches and twigs, sipping hot tea. The women were clearing a few pots and pans from a cloth spread on the side of the road. Daddy had stopped the car and told us to wait inside while he went to see if they objected to talking with us. Mummy was to stay out of sight because seeing a foreigner might make them hostile, for it was well known that foreigners had from time to time fomented unrest among the tribes and instigated uprisings against the central government. The tribes were wary now not only of foreigners, but of all outsiders.

We had watched as Daddy approached the seated Bakhtiaris, one hand held over his heart, his head bowed deferentially. We could not hear what was said, but after a few minutes he had returned to the car and told us we could get out. The Bakhtiaris would extend their hospitality to us, even though one of us was a blue-eyed, fair-haired foreigner. They had risen to greet us and asked us to join them, while the women rushed to spread a blanket on the ground for us to sit on. Nearby a flock of goats had grazed. One curious goat had come warily close to us, but had bolted as soon as I stretched my hand out to it, the bell around his neck jangling as he frisked away. He had bleated loudly, and other goats in the herd had responded by bleating also.

Offering us traditional nomadic hospitality, the women had rinsed out small, narrow-waisted glasses with hot water and served us tea. They had gathered around us and looked with fascination at Mummy's blond hair and fair complexion, which stood out against the rustic, tanned appearance of the tribesmen and women. They had seemed as interested in our clothing as we were in their multilayered ankle-length skirts sparkling in the sunlight and in their head scarves embroidered with metallic thread. Strings of silver coins were wrapped around their foreheads, oversize earrings dangled down almost to their shoulders, and hammered gold necklaces hung loose and long over their chests. Years later, after they had fallen on hard times, much of that jewelry started showing up in the great bazaars, where it was sold to tourists at greatly inflated prices. Still later it would become difficult to find so much as a single piece of the exotic ornaments as they were snatched up by hordes of tourists or shipped out of the country to expensive boutiques, where they fetched exorbitant prices. But back then the Bakhtiari women had proudly worn their jewelry, which, along with the men's rifles and ammunition, some tea, sugar, and cotton fabric, were among the few articles they bought for cash. Their flocks of goats and sheep had provided their other needs—wool for tents, blankets, and rugs, and milk, butter, and cheese for food. Although Muslim, the women were unveiled, for few nomadic tribal women veil themselves unless they settle in a city.

One young girl, who seemed just a few years older than I, had been nursing her baby, while a toddler tugged at her skirt. Mummy had been immediately drawn to the children, but had taken care not to admire them openly. The young mother answered Mummy's questions shyly and appeared surprised that this *farangi* woman could speak Persian. Mummy later told me how the nomads accommodate a birthing during a migration. The tribe stops just long enough for a mother to deliver a child, cut its umbilical cord, clean it, and swaddle it, without benefit of midwife or anesthetic. After a few hours' rest the mother is helped up onto a horse, with her baby in her arms, and off they all go again. This practice was in striking contrast to the birthing customs of women in the urban areas, who were confined to bed for at least ten days after a delivery.

Many years later the Shah would enact the White Revolution, as part of which he would establish a system of traveling instructors to accompany the tribes on their migrations and to teach the children how to read and write. Their classrooms would consist of portable blackboards set up outdoors, with the children sitting in rows on the bare ground. But on that trip long ago when I first met the Bakhtiaris, most of the women and children were illiterate.

On that day Mummy and Daddy had tried to coax the women into doing a Bakhtiari dance for us, but they had giggled and shaken their heads in refusal. My parents had finally given up and, after thanking their hosts for their hospitality, had herded me and my brother back into the car, and we had continued on our journey.

As I passed through this landscape with Mrs. Cook and the members of the dance troupe in 1947, I regretted that we were not close enough to the migration route to see any Bakhtiaris.

New Dreams

Now hearken: the story of Suhrab I'll tell,
And the strife which 'twixt him and his father befell.
—Ferdowsi, *Shahnameh*

AFTER OUR SUCCESSES in Abadan Mrs. Cook's imagination knew no bounds. Buoyed by our warm reception, she envisaged ever greater and more ambitious projects. We would go, she dreamed, on a grand tour of Turkey, Greece, India, and other places, presenting to amazed audiences the world over the glories of ancient Persia molded into a new spirit of modernity. Antique splendors grafted onto the sensibilities of a modern Iran, the old blended with the new, folk dance melded with ballet—it all spoke to the ethos of the times. There would be nothing to stop us from eventually performing in the United States, where we would surely enrapture an adoring public with the beauty and pageantry of our performances. Like Sheherazade, we would spin tales of enchantment, only we would use the languages of poetry, music, and dance instead of words alone.

Looking back, I am astounded at the expansiveness of Mrs. Cook's vision and the magnitude of her accomplishment. Admittedly, the political climate was favorable to her endeavors. The Iranian government had been pursuing a program of modernization and also deliberately cultivating the United States in an attempt to balance its power against that of the Soviets and the British so as to minimize the traditional Soviet-British interference in Iranian affairs. The popular perception of the United States was particularly favorable at this time because the Americans had exerted diplomatic pressure to help bring about the withdrawal of Soviet troops from Iran's northern provinces after World War II. Iran was also anxious to win American financial aid and technical military assistance. The prime minister, Ahmad Qavam, agreed to subsidize the Studio for the Revival of the Classical Arts of Iran under the Department of Propaganda and Radio and to send the group on tour abroad as a cultural mission.

By now I was fifteen and in my second year of high school. Aida and Wilma were one or at most two years older. We were entering crucial years of schooling, and our parents, concerned about our studies, did not readily take to Mrs. Cook's grandiose plans and objected that two months out of school would set us back, perhaps make it impossible for us to catch up. Although I was excited at the idea of traveling and performing abroad, I knew it would not happen without the consent of our parents. I waited and watched. Mrs. Cook, I knew, had a persuasive way and a charmed tongue. She seldom took no for an answer; maybe she would be able to work it all out.

And so she did. She offered to hire a tutor who would travel with us and help us keep up with our schoolwork. All we had to do was bring our textbooks along. Of course, each girl would also be accompanied by a parent to protect her reputation. After much discussion and debate, Aida's parents and Mummy agreed. Mrs. Cook would hire a tutor, Mummy would accompany me, and because Aida's mother was expecting a baby and was in no condition to travel, her father would accompany Aida, taking leave from the bank where he worked. Wilma's parents, however, flatly refused to allow her to go. I could not understand why and worried that this refusal might throw a monkeywrench into the entire plan.

Undaunted, Mrs. Cook found someone to take Wilma's place, a young woman who had studied folk dancing at the Janbazian Dance School, which specialized in Central Asian and Caucasian folk dancing. In this type of dancing there is much emphasis on rising onto the toes (without benefit of toe shoes) and much bravura stomping, but also delicate arm, head, and facial movements, so this young woman turned out to be quite a catch. She not only ably replaced Wilma, but contributed invaluable suggestions to Mrs. Cook's choreography. To preserve a measure of anonymity she used the stage name Sheherazade. A divorcée, she was somewhat older than Aida and I, so we had little in common with her other than our interest in dance. Mrs. Sadeq, our costume designer, agreed to act as her chaperon, for even divorcées had to protect their good names.

We continued to practice and rehearse, all the while adding new dances to our repertory in preparation for the foreign tour. Mrs. Cook was still working out the choreographic details of *Rostam and Sohrab,* a dance based on an ancient legend in which the great warrior Rostam unknowingly kills his own son, Sohrab. As recounted in Ferdowsi's *Shahnameh,* Rostam and Tahmina, the beautiful daughter of his enemy the king of Samangan, secretly and hastily marry. After spending only one passionate night together, the lovers never see each other again, nor for years does Rostam see his son, who is born nine months later. When father and son do finally meet, it is as members of opposing armies, their identities concealed for reasons of security. In truth, Sohrab has gone to Iran to find his father, intending to go over to the Iranian side if he finds him. As fate would have it, however, father and son engage each other in mortal combat not knowing their relationship to one another, and the stage is set for tragedy.

In choreographing *Rostam and Sohrab* Mrs. Cook drew inspiration from the House of Strength (*zurkhaneh*), a form of martial arts. Usually practiced by religiously fervent men, this sport—involving synchronized movements with clubs, chains, and weights—is meant to develop the participants' minds and spirits as well as their bodies. Spectators are allowed to watch. I had once seen such a performance and had been fascinated by its rhythmic martial arts movements, clearly designed to display strength, yet reined in by patterned choreography and poetic narrative, all imbued with a strong spiritual component. I had watched with fascination as the men entered the hallowed ground of the pit (*gawd*), dressed in knee-length embroidered breeches, their chests bare. A leader (*morshed*), had tapped the drum and chanted verses from Ferdowsi's *Shahnameh,* in particular the heroic exploits of Rostam in defense of Iran. The men had strained and sweated as they moved in unison to the call of the *morshed.* The rhythmic movement, the tapping of the drums, the recitation of verse in chant or song, combined with rippling muscles and physical prowess, had made for a powerfully stirring spectacle. The exercises had been followed by prayer.

In Mrs. Cook's *zurkhaneh*-influenced *Rostam and Sohrab* the fatal battle between father and son was brought to life on the stage by two young men who were highly skilled acrobats. A rousing reading of lines from Ferdowsi's Persian epic added pathos to the tragedy being enacted by the dancers:

The story of Sohrab and Rostam now hear:
Other tales thou hast heard: to this also give ear.
A story it is to bring tears to the eyes,
And wrath in the heart against Rostam will rise.

As the music played, two dancers circled each other warily, their eyes watchful, their bodies tensed, like panthers ready to spring. Bare-chested and wearing embroidered knee breeches, they held their arms akimbo, ready to wrestle each other in a fight to the death. They feinted, drew back, attacked, repelled, retreated, advanced, all the while leaping and springing backward into multiple handstands with dizzying speed, each time landing with the nimbleness of a cat. Their muscles rippled as they arched, bent, spun, darted, rolled, and finally struggled in a lethal embrace. Above the music, the sonorous reading of the epic poem continued: "Death's breath doth resemble such pitiless fire, / Consuming alike both the son and the sire."

Finally, picking Sohrab up and holding him over his head, Rostam spun him around in a dizzying, triumphant spin. The audience held its breath. He stopped abruptly, legs spread, arms aloft, and sent Sohrab crashing to the ground. The dancer on the ground lay still. Rostam was triumphant. He had vanquished his enemy. The audience, knowing what Rostam did not know—that it was his own son who lay dying at his feet—reacted to the tragedy with exclamations of *"aakh,"* "the pity of it," and "alas, alas." They applauded, moved to tears by the scene so exquisitely heightened in its pathos by the blending of poetry, music, and dance.

One day as we were rehearsing, I saw a young man, a stranger to me, watching the two acrobats leaping and tumbling. Of swarthy complexion, with piercing eyes and a demeanor so serious as to be intimidating, he waited until the dance was over, then went up to the two dancers and shook hands with them. Amir, the acrobat who played the role of Rostam, took him by the arm and introduced him to Mrs. Cook. The young man was a relative, Amir said, a distant cousin who was a student at the Faculty of Law, Political Science, and Economics at the University of Tehran, and was interested in the possibility of accompanying the troupe as our tutor. He had never traveled abroad and would welcome the opportunity to do so, and because the university system in Iran did not require attendance at classes, being a student was no obstacle to his taking off a couple of months to travel.

Mrs. Cook talked to the young man at some length, then introduced him to Aida and me. "This is your new tutor," she said. "He will go on tour with us and help you keep up with your studies." Mrs. Cook introduced him by his family name, as was customary, and that was the way I addressed him for many years to come. There was nothing in this first meeting to suggest that I would ever address him in any other way, and if anyone had hinted at such a possibility, I would have laughed outright. Little could I guess how closely our lives would eventually intertwine.

The thought of going on tour in a foreign country gave me butterflies in the stomach. I was delighted but also apprehensive. Sometimes it seemed I must be dreaming. That I should dance before large audiences in far and distant places had always been such an unlikely prospect that I had never dared even hope for such a possibility. Yet just such a fantasy was fast becoming a reality. Although I dreamily contemplated adventure, romance, and many curtain calls, I also wondered how well I would do. Foreign audiences, after all, were more discriminating than the ones we were used to; they had probably seen ballet companies from all over the world. Perhaps they would be more critical.

Mummy, on the other hand, had no apprehensions. She was sure audiences abroad would love our dances. She looked forward to the trip as a diversion from the daily routine. We would be going first to Turkey. After that, perhaps—Mrs. Cook never quite spelled it out—we would go on to Greece, Lebanon, and then maybe India. The plans were all very vague. Perhaps we should have realized that Mrs. Cook's projected "two months" was an extremely loose and elastic time frame. Instead, we took her at her word.

Also joining the company was a dwarf no more than four feet tall. A skilled comedian with a powerful voice, Hojatzadeh was to sing in front of the curtain and sometimes tell ribald jokes as the entr'acte while we dancers made hurried costume changes. We also had a young woman singer, a university student named Qodsi, along with an electrician, a cook, and an army band of eight musicians—all conveniently placed at Mrs. Cook's disposal. Mrs. Sadeq had agreed to accompany us as chaperon and dressmaker, and Nejad would serve as assistant, organizer, director, squire, and treasurer all rolled into one.

A plane that could have whisked us to Istanbul in a matter of hours would have been a costly business. Instead, three lumbering buses weighted down with our suitcases, our costume trunks and makeup kits, the stage props, and all our other paraphernalia carried us out of Tehran across open plains, not pausing until we arrived in Qazvin, our first rest stop. A dilapidated, neglected city, Qazvin had twice been a flourishing metropolis—under Shah Tahmasp in the fifteenth century and then under the Qajars in the nineteenth—but there was little left of its former splendor, and we stopped only briefly for refreshments and rest.

The mountains loomed large in the distance long before we started the steep ascent into their rocky and forbidding passes. From time to time a rise appeared far off, on top of which the bulbous dome of a miniature shrine stuck out incongruously. Small, spare structures, devoid of any ornament, these repositories of human hopes and prayers were minimal, stripped-down copies of the grand structures to be found in cities across the country. For the most part they were the only indications of the presence of humans along the way; the terrain was rough and unyielding, and for miles we saw no villages. It was difficult to imagine that men had labored atop those forbidding heights to build these singular expressions of devotion and faith, or that others would climb those sun-bleached cliffs to pray at the shrine or to plead for relief from some unbearable burden.

Gradually, the road became less steep, the villages more frequent, the scenery greener, until finally the land was cultivated as far as the eye could see. South of the Shibli Pass, some forty miles from Tabriz, we caught a breathtaking view of Mount Sahand, standing proudly at 12,200 feet, surrounded by rolling hills.

By the time we arrived at Tabriz, our second rest stop, we were tired and hungry and more than pleased to accept the accommodations the mayor of the city had arranged for us in the local town hall. Mummy and I were housed in an office temporarily converted to a bedroom by the placement of two cots along one wall. Its windows looked out over a sprawling, drab, and unattractive city. Glancing out, I saw storks nesting in the rooftops and a hodgepodge of *doroshkeh*s, donkeys, carts, bicycles, and an occasional car crowding the streets below. Similar rooms had been readied for the other girls and their chaperons, but all the male members of the troupe—dancers, singers, musicians, the tutor, and various assistants—found themselves herded into an enormous reception room in the same building. Except for a grand piano standing in one corner, a

With Qodsi *(left)* and Aida *(right),*
being silly in the park in Tabriz.

number of huge crystal chandeliers hanging from the majestically high ceiling, and the elegant Persian carpets covering the floor, it was devoid of furniture. Bedrolls had been spread on the floor alongside one wall for the men.

That evening the mayor, displaying traditional Persian hospitality, provided us an elaborate dinner of *chello kabab*—mountains of fluffy white rice and skewers of charcoal-broiled lamb—served in the reception room on clean white cloths spread on the floor. Later, when the cloths were whisked away, the room reverted to a dormitory for the men of the troupe.

Tabriz is the second largest city in Iran, the capital of Iranian Azerbaijan, the northwest province. Just a year earlier there had been fighting in the streets here when government troops quelled a Soviet-backed rebellion seeking autonomy for the province of Azerbaijan. Colleges, monasteries, mosques, palaces, and gardens had been built in the city at the turn of the thirteenth century, when Tabriz was the Mongol capital. The city had flourished again in the fifteenth and sixteenth centuries under the Timurids and Safavids, when it contained twenty-four caravanseries, fifteen hundred shops, and thirty thousand houses. It had boasted two hundred reciters of the Koran, four hundred scholars and theologians, one thousand students, and a mosque with the largest brick vault in the world. Historians write of Tabriz's marble columns, bronze lamps inlaid with gold and silver, latticed windows with gold-etched glass, metallic lustre faience, water-spouting lions, bubbling streams, huge lakes, hospital, library, academy of philosophy, and palace with twenty thousand rooms. But earthquake, war, and neglect had taken their toll, and when we saw Tabriz, little remained of those splendors. All that was left was the imposing mass of the citadel's 120-foot sheer brick wall, the sad ruins of the Blue Mosque built by Shah Jahan in 1465, and a large lake, its waters now slimy and green, in the center of which crumbled the ruins of a once-magnificent palace. Disappointed, we turned our attention to the modern city of Tabriz.

Featureless, nondescript, and utterly lacking in charm, its drabness was relieved mainly by an impressive bazaar and a large park with a huge reflecting pool, where Aida, Qodsi, and I snapped shots of each other in various silly poses. Wherever we went, we found we could not understand anyone, for the people here spoke in a Turkish dialect, not Persian. The tribal groups who had settled Azerbaijan are ethnically Turkish, although Iranian nationals, but the Azeri Turkish they speak is different from that of neighboring Turkey, as we would soon find out. To my surprise I learned that Nejad could speak both. Once again I had the feeling of being in a foreign land even though I was still in Iran.

As we resumed our journey toward Turkey, steep mountains rose before us, and the buses whined and groaned on their way up the winding road. Deep gorges dropped away on one side, while craggy boulders jutted precariously from the sheer cliffs that towered above us. The trip seemed interminable, and the lurching of the bus made my stomach queasy. On and on we drove until finally, off in the distance, we saw a sentry post on the side of the road and a fence barring our way. Beside it stood a forlorn and rickety building that looked as if it might collapse as it squeaked and trembled in the gusting wind. We had reached the customshouse on the Turkish border.

Where East Meets West

Neither quite this nor altogether that, terrifically itself yet
perpetually ambiguous, Turkey stands alone among the nations.
—Jan Morris, introduction to *Turkish Reflections*
by Mary Lee Settle

WE ENTERED THE CUSTOMSHOUSE in Turkey to find ourselves in a large room furnished with nothing but a worn desk and a few wooden chairs on the verge of collapse. Knowing full well what petty tyrants border guards could be in their own domain, Mrs. Cook turned on her charm. She beamed as she shook hands with the head customs inspector, and I saw something in the palm of her hand pass to the palm of his hand—the customary *bakhshesh,* I imagine, for *nothing* was ever accomplished without a "tip." Demonstrating unusual patience and civility, she sat in one of the chairs and accepted a dainty glass of tea. With Nejad serving as translator she engaged the headman in small talk and did her best to impress upon him that we were on a cultural mission on behalf of our government and that we held diplomatic passports. Smiling sweetly while pulling rank, she let him know that Princess Ashraf was our sponsor, for she knew the customs inspectors would be going through all our luggage in the most meticulous manner and might easily manufacture pretexts to confiscate our goods or hold us up interminably while waiting for a bigger bribe.

We milled around and waited and before long saw for ourselves how limitless was the power of the border guards. Schooled in a long-established system of hierarchy and authority, and located miles away from supervision by the central government, they were demigods here. Mercifully, we were not the targets of their wrath.

Our trunks had been unloaded and carried into the customshouse, and several inspectors were going through them. The huge containers stood upright with their doors ajar, displaying tulle, chiffon, and shimmering brocade, but the inspectors had obviously had their orders. They barely passed a hand through the tulle skirts before passing on to the next trunk and the next. At the same time, however, they vented their fury on an unfortunate villager. The poor man's worn jacket and cotton pants hung loosely on his body, and the bones on his back stuck out like wings. His meager belongings were wrapped in a large cloth bundle. Pointing toward the *boqcheh* with disdain, the chief inspector barked something at the villager, in response to which the old man opened his bundle and spread its contents out on the floor. I could not, of course, understand the command, for it was given in Turkish, but the sequence of events and the inspector's gestures and gruff tone of voice made clear exactly what was going on.

A pair of shoes—shiny, new, and conspicuous for being at odds with the frayed shoddiness of the other articles—immediately attracted the inspector's attention. With a scowl he picked up one shoe while taking a penknife out of his pocket. "What do you have here?" he demanded. The villager lifted his deeply lined face and looked beseechingly at the inspector. His voice trembled as he spread both hands out and whispered "nothing." As Nejad explained to us later, the poor man had bought the shoes in Tabriz and was taking them back to his village as a gift. He looked on helplessly while the inspector took his blade and first ripped off the heel, then the sole of the shoe, looking ostensibly for drugs. The inspector pulled out the lining on the inside to make sure he had missed nothing, while the villager pleaded with him, on the verge of tears. He methodically slit open the other shoe, similarly finding nothing concealed there. He shrugged. By now all the members of the troupe had gathered around, and Nejad started translating for Mrs. Cook. "The inspector says there are so many people smuggling opium across the border these days, one cannot be too careful. His duty is to outsmart drug dealers and hooligans." The miserable villager was now weeping uncontrollably, and the inspector, losing patience, roughly grabbed him by his collar, shoved him out of the customshouse, and barked some orders at one of his lieutenants.

Then he turned back to Mrs. Cook, all smiles and courtesy. She, after all, was the head of a group of traveling diplomats. The diplomatic passports Mrs. Cook had managed to secure for every one of us—dancers, musicians, singers, electrical technicians, and stage hands—worked their magic. Meanwhile, the inspector's underling picked up the remnants of the new shoes, tossed them back into the *boqcheh,* knotted the bundle, and threw it out the door after the unfortunate villager.

How many hours we spent there I do not know, but it took a long time for the inspectors to go through our luggage even superficially. Eventually, however, the trunks were loaded back onto the buses, and we crossed the border into Turkey. We still had many more miles to cover before we would arrive in Istanbul, but we were well on our way.

Rudyard Kipling was wrong, of course, when he said, "O, East is East and West is West and never the twain shall meet." Since time immemorial, Turkey has been a land where distinct cultures have simultaneously resisted and blended, confronted and accommodated each other. Neither completely Eastern nor completely Western, this country resonates with the echoes of the past, its history permeating every aspect of its psyche.

Known for hundreds of years as Constantinople, the city we were headed for was renamed Istanbul after the Turks conquered it in 1453. Straddling the point where two continents touch, this extraordinary metropolis is the very embodiment of the physical and cultural meeting of East and West. Part of it lies in Europe and part in Asia, the two segments divided by a body of water known as the Golden Horn and joined together by bridges.

I was not prepared for the spectacular skyline of domes and minarets silhouetted against the waters of the Golden Horn and the Bosporus, and I caught my breath at the sight. Round domes, needle-thin minarets, and slender spires jutted upward from the crests of rolling hills. Banked up one behind the other and illuminated by the glow of the setting sun, they turned golden, pink, and finally deep mauve as the sun, by now a red ball of fire, sank into the water. Layers of history spread out before us in its many permutations—peace and war, conquest and resistance, victory and defeat, faith and skepticism, dedication and betrayal. As I watched, lost in thought, I was blinded for a moment by the light glancing off myriad windows—glittering panes of gold flashing across the now darkening waters. A moment later the scene faded into darkness, then gradually sparked back to life as lights started to twinkle and sparkle in the blackness of the night, like jewels strung out on a canopy of dark velvet.

We were lodged in the Asian part of the city, known as Beyoglu, near Taksim

Photographed in front of the
Bosporus, flanked by our tutor
Ramezooni (Ruhi Ramazani) *(left)*
and Nejad *(right)*, with Hojatzadeh
kneeling in front.

Square, which was packed with international hotels, business offices, and shopping quarters. That night we saw the cafés, clubs, and bars come alive, and we walked by many restaurants that catered to an ever-changing clientele.

As usual, we girls, Mummy, Mrs. Cook, and Mrs. Sadeq were lodged separately from the men, except for Nejad, who, as Mrs. Cook's manager and man Friday, got away with breaking all the conventions. We occupied one floor of a modest hotel, where each of us shared a private room with our personal chaperon—except for Sheherazade and Qodsi, who doubled up with Mrs. Sadeq, their chaperon. The other men in the troupe were put up in the dormitory of a local boys' school some distance away.

Because none of us had private baths and the hotel facilities were inadequate at best, Mrs. Cook arranged once again to take us to the public bath. We followed her down narrow, winding back streets until we came to a large domed structure. This edifice must once have stood in splendid isolation, but was now hemmed in on every side by buildings. Built in 1454 for Fatih Sultan Mehmet, the Aga Hamami bath had been restored and was once again in use as a public bath. Mrs. Cook left us there, choosing not to join us inside.

The rest of us went in, looking at our surroundings with wonder, for nothing in our previous experiences had prepared us for the grand opulence of the Turkish bath. The attendant ushered us into the changing room, handing each of us a large cotton wrap and a bag for our clothes. Turning our backs on each other for privacy, we undressed and draped ourselves with the wraps, twisting the ends and knotting them together just above our bosoms.

We would not have the wraps on for long. Following the bath attendant down a hallway, we removed our cotton covers at her bidding and hung them on pegs before stepping into the inner sanctum, a large central chamber, where ended all resemblance to any previous *hamam* we had ever seen. The cavernous interior was similar in size to that of a mosque, covered with a great vault surrounded by lesser vaults, the whole spanning a huge hall with evenly spaced, recessed vaulted shelves and marble basins projecting from the circular wall. In the center was a small raised pool, with steps leading away from it down to floor level. From numerous glass bubbles in the ceiling shafts of light pierced the clouds of steam, illuminating the marble interior and the nude bodies standing, crouching, bending over the marble basins, or reclining on pale white steps.

Repressing my embarrassment at walking along naked, I covered my pubic area with one hand as I saw the others doing. Mrs. Sadeq and Sheherazade positioned themselves near a marble basin protruding from the wall and took turns pouring water over each other's heads. Aida's and Qodsi's long tresses were soon dripping wet and ready for shampooing. Mummy poured water over me. Taking us in hand, the bath attendant led us one by one to the wide steps at the base of the central pool to sit or recline as she scrubbed us down before shampooing our hair. I watched as she exfoliated Aida with a coarse mitt, marveling at the soft fullness of Aida's breasts and the gentle curve of her buttocks. As Aida caught my gaze on her, I quickly lowered my eyes, embarrassed at my indiscretion. I would certainly not have liked to have anyone watch me being washed.

Soon it was my turn. The attendant had me recline on a marble slab. Her touch was not gentle. As she scrubbed me and shampooed my hair, she jerked my head this way and that. She led me to a basin where she used the copper bowl chained to the faucet to pour water over my head and rinse off the shampoo. Turning her attention then to Mummy, she found that my mother had already taken care of herself, for she had short hair, unlike our luxuriant locks, which hung down well below our waists.

At the first opportunity after our baths we set out to explore our surroundings. A tram took us to the waterfront, where we strolled by the Misir Carsisi, the spice market, with its mixture of delicate and pungent aromas. Coriander, cumin, cinnamon, and fenugreek perfumed the air. There were endless varieties of pepper—black, green, red, white; sacks of turmeric, ginger, and dried lime; as well as jars of saffron, dill, paprika, mint, and thyme.

Nearby we admired the flower market and moved on to the bird market. Although the parrots, parakeets, and other brightly plumed birds were handsome, it distressed me to see them imprisoned in their cages. "Poor things," I thought, trying to imagine what it must be like for them never to be able to fly. "I wonder how they can stand being cooped up in a tiny cage all the time." I mused on how I would feel if I were never able to dance again.

As we approached the Karakoy end of the Galata Bridge, we were met by stall after stall of fresh fish, the likes of which I had never seen before. Large fish with blue spots, small fish with yellow stripes, flat fish with two eyes on one side of the face, bloated fish with turgid bellies, and some enormous round fish that were as flat as pancakes and flecked with orange. Crossing Galata Bridge, we looked down on dozens of little boats tied up on the waterfront, bright daubs of red, green, and blue. They doubled as floating snack bars, for here passersby could buy fried fish served with bread and onions. "In England they would be selling fish and chips," Mummy said, as she insisted on stopping to buy some.

By now we were already starting to divide into small groups. Mrs. Sadeq and Sheherazade were inseparable; Aida and her father stayed fairly close to Mrs. Cook and Nejad; and Qodsi and I were often together because we had struck up a friendship, one that flattered me enormously, for she was a university student and I a mere schoolgirl. We were usually accompanied by Mummy and, more often than not, by the tutor, whom we now called Ramezooni—a version of his surname, Ramazani—which indicated a certain measure of friendliness but fell short of familiarity.

Sometimes Ramezooni would join Aida's group, holding long conversations with her father, but then would gravitate back to us, often attending gallantly to Mummy and chatting with her. None of these groupings was static but, like the particles in a kaleidoscope, came together, separated into disparate parts, then regrouped in a different pattern. Whenever there was a new sight to see, we all crowded around Mrs. Cook, who could be counted on to enlighten us—without benefit of guidebook, map, or note—on the history, background, and mythology of whatever historic marvel we were admiring.

She led us through St. Sophia, a magnificent cathedral built by the Emperor Justinian in the sixth century A.D., but converted to a mosque by the Turks after they conquered Constantinople. Now a museum, the structure dramatically embodies the layers of history and competing cultures that mark Turkey's uniquely diverse past. Awed by the sheer size of the interior and moved by its multiformed beauty, I craned my neck upward and listened attentively as Mrs. Cook sketched the history of this remarkable structure and pointed out the now coexisting Christian frescoes and Islamic calligraphy and tile work.

Nearby stood the lovely Sultan Ahmet Mosque, also known as the Blue Mosque because of the dominant color of its tile work. It is the only mosque in the world with six minarets. Removing our shoes, we stepped onto the luxuriant carpets spread in the interior. In the great central hall with its fine tiling, people were praying, standing, or kneeling, with head bowed or touched to the floor, indifferent to the tourists quietly milling around, for the Sultan Ahmet is a functioning mosque. Some members of our troupe dropped to their knees and joined quietly in the prayers.

A short distance away stood the Underground Palace, a cistern built by the Romans in the sixth century to store water brought hundreds of miles by aqueduct from the Belgrade Forest. As I stepped into its gloomy subterranean darkness, I looked out over a great expanse of water, out of which jutted 336 massive Corinthian columns spanned by a vaulted ceiling. The smell of rot and mildew, the somber massiveness of the vaults and pillars, the stillness of the black waters filled me with an almost uncontrollable panic. It was a relief when we went back up into the daylight.

Of all the sights I saw that day the Topkapi Palace was the most memorable. This labyrinthine structure was for more than four hundred years the residential palace of the Ottoman sultans. Here they lived, maintained their harems, and ruled their vast, polyglot empire. Here they practiced fratricide, and often when a sultan acceded to the throne, all his brothers were strangled with a silk cord to avoid the chaos of a contested sultanate. Here Süleyman the Magnificent ruled half the civilized world, from 1520 to 1566, when the Ottoman Empire reached its apogee in territorial conquests, art, and culture. Here Sultan Süleyman brought his favorite wife, Roxelana, and his harem attended by eunuchs, unwittingly setting into motion the palace intrigues that eventually undermined the regime.

I had never before realized how far Hollywood portrayals of harems were from the reality. Although very little of the harem proper was open to tourists, for it was not yet fully restored, I received a fairly clear picture of a grim existence for its inhabitants. Like the caged birds whose imprisonment had troubled me, the phantom presence of thousands of young wives and concubines cooped up in suffocatingly enclosed spaces, incarcerated for life in gilded rooms, filled me with pity bordering on horror. The display of assorted whips used to exact obedience and to discipline rebellious inhabitants of the harem left me with a hollow feeling in the pit of my stomach. Stained-glass windows, which in another setting might have elicited rapture, here filled me with gloom, for they shut out the outside world as effectively as prison bars. The decorative tendrils and curlicues that graced the walls would ordinarily have excited my admiration, but here only suggested entrapment as they swirled upward and collapsed back on themselves in an intricate tangle, forming an endless unbroken circle from which there was no escape.

The harem's structure and architecture conjured up images of sultans, eunuchs, and odalisques. They bore witness to opulence and tyranny, as well as to a limited existence for hundreds of women who shared one man and for hundreds of children whose father barely knew them. The walls whispered tales of parents so poor they gladly brought their daughters to live here, receiving in return a stipend for life, and of others so wealthy they brought their daughters here so as to secure their own status and privileges. The walls spoke of women entrapped, unable even to watch the world go by. I pondered this page of history and was glad I had not been part of it; I did not think I could have borne it. To my surprise, however, Mrs. Cook did not seem perturbed at the sight of the harem, but emoted eloquently on the benefits, security, comfort, and leisure the selected girls and their families had enjoyed.

The palace, of course, was more than just a harem, and we found much in it to impress us—the exquisite porcelains in the palace kitchen, the library of Sultan Ahmet III, the audience hall where sultans used to receive emissaries, and the displays of silken caftans, tapestries, artfully decorated swords and daggers, and jewelry so opulent and large as to look almost fake. In the Pavilion of the Holy Mantle we examined with some skepticism the sacred relics supposed to have belonged to the Prophet Mohammad and questioned their authenticity.

Leaning over a display case containing diplomatic correspondence between the sultans and their satraps, I found Ramezooni at my elbow as I studied the flowing script of the missives. He started reading some of them out loud and commenting on them, revealing a vast knowledge of the history of the empire and its relations with Iran. The rest of the troupe gathered around and listened. Turkish tourists, too, started milling around us, fascinated by our ability to read the texts, which were written in Persian, the court language of the time. Ramezooni explained that Turks of our day could no longer read the Persian or Arabic script because the founder of modern Turkey, Kemal Ataturk, in his unrelenting drive to modernize Turkey, had converted the Turkish script from the Arabic to the Latin. "What a loss," I could not help thinking as I deciphered the elaborately ornamental calligraphy that decorated so many of the artifacts we were admiring. Later, as Ramezooni strolled by my side, we considered the pros and cons of such a radical change and its effect on the psyche of a nation. We could not imagine such a thing happening in Iran, where everyone was a poet, where the language was almost sacrosanct and calligraphy elevated to a high art form. We compared Reza Shah with Ataturk, both of whom had sought to modernize and reshape their respective countries, and found Reza Shah lacking by comparison with his more radical, bolder contemporary. At the same time we felt that perhaps Ataturk had gone too far in his modernizing zeal.

Before this trip to Turkey I had never even heard of Mustafa Kemal Ataturk. After arriving there, I was literally bombarded with information about him. Giant posters of his likeness were plastered over city walls; his portrait could be seen hanging in shops, restaurants, and offices everywhere. Before this extraordinary leader came to power, what we call Turkey today was part of the Ottoman Empire and was ruled by sultans, but as the empire tottered and collapsed, Ataturk almost singlehandedly carved out and created a unified republic in 1923. As Turkey's first president (and virtual dictator), he instituted a series of radical reforms over a ten-year period (from 1924 to 1934), completely transforming Turkey. Declaring religion a matter of personal conscience, he abolished the caliphate and secularized the state. He outlawed polygamy and introduced a new legal code based on Swiss law. He banned the veil and the fez—

the traditional headgear of the Ottomans—and laid the foundations of an infra-structure that would enable the country to compete economically in the markets of Europe. His revolution was based on six principles: the "six arrows" of secularism, statism, republicanism, nationalism, populism, and revolutionism.

As I peered up at Ataturk's angular jaw and bushy eyebrows in an omnipresent portrait, it was clear to me that here was a national hero of mythical proportions. We would be hearing a great deal more about him during our months in Turkey.

The Special Devotion of Love

I once had a thousand desires,
But in my one desire to know you
all else melted away.
The pure essence of your being
has taken over my heart and soul.
—Jalal ad-Din Rumi,
"All My Youth Returns"

ISTANBUL WAS A CITY full of sights, old and new. Not only was it dotted with more than its share of churches, mosques, palaces, and other remnants of its many-layered history, but it boasted a modernity that was relatively advanced for that part of the world—certainly far more sophisticated than anything we had seen in Tehran.

Here streetcars ran on time and whisked riders to far-off destinations with dispatch and at low cost. Elegant storefronts, with mannequins draped in the latest fashions, displayed merchandise artfully, a striking contrast to the jumble of goods indiscriminately crammed into Tehran's store windows. Sidewalk cafés abutted pastry shops where fashionably dressed clientele conversed at a leisurely pace while sipping coffee and eating dainty cakes. All the glitter and glamour of a major Western metropolis vied for attention with historic monuments.

Seduced by the displays, we girls longed to go into those enticing stores and explore their offerings, but none of us had much money to spend, for the need to protect our reputations required that we preserve our amateur status. It was understood from the beginning that we were on a cultural mission on behalf of the government of His Imperial Majesty the Shah of Iran. Because our endeavors were purely artistic, salaries were out of the question. Mrs. Cook, however, had given us to understand that she would provide each of us with "spending money," a sum sufficient to meet our necessary personal expenses.

The enormous costs of feeding, housing, and moving such a large group of people had not yet begun to wear Mrs. Cook down. She parceled out a modest sum of money to each member of the troupe and promised that more would be forthcoming at the beginning of the following month.

Tempted by the tastefully displayed wares in the stylish storefronts, Aida, Qodsi, Mummy, and I set out to do some shopping. Mummy, of course, had seen fancy store windows before, so she was circumspect, but the rest of us were enchanted at finding silk stockings of a filmy texture guaranteed to flatter all but the ungainliest of legs. We each bought a pair of dress shoes and several pairs of stockings, and later, when the inevitable runs appeared in our stockings, we took them back to the store to be repaired.

We had a two-week run of performances ahead of us, however, and soon enough were eagerly rehearsing. The male members of the troupe were housed in the headquarters of the Khalq Ferqisi, the nation's sole political party at the time. A large assembly hall in this building also provided the perfect place for rehearsals. Cleared of chairs, it was placed at our disposal, and Mrs. Cook started pressing everyone into service, appointing Mummy to supervise the cook, to send out the laundry, and to help with costume changes and makeup, and Ramezooni to recite the epic poetry that accompanied our dances, for it was obvious by now that he would not be spending much time tutoring us. His powerfully resonant voice brought an added richness to the poetic backdrop against which we dipped, circled, and soared.

We practiced and rehearsed many absorbing and exhausting hours each day and gradually learned to take it in stride when Mrs. Cook flew off the handle. It was not amusing to see a grown woman having temper tantrums like a child, even if her ire was mostly directed at the musicians and electricians, and behind her back we laughed at her odd behavior and dismissed it as the ranting and raving of an eccentric.

We spent our free hours taking in more of the sights of this picturesque city, forming new alliances among the members of the troupe and then breaking them. Nejad flirted by turns with Aida and then with me. I, for one, gave him no encouragement, but he was brazen and persistent, and pursued both of us with equal determination.

One morning I heard a knock on the door of the hotel room Mummy and I shared. Mummy had already left to do some errands, and I had been sleeping late. I thought it was a chambermaid knocking on the door and called out "come in" in one of the few Turkish phrases I had learned. To my astonishment Nejad opened the door. A few strides and he was at the edge of the bed, leaning over me. Alarmed, I sat bolt upright, clutching at the covers and pulling them up to my neck. "What *are* you doing here?" I asked, aghast at his audacity. "But you yourself told me to come in," he taunted, laughing at my embarrassment. "You must have known it was I." He pushed me back against the pillow, pinning me down with his chest. I struggled to free myself, stubbled cheek chafing mine, revulsion and horror welling up inside me. Still in my flimsy nightgown, I could not leap out of bed. "Give me a kiss," he said. "Just one kiss and I will leave." Painfully aware of the need to keep my voice low so as not to be heard by anyone passing by, I chided him for his effrontery. "Get out," I whispered. "You have no right to come into my room. You'd better leave quickly before Mummy gets back and finds you here." We struggled some more, until finally the pressure of his chest on mine eased. "Quick," I said. "You know how bad it will be for both of us if Mummy finds you alone here with me. Now go—*please.*" A flash of realization crossed Nejad's face, and he stepped back and quietly left, pulling the door shut behind him. From then on he turned his attentions more assiduously to Aida.

Mrs. Cook had assigned me a solo dance based on a beautiful lyric poem by Hafez that spoke of the great love between a rose and a nightingale. It was a dance of great delicacy and charm that required much facial movement—a rapid lifting of eyebrows, winking of eyes, and seductive tilting of the head. It was a role I thoroughly enjoyed.

On the evening of our dress rehearsal I felt the tutor's eyes on me as he stood in the wings ready to recite Hafez's lines. The heavy velvet curtains drew open, and the spotlight focused on me as I lay on a raised dais, my head buried in my arms in imitation of a sleeping rose. As I slowly unfurled my petals, my shimmering green skirt flared out and dropped away from my waist over the edges of the dais. Stretching my arms, I gradually awoke—to a beautiful morning, to love, the love of the nightingale. As my arms extended above my head, I separated my fingers, mimicking the unfolding of the tender petals of a rosebud, while Ramezooni's voice rang out: "The rose has flushed red, the bud has burst, / And drunk with joy is the nightingale—."

My bodice was a bright red, for the Persian word for *rose* is *gol-e sorkh,* literally "red flower." Long sleeves hung loosely from the elbow so that when I raised my arms, the freely floating fabric created the effect of red petals. As I twirled and leaped, my green skirt swirled around me, glinting in the soft light of dawn. Preening and beautifying myself so as to attract the nightingale to my brilliant color and sweet nectar, I indicated the nightingale's presence through mime and gesture.

During a break in our rehearsal Ramezooni asked me if I knew what this particular dance was about. "About love, of course," I responded with the assurance of ignorance and youth. He smiled and agreed that, indeed, at one level it was a love story. But, he went on, his face more serious now, at another level it must be understood as an expression of *erfan,* the Sufi mystical belief that through the special devotion of love one can meet the Divine Beloved in the present world. "So when Hafez refers to the 'lover' and the 'beloved,' he is speaking of the devotee's love of God and his yearning for union with God." It is this union that brings ecstasy and imparts the mystical knowledge of the true world that Sufis strive to achieve, he explained. They arrive at that state through the collective repetition of the name and attributes of God, sometimes accompanied by music and dance. I was silent. I had not had the remotest inkling that there was anything more to the poem and to the dance than a simple love story, a metaphor for human love—but divine love? Ramezooni went on to explain that Sufi tradition often uses the metaphor of the nightingale to represent the soul and the rose to portray the perfect beauty of God. I pondered this connection for a long time, bewildered that this simple love poem could actually involve something deeper and more profound—a mystical religious experience.

Some time later Ramezooni pointed out that another dance in our repertory also had links to Sufi mysticism, based as it was on a poem by the thirteenth-century poet Jalal ad-Din Rumi, known to Turks as Mowlana, "the Master," and to Iranians as "Mowlavi." Ramezooni filled me in on the great poet's life story, explaining that he was the founder of the order of the Mowlana dervishes, known to the outside world as the "dancing dervishes." His followers

Preening as a rose preparing to attract a nightingale in the Dance of the Rose and the Nightingale.

chanted and danced and spun themselves into a state of ecstasy until, touched by the all-enveloping Divine Presence, their souls floated on the edge of altered consciousness, illuminated by intuitive knowledge and at one with the universe.

In our interpretation of Rumi's poetry Aida and I were *paris*, or angels. Attached to the backs of our bodices were large translucent wings made of sheer fabric stretched out on thin metal frames. Nejad, dressed as an old man with a long white beard and all-enveloping sackcloth coat, moved haltingly across the stage, leaning on a staff, while Aida and I cupped our ears to hear the words of wisdom passed down through the ages. "Said M-o-s-e-s," sang Hojatzadeh from the wings. He stretched out the *Moses* in a singsong recitative, as we cocked our heads, listened, and slowly turned, our skirts of blue chiffon billowing outward like those of whirling dervishes. Then, again, "Said M-o-o-o-s-e-s," with improvised melodic rubatos, his voice quivering in the throaty manner of Persian classical singing as it rose and fell. Aida gave expression to sorrow and remorse by kneeling, her hand to her forehead, while I stood over her, holding her other hand in a comforting gesture. Then, once more, "Said M-o-o-o-s-e-s . . ." And this time the song went on, "Oh, stubborn, unbending ones; hardly yet fully Muslim, already you are Kaffirs."

Until my conversation with Ramezooni I had no idea what this dance really meant. Now I started to understand, even if only dimly, the significance of Rumi's poetry in terms of Sufi philosophy. This dance would probably be particularly well received in Turkey, my tutor surmised, because Turkey claimed Rumi as a great *Turkish* poet. Baffled, I countered, "But I thought Rumi was a great *Persian* poet and that in our dances we were interpreting *Persian* poetry." "Yes," he explained, "But the Turks claim Rumi was Turkish, and the Iranians claim he was Iranian—a long-running debate that will probably never be resolved." He went on to elaborate that the great poet's very name reveals the ambiguity of his status, for Rumi means "of Rum," or Asia Minor, where the greater part of the poet's life was spent.

Born in Balkh (now located in Afghanistan, then part of Persia) in 1207, Rumi wandered with his family in forced exile for eleven years before finally settling in Konya in Asia Minor, currently Turkey, where he spent the rest of his life. His early studies were chiefly with his father, then later with a former pupil of his father, who instructed him in the mystic lore of "the Path" and after whose death he received further esoteric teaching from Shams-i-Tabriz, a mystic who believed himself to be God's spokesman.

Rumi's great works, the *Mathnawi* and the *Diwan,* are considered to be Persian poetry of a very high order, but are also acknowledged to be singularly abstruse. The former is commonly said to be "the Koran in the Persian language," and the author himself describes it as containing "the Roots of the Roots of the Roots of the Religion, and the Discovery of the Mysteries of Reunion and Sure Knowledge." "Clearly," Ramezooni said, "the cultural influences on him were Persian—the language of his poetry is Persian, his origins were Persian—but he spent the greater part of his life in Turkey. Thus, both countries in a sense have a legitimate claim to him." He went on to outline the profound impact of Sufi philosophy on the Iranian soul and added, "Every Iranian is to some extent a Sufi at heart."

That evening I was in a strangely contemplative mood as I slipped into my *pari* costume, making certain the wings were in place and properly secured. I pondered the mysteries of the Sufi mystics' inner peace and felt strangely calm, free of the usual apprehensions and anxieties I normally experienced during a dress rehearsal. My limbs seemed suffused with warmth as I floated onto the stage, as though suspended in midair, feeling light and free, and moving like quicksilver. Then, like fire, I was everywhere at once, darting, flashing, twirling, leaping. A tornado inside spun me across the floor in an explosive burst of energy, wild and furious, while the eye in the center of my storm remained controlled and calm. Afterward Aida looked at me with questioning eyes and wondered what had come over me. I offered no explanation. I had none to give her, but to myself I thought perhaps, after all, this feeling was what *erfan* was all about—this mystical sense of otherworldliness, of being merely spirit, so suffused with joy as to be able to fly, to touch the outer rims of the universe, to melt into and become one with it. That evening I felt transformed by an inner light. I felt unusually serene and looked forward eagerly to the following night when the curtains would rise on our first performance.

Opening night presented more than the usual problems. The stagehands were having difficulty assembling the Bridge of Isfahan backstage, the electrician was having trouble with the lights, and we were unable to start on time, adding to the tension. As the minutes ticked by, the audience gradually grew restive, and after half an hour we heard occasional yells and whistles from the audience, then an increasingly loud murmur of voices. Mrs. Cook was furious and vented her frustration backstage on anyone who crossed her path. We dancers stood ready in the wings, makeup and costumes on, trying to keep our muscles warmed up by bending and stretching. But we stayed out of Mrs. Cook's way, for at such times it took little to make her lash out. Occasionally we would stop and take a peek at the audience from behind the curtains. It was a huge hall, and hundreds of people were seated in rows—waiting to be entertained, ready to condemn or approve our efforts. The gilded presidential box was empty but conspicuous in its elegance.

We seemed to be off to a bad start, but finally the last touches were put to the scenery, the lights were dimmed, and the orchestra started playing. We took our places, and the curtains slowly drew back to reveal a fairytale land of art and illusion. We were on! Thrilled to be performing before a foreign audience, we outdid ourselves, bringing a heightened verve and vigor to our performance. The audience in turn expressed its appreciation and forgiveness with long applause. We took numerous curtain calls. "Bravo! Bravo!" they shouted. Bouquets were thrown onto the stage as we bowed and curtsied again and again.

The next morning we awoke to rave reviews. Mrs. Cook triumphantly brandished a handful of newspapers filled with photographs of our performance and commentaries. Nejad translated for us many glowing articles praising the delicacy, charm, and pageantry of the Iranian Ballet Company's expositions of Persia's rich heritage. We laughed and hugged each other, basking in our success.

From then on, everywhere we went, we were besieged by reporters. They took our photographs, requested interviews, and occasionally asked for an autograph, although Mrs. Cook did her best to keep the reporters from talking to us directly, which was not too difficult because we did not speak Turkish. With Nejad serving as her translator, she gave what information she wanted them to hear, sometimes manipulating it for her own ends. She told the reporters Aida was "self-taught from childhood," a piece of misinformation meant to enhance the audience's amazement over Aida's exquisite technique. Another reporter cornered me, though, and learned that in fact Aida had been taught by a Russian ballet teacher. "Self-taught" might have been true for Sheherazade, but it was certainly not true for Aida. Clearly, Mrs. Cook was trying to deny Mme. Cornelli any credit for our training, but to what end I could not understand. Was it because our teacher was Russian? Or did Mrs. Cook want to deny any foreign influences on us to make us seem more authentic? I do not know. She was livid when she learned that it was I who had revealed the true source of Aida's fine technique; pouting and sulking, she refused to speak to me for several days. She was not used to being thwarted.

The reporters and reviewers were genuinely surprised that there was such a thing as a Persian ballet company. They had thought that Iran was too "backward" and "underdeveloped" a country to have a dance company, in particular one with female performers. They had thought that Iranian women remained veiled and secluded. Yet here, to their astonishment, were Persian girls dancing on the stage. As modern as Turkey was at that time, it did not have a native dance company, and, indeed, another decade would pass before it was to get one. The reporters were impressed. One of them summarized the essence of our performances:

> The Persian Ballet, in its distinctive character, is a remarkable formation achieved by the melting together of historic, literary, and folkloric values on the one hand and a sound theatrical knowledge and genuine talent on the other. It has known what to take from the West and how to take it, without losing its own Persian individuality and character, however fine a use of Western techniques is displayed. We . . . have much to learn from the Persian Ballet.

When the Iranians set out to modernize their music and dance, they held their rich literature and history and the folklore of their country in the place of first importance. Bringing their own genius for beauty into play, they succeeded in creating a ballet truly Iranian and Oriental. Thanks to this guiding principle, the ballet has avoided the danger of being merely a Western imitation and has emerged as a remarkable entity fully retaining its Oriental character, to be valued as such all over the world. Iran has entered the international scene with still another great art form. *(Aksham* [Istanbul], November 5, 1947)

We danced nightly for an adoring public for two weeks. At the end of each performance we chattered excitedly backstage over that day's mishaps and successes, while Mummy and Mrs. Sadeq helped us undress, remove our makeup, and put our costumes away. Our exhilaration would take a long time to wear off, and it was often difficult for us to calm down. Over a very late dinner we would review every little detail of the evening—as though the audience knew the difference between five or six turns in a sequence or could possibly have noticed a slight wobble during an arabesque.

As we rehashed the triumphs and calamities of our performances, we picked at the traditional *meze* spread before us—delicate grape leaf *dolma* filled with pine nuts and rice, flaky *borek* stuffed with feta cheese or meat, vegetable cutlets sprinkled generously with thyme, or eggplant and tomatoes dripping with olive oil. Other times we would feast on *doner kebab* served on a bed of spiced pilaf, or *taze fasulia* smothered in onions, or shish kebab, or tiny lamb chops, and always tasty bread (*pide*), and yogurt on the side.

One night while we were reviewing the events of the evening, Mummy suggested that we should shorten *The Prayer of Darius.* "It is too long and repetitious," she said, "and would benefit from being cut." Mrs. Cook's eyes narrowed, and she scowled at the unsolicited advice, but said nothing and kept on eating. She was a vegetarian—not out of conviction, but on doctor's orders because she suffered from high blood pressure. It was not the first time Mummy had expressed an opinion Mrs. Cook did not like. Perhaps Mummy was right. Perhaps to Western tastes *The Prayer of Darius* did seem monotonous, but, to be fair, it was true to its origins and, like the religious rituals that inspired it, relied for its effect in part on a seemingly endless cycle of repetitions.

Ramezooni jauntily walking
down a boulevard in the port city
of Izmir (Smyrna).

A reception was held in our honor one evening at Robert College, a well-known American institution set in an idyllic location high up on a hill overlooking the Bosporus. We arrived at sunset, when the sky was flushed with pink and the Bosporus glistened like burnished gold. The heartbreakingly romantic view from the hilltop made us catch our breath. Several students of the college were at the reception, and one of them—a young man from Kansas, with blue eyes, fair hair, and a Grecian profile—singled me out for attention. Smitten with his good looks, I accepted his invitation to go to the movies with him.

A couple of nights later we sat in a theater, holding hands. It was a costly evening for the young man because he not only had to pay for the movie tickets but for a taxi to take him all the way back to Robert College. The trams and buses stopped running fairly early, and we had spent a couple of hours after the movie sitting on a park bench, talking. With some embarrassment he confessed to me that he did not have enough money to see both of us back to our quarters and asked if I could lend him some. He would be sure to repay me by the end of the week before we departed for Izmir. He would come by the hotel in person and repay it. "But of course," I answered, my heart going out to him in his embarrassment. I pulled out my few remaining Turkish bills and pressed him to take

In a park in Izmir with *(left to right)* Ramezooni, Mummy, Hojatzadeh, and Amir.

them, certain that I would see him again and that he would return the money. A few days later, however, I was on board a ship heading south along the Mediterranean coast without having seen either him or my money again.

Barely a ripple disturbed the glasslike surface of the water of the Aegean, a vast stretch of turquoise mirroring the blue of the sky above. Joined at the horizon, the sky and water seemed to form a blue cocoon around our boat as it rocked gently back and forth. The sound of the waters lapping against the hull lulled me into a dreamily romantic mood; leaning against the railing of the deck, I gazed out at the seemingly endless sea. As the water splashed upward and caught the glint of the sun before dropping back into the dancing waves, I felt a deep sense of longing—although I could not say for what. Gazing up at the birds circling the ship, I yearned to be able to fly like them; looking down at the schools of fish darting away from the prow, I wished I could flash and leap as they did. I sensed someone nearby and turned to find Ramezooni quietly standing beside me. We looked out over the rippling velvet stretched before us and stood silently, as though in a reverie. After a while we started talking. "What do you think of when you look out over the sea?" he asked. After some hesitation I answered, "Eternity," as the waves swirled against another row of waves and another and another, endlessly circling outward. We talked about the concept of eternity and about the transience of life. Then, still looking out over the sea, Ramezooni recited some quatrains from Omar Khayyam's *Rubaiyat:*

Visiting a girls' school in Izmir *(front row, left to right):* Aida, Qodsi, me, Mummy, Mrs. Cook with poodle on arm, school official, and Nejad. Other members of the troupe are behind us.

Alas, that Spring should vanish with the Rose!
That Youth's sweet-scented Manuscript should close!
    The Nightingale that in the Branches sang,
Ah, whence, and whither flown again, who knows!

While the Rose blows along the River Brink.
With old Khayyam the Ruby Vintage drink
    And when the Angel with his darker Draught
Draws up to thee—take that, and do not shrink.

I stood entranced. The musical resonance of his voice swept over me, evoking wonder and awe, tenderness and warmth. Like the splashing sea spray, my heart leaped as I caught my breath, overcome by the beauty of the language, the timbre of his voice, the romance of the moment. I turned and looked at his profile as he faced the sea—strong and self-assured. The cadence of the verses seemed to reflect the rhythm of the waves, the pulsing of my heart. When he finished, we stood together in silence, just watching the waves as they rose and fell.

The next day we arrived in Izmir, once considered the pearl of the Aegean. Historically known as Smyrna, this city was the site of the acropolis of the capital of the Aeolian League in Homer's time, and here one can still see the ruins of a Roman agora built under Marcus Aurelius. It was here King Richard the Lionhearted landed during the Crusades; here that Lord Byron found the inspiration for *The Bride of Abydos;* and here that a 2,500-year Greek presence in Asia Minor came to an abrupt and bloody end when in 1922 Turkish troops drove the Greeks out of the city.

In Ephesus, Ramezooni jotting down notes.

We found modern Izmir to be a waterfront and boulevard city, with charming open-air cafes and inviting restaurants. In the evening family groups came out on the boulevard to stroll, eat, or watch the sun set. Nearby stood a spacious park built a few years earlier to accommodate a World Trade Fair. In an old album photographs record our excursions: Mummy, Qodsi, Ramezooni, and I—on the boulevard, in the park, in a café, at a girls' school. We look very relaxed and very young.

After two weeks in Izmir, we boarded a bus for the hour and a half drive to the ancient ruins of Ephesus and Bergama. Ephesus's main attractions are its Greek ruins. Considered to be one of the world's most stupendous archaeological excavations and reconstructions, the sight transported Mrs. Cook. As we wandered around the ruins, unparalleled for sheer magnitude, she walked as though in a dream, stopping once in a while to give us a running commentary on the history of the site and the mythology and significance of the numerous statues, columns, pedestals, and capitals strewn and scattered along the marble-paved Arcadian Way. At one time a grand promenade lined with shops and arcaded colonnades, the site was now littered with smashed pediments and the broken arms and heads of statues, only an occasional column standing upright in solitary splendor. I listened intently as Mrs. Cook commented on the various

Touring the ruins of Ephesus with
(left to right) Mrs. Sadeq our dress
designer, Sheherazade behind
statue, and Aida.

gods and goddesses we encountered along the way and was humbled by her vast knowledge of the subject and by her fluency in Greek that enabled her to read to us the inscriptions carved into some of the stones.

From time to time we would stop to admire a particularly voluptuous Greek goddess or cluster around a standing statue for a photograph, while some members of the troupe snickered over the nude statues and whispered to their comrades behind cupped hands. To cover up my embarrassment I feigned sophistication, as if I had seen many such statues and found in their nudity nothing remarkable. We posed for photographs, with the members of our troupe lining up in front of the remnants of the ancient library (second in size only to the one in Alexandria); smiling in front of the public lavatories, the baths, and the brothels (more snickers here); and standing in the agora, where public discussions, transactions, and commerce took place. Finally, having climbed to the highest tier of the 24,000-seat theater carved into the side of Mount Pion, we caught our breath at the panoramic view at our feet, while Ramezooni, at the bottom of the steps on the arena stage, tested the acoustics. First declaiming loudly, he gradually dropped his voice to a whisper; as expected, we could hear him clearly and wondered at the ingenuity of the ancient Greeks.

In Bergama (ancient Pergamum) we walked through chambers where the Romans used music as a soothing antidote to sadness, depression, and insanity and where invalids came from distant parts of the country seeking cures by the god Asclepias and his priests. It did not surprise me that the Romans should have considered melodious sounds to be restorative, for I myself had always found music calming and uplifting.

But we had upcoming performances in Mersin and Adana, and we moved

In Ephesus *(left to right):* Hojatzadeh, Daneshvar, and Ramezooni.

on. Of these port cities, I recall little other than the beautiful backdrop of the glittering sea, against which Ramezooni kept photographing me—full face, in profile, over the shoulder. He was fast becoming Mummy's and my frequent companion.

By the time we finally arrived in Ankara, the capital of Turkey, we had already been on tour for much longer than the projected two months, and the end was nowhere in sight. After our two-week engagement here we were scheduled to return to Istanbul for another two weeks. Each fortnight of performances meant another fortnight of traveling, rehearsing, and preparing. The tour was taking much longer than any of us had expected. By now Aida's father had been away from work for four months, far longer than he had anticipated. Becoming more and more disgruntled, he felt he absolutely had to return home. At the same time he was reluctant to leave Aida without a chaperon, so Mrs. Cook offered to take over the role, assuring him that she would look after his daughter. The new arrangement, however, put Aida in much closer contact with Nejad, for he was always by Mrs. Cook's side. From then on the three of them were inseparable.

At a large reception held in our honor at the Iranian embassy we were surprised to find that our hostess, the ambassador's wife, was a former fellow student at Mme. Cornelli's ballet school. With her elegant dress, her hair stylishly swept up into a pile on top of her head, and her mature self-confidence, she was hardly recognizable. We exchanged hugs and kisses and learned that she was receiving private ballet instruction at home because it would be inappropriate for a married woman to perform in recitals or for an ambassador's wife to attend

Posing for photographs in
Mersin, Turkey.

ballet classes. We all knew society's rules and did not think to question them. We all assumed that when we married, we too would have to give up performing and probably dancing. By a strange twist of fate, however, the only one of us to continue her *performing* dance career after marriage was the one who stayed in Iran and married an Iranian—Aida.

On opening night in Ankara the atmosphere fairly crackled with excitement, for we had been told that the president of Turkey himself, Ismet Inonu, and his entourage would be attending. I could hardly believe it. It all seemed like a dream. Here I was, touring Turkey, dancing on the stage night after night, receiving ovations and fantastic reviews. On top of that I would now be dancing for the president of Turkey! I was ecstatic and scared at the same time. President Inonu was Ataturk's successor, and his presence would be a great honor.

That evening a strange and singular event occurred. As I, the rose, was preening my petals, a bat flew into the lights, swooped toward me, then turned away and soared upward, only to dart down again. The timing was extraordinary. I reached toward it as toward an imaginary nightingale and found its movements and mine miraculously synchronized. It created the illusion of a nightingale fluttering around me, seemingly resulting from clever lighting effects. After my dance was over, the bat disappeared, and we never saw it again.

On another night while dancing *Caravan,* I felt a sharp, piercing sensation in my foot. Dancing barefoot, I had stepped on a nail that had not been swept up after the Bridge of Isfahan was mounted. I had to contain an impulse to scream, to pull out the nail, to cry and go running off the stage in full view of everyone, but I knew I had to keep on dancing. "I cannot stop now," I thought. "I just have

Crossing a bridge with
Ramezooni in a park in
Ankara, Turkey.

to keep going." And I did. Fortunately the incident occurred near the end of our dance. As the last strains of the music died away, Aida, Sheherazade, and I in silhouette stepped slowly off the stage, and the curtains came down to thunderous applause. When we reached the wings, I burst into loud sobs. Aida and Sheherazade looked at me with amazement, for they had been unaware that there was anything wrong. Crying, I lifted my foot and plucked out the offending nail, holding it up for all to see. The applause was continuing, so they dragged me out for a curtain call, where I curtsied and managed to smile through my tears. Within minutes a doctor arrived on the scene, cleaned and bandaged my foot, gave me a tetanus shot, and pronounced me ready to go on with the rest of the performance. I changed costumes, put on a soft ballet shoe, and went back on, stepping gingerly on the injured foot. Later that evening Aida and Sheherazade rewarded me with new looks of admiration and respect.

Ankara was largely a new city, built onto the old city in the 1920s to be Ataturk's capital. Compared to Istanbul, it offered little of sightseeing interest, but we paid a visit to the Ataturk Mausoleum high on a hillside, where we had a superb view of the city and where Ramezooni expounded on the significance of Ataturk's accomplishments. To my surprise he painted the picture of a man beset by vices. "He drank heavily," he said. "He was a gambler and womanizer as well." But Ramezooni went on to relate how Ataturk had largely succeeded in fulfilling his vision of creating a modern nation-state out of the remnants of the Ottoman Empire. I wondered how a great statesman could be so lacking in virtue in private life, so Ramezooni and I ended up in a long discussion on whether there was any correlation between public greatness and private virtue. Disillusioned but a little wiser, I conceded reluctantly that the evidence did not seem to substantiate any link between the two.

One of our favorite spots for outings was a lovely park centered around a huge lake made from a former swamp on Ataturk's orders. Here shrubs and trees lined paths and walkways, and graceful bridges spanned the banks of flowing brooks. I have a snapshot of Ramezooni and me in that park. We look very young. We are both smiling as we walk across one of those bridges.

Revolt in the Ranks

Come, fill the Cup, and in the Fire of Spring
The Winter Garment of Repentance fling:
The Bird of Time has but a little way
To fly—and Lo! the Bird is on the Wing.
　　　　　　　—Omar Khayyam, *Rubiayat*

BY THE TIME we returned to Istanbul, we had been touring for five months. As I looked out over the soaring minarets and rounded cupolas of the city's distinctive skyline, my heart embraced it like a familiar friend. At the same time I knew it would be only a temporary reunion, for I would soon be moving on, either to dance in Athens or to return home to Tehran. Signs of revolt were increasingly evident among the members of our troupe. I could sense it in the grumbling and muttering in quiet corners, the turned backs, the closed circles—especially among the musicians. One could hardly blame them. They had wives and children back home and had not expected to be away for so long.

Besides, Mrs. Cook was getting more and more irascible. Her demands were increasingly unreasonable, and she was working everyone to the point of exhaustion. Rehearsals went on until late into the night, and no one's thirst, hunger, or fatigue seemed to be of any consequence to her. Like a petty tyrant lording it over her fiefdom, she pushed us hour after hour. We girls did not mind too much because we loved to dance and because most of the time she remained courteous to us, but toward the musicians and stagehands, who were not there of their own volition, she had dropped all pretense of civility. She yelled at them for the most trivial offenses, using unbecomingly foul language.

Early sporadic complaints gradually gave way to a groundswell of anger and

224

resentment. "Two months. She said two months. We have been gone nearly six months, and now she's talking about going on to other places!" "My wife was expecting a baby when I left. I don't even know whether she has had it yet or if it is a boy or a girl. I need to go home!" Whenever Mrs. Cook approached, small clusters of whispering members of the troupe would suddenly fall silent. Here she was, they thought, casually talking about our going to Greece for a few months and then perhaps on to India. Even an elastic definition of Mrs. Cook's "two months" could not have prepared us for such an extension of time. She was used to getting her way, though, even if it meant riding roughshod over others' needs and inclinations. Against all odds she had created something remarkable and had no intention of giving it up now, no matter what the cost.

As for myself, I loved traveling. I thrilled to the excitement of the footlights and was certainly not eager to return to school. I adored the bustle of Istanbul, its trams, shops, and sidewalk cafés, as well as the domes and cupolas that stood as an ever-present reminder of a past that covered the full range of human experience—blood, sacrifice, greed, treachery, power, pomp, glorious conquests, and the extraordinary creation of a great empire.

I had also just seen my first opera. Standing with Ramezooni in the highest tier in the opera house through the entire performance, I was utterly transfixed as the singers sang *Madame Butterfly* in Turkish. On the wings of Puccini's melodies, my heart soared to the outer reaches of ecstasy, then plunged to the depths of despair. I wept for Madame Butterfly. I had never seen or heard anything so beautiful in my life. Had I not been in Istanbul with the ballet troupe, I would never have seen this opera.

Nevertheless, somewhere in the farthest recesses of my mind I was starting to feel uneasy about missing so much schooling. My books remained unopened, yet somehow I would have to take the final exams at the end of the school year. Geometry, in particular, worried me. What if I were to fail? The thought put me in a somber mood. Perhaps after all it was time to go home. Besides, I was starting to tire of Mrs. Cook's eccentricities, as she wound up tighter and tighter under the strain of the venture she had undertaken.

Mummy's anxiety was increasing by the day. She had no idea whether the tenants were paying the rent or the electricity and telephone bills, and she feared for the condition of the house, with no one there to look after it. "I would never have agreed to our going on this trip, if I had known we would be gone so long," she complained. Sightseeing and traveling were all very well, but this was going too far.

Even more pressing was the matter of money. After the initial pocket expenses Mrs. Cook had given us at the beginning of the trip, we had not received another penny. Most of us had by now spent it all, some on frivolities, but mainly on necessities—bus and taxi fare, occasional meals out, museum entrance fees, and the like. Ramezooni was the only one among us to have carefully husbanded his money and not spent it. One morning, though, he woke up in the men's dormitory to find his wallet missing. "I know who took it," he said, barely able to contain his anger. "But I have no way of proving it. If I confront the bastard, he will just deny it." So now none of us had any money, and those were the days before checks and wire services and long-distance bank transactions—at least in that part of the world. The only credit Mummy and I had ever known was the account the corner grocer kept for us—carefully hand recorded in a notebook—which she paid up at the end of each month. All other transactions were strictly cash and carry, and now we had no cash. We could not buy a ticket for a plane or train or even bus to take us home. Mrs. Cook had us over a barrel.

The army musicians were in the most difficult position of all. They were lowest in the hierarchy of the troupe, received the least consideration and the worst treatment, and were the most unhappy about being away from their homes and families. They grumbled and cursed, but knew there was very little they could do to alter their situation. They had been put at Mrs. Cook's disposal and that was that. The flutist Naraqi, however, was a free agent and not a member of the army band. He too was anxious to return home and so joined our small group of would-be protesters. As for Ramezooni and Qodsi, they both needed to get back to the university, but Ramezooni was the one most intent upon it and most inclined to take matters into his own hands.

When I discussed these troubling matters with Aida, however, she only became upset that any of us could even consider letting Mrs. Cook down after all she had done to build the company. "How can you even *think* of leaving?" she exploded. She would take care of her schoolwork when the time came. For now, she was looking forward to going to Greece and possibly India. "This is an incredible opportunity!" she said. "And how can Mrs. Cook do without you? How can she possibly replace you?" What Aida might have added, but did not, was that Nejad had been quietly courting her. The two of them could frequently be seen whispering together, brushing hands, bumping shoulders, giggling over some private joke, lingering on until everyone else had left. Their courtship was an open secret. A gulf opened between us. We became distant, our conversation strained, our interaction correct but cool.

Meanwhile, Ramezooni spent more and more time with Mummy, and I watched as the two of them fanned the flames of resentment among the dissident members of the troupe. A sense of injury linked them, drawing them together into a sort of conspiracy. When Ramezooni suggested it was time for us to speak to Mrs. Cook, the rest of our group of rebels readily agreed. It would not be easy, for we not only had to inform Mrs. Cook we were parting ways with her but had to persuade her to provide transport for us, something she would surely refuse to do. Our departure would deal a major blow to the ballet company; I was one of its principal dancers, so it would be difficult to replace me. But Ramezooni was unflinching in his determination, and the rest of us drew courage and inspiration from his resolute fearlessness.

I imagine Mrs. Cook had an inkling of the looming confrontation. We arranged to meet with her and found her sitting on a couch with her little poodle cuddled to her chest, her feet planted firmly and defiantly on the floor, Nejad by her side. "I need to return home and take care of my house and tenants," Mummy said. "And Nesta needs to get back to school. You told us the tour would take two months. Here it is now six months, with no end in sight and no telling how much longer this will all take. We simply *have* to get back." Ramezooni, in turn, spoke of his need to return to his studies at Tehran University, emphasizing that he never would have agreed to go on tour with the troupe had he known how long he would be away. "You misled us," he said, looking her in the eye without flinching, his voice calm and controlled. "And it is your responsibility to provide for our return."

Mrs. Cook turned white, then red. Her eyes grew round and large, then narrowed into daggerlike slits of violet. Turning on us in a rage, she snarled, "You troublemakers. I know you have been going around hatching plots against me." Dropping her poodle onto the couch, she stood up and stomped one foot on the floor, shaking her fist combatively. "You traitors," she spat out, "ingrates, turncoats. After all I have done for you, you turn around and stab me in the back?" Her voice, at first rough and low, rose in a crescendo and finally exploded with the force of thunder. "How *dare* you talk about leaving the troupe? I won't let you." I drew back, for much of her anger was directed at me. Suddenly, though, she seemed to be having trouble breathing. She gasped and clutched at her throat as though choking, then unexpectedly crumpled to the floor in a faint. I was alarmed to see her corpulent body stretched out limply on the bare tiles, while Nejad fanned her face and tried to lift her up. "Now look what you have done," he scolded, "after all she has done for you, after all the success and renown she has brought to every one of you."

I was deeply distressed as I watched Mrs. Cook slowly coming to, looking around her and whispering, "Where am I?" With Nejad's help she dragged herself up, sat heavily back onto the couch, turned her back on us, and refused to speak another word. Nejad hustled us out. Later Mummy, Qodsi, Naraqi, and Ramezooni laughed over the incident, convinced the fainting spell was nothing but histrionics on Mrs. Cook's part. Perhaps I was being naïve, but I believed she really had passed out.

From then on, it was open war. Mrs. Cook snubbed those of us who had declared our intention to return home. She was particularly irritated with me and took every opportunity to express her annoyance. To forestall any protest on the part of the troupe's musicians she gave them to understand emphatically that they had no recourse but to go along with her and that complaining was going to get them nowhere. They were in her employ and in her absolute power. They glumly acquiesced. An uneasy truce enabled us to go on with the two-week show that had been scheduled for Istanbul, but there was a definite coolness between Mrs. Cook and our faction. She showered Sheherazade and Aida with attention but treated the rest of us like outcasts. We stuck together, though, keeping a little apart from the rest of the troupe.

On an outing to Buyuk Ada, an emerald island set in the tranquil waters of the Bosporus, where the principal means of transport was by horse-drawn carriage, our rebel contingent rode in a separate conveyance. Now the groupings of the troupe never changed. On a boat ride one moonlit night Mummy, Qodsi, Ramezooni, the flutist Naraqi, and I stood at the railing at opposite ends from the rest of the company. As we sailed down the Bosporus, Ramezooni again stood next to me, and we silently watched the moonlight glittering on the breaking waves as the waters parted before the bow of the gliding boat. Then, turning to me, he started to sing, and soon Mummy, Qodsi, and I joined in. "I am drunk, I am drunk with love," we sang boisterously in the Gilaki accent of one of the folk songs we knew so well from our nightly performances.

Mrs. Cook seemed to think we had no alternative but to go along with her grand plans. She certainly had no intention of supplying us with transportation home, but what she had not counted on was the ingenuity and resourcefulness of our tutor. Trained in the law, he knew what the rest of us did not—that because we held diplomatic passports, the Iranian embassy in Turkey had a legal obligation to provide those of us who wanted to return to Tehran with the means to do so. At the end of our two weeks of performances in Istanbul, with Mrs. Cook making plans to travel on to Athens, he made an appointment for the rebel faction to see an Iranian consular official.

We stepped into a spacious office carpeted with the finest of handwoven Kashans, the spires of Istanbul's minarets magnificently framed in a large plate-glass window. The consular official was courteous and attentive. After all, we held diplomatic passports, even though three of us were students, one a housewife, and one a professional musician. Briefly and politely Ramezooni presented our case. He made it clear that he knew both what our rights were and what the embassy's obligations were under the law. We realized the troupe's mission had been a diplomatic coup, and we did not mean to sabotage it, but we had made no commitment beyond two months and had greatly overextended ourselves. He stressed that Mrs. Cook had clearly misled us; she would have to do without us if she insisted on continuing onward. Mummy and Qodsi added a few words of their own, and we left with assurances that the official would do everything he could to help.

A few days later, as the troupe was getting ready to depart for Greece, Mummy and I packed our bags in preparation for the long trip home. Although deep down I regretted not being able to continue on with the troupe, I was by now resigned to the inevitable and knew I had to get back to school. I was also sufficiently caught up in the fervor of revolt against Mrs. Cook that I shared some feelings of triumph and solidarity with the other members. We met Qodsi in the lobby, and before long Ramezooni, Naraqi, and a couple of the stagehands joined us. A bus drove up to the front door of the hotel, and we boarded it. We were returning home. There were no good-byes, no parting courtesies. I felt uncomfortable about letting Mrs. Cook down and about leaving her in hostility rather than friendship. I knew I had no alternative, even though I suspected our parting of ways meant the end of my dance career.

We were now in the depths of winter. Istanbul had been uncomfortable enough the last few weeks, with its damp cold that chilled me to the bones and made me shiver, but the mountain passes we now traveled through were colder still, and the bus was not heated. Of course, we did not expect it to be, and we simply put up with the cold, as we were used to doing. Our endurance was sorely tested as we journeyed through the stark and frozen landscape.

For days we drove along mountain roads so narrow and twisting that I feared we might tip over the edge and plunge down steep ravines. Instead of the tawny golds and browns streaked with purple we had seen on our journey six months earlier, the landscape was endlessly white. Deep snow drifted and piled as far as the eye could see, carving strange and beautiful shapes. Occasionally, as the sun glinted off a crusty glaze, the colors of the rainbow played over the snow's iridescent surface. At times the road was barely visible or completely blocked, and the driver and his assistant would have to get out and shovel before we could continue on our way. Several times the chains on the bus broke, and we waited while the driver repaired them. When he stopped in a small mountain village for gasoline, Qodsi, Mummy, and I went inside a ramshackle store not much larger than a cubbyhole, hoping to warm our numbed feet, but, if anything, it was colder inside than out. The only heat came from a tiny charcoal brazier on the dirt floor, around which we crowded. Its meager embers did little to warm us, and we soon decided we would be better off standing out in the bright sunshine.

Boarding the bus again, we stomped our feet, blew on our gloved hands, and distracted ourselves from our discomfort by singing songs, most of them still fresh in our minds from our dance repertory. "Lulla-lullaby," Qodsi and I sang together, "Oh, my tulip flower. Where, oh where has your mother gone?" Occasionally we would croon a popular American song, and the two of us tried singing "An Indian Love Call" in harmony. "When I'm calling you-ou-ou-ou, ou-ou-ou. Will you answer too-oo-oo-oo, oo-oo-oo," we warbled, collapsing in peals of laughter. But neither of us really knew how to harmonize, and after a while the others on the bus became irritated with our silliness. Their acerbic comments finally quieted us.

From time to time we would change seats, and sometimes Ramezooni would sit next to me, engaging me in long and absorbing conversations. We argued passionately over whether suicide was a brave or a cowardly act, whether there was life after death, whether there was a God and, if so, what the evidence was. At every turn I found myself checkmated in my arguments by my tutor's superior knowledge of philosophy, history, psychology, law, and literature, and I vowed silently to myself to learn more about those subjects. Yet in spite of my disadvantage in these discussions I found myself pondering the questions we raised, my mind stimulated and deeply engaged.

Ramezooni and I had up to this point kept a distinctly respectful distance between us, as was only proper between a tutor and a student, and we had never discussed matters of a personal nature. Now, once in a while, Ramezooni would talk about himself and his family. He confided that it was his interest in the theater that had led him to accept the tutoring job with Mrs. Cook's ballet company. Ever since his early teens he had been putting on plays at his high school, where he had scrounged to find old sheets to set up as curtains, used his imagination to devise a stage, and battled the disapproving principal every step of the way. He had not only produced and directed the plays, but also held the leading roles in them, performing in both comedies and tragedies, reveling in his ability to move the audience either to laughter or to tears.

He confided, however, that an additional reason for his taking the tutoring job was to get away from Tehran and the still painful memories of his mother's premature death. "I loved her more than anyone in the whole world," he said, "and she died in my arms." He had found it difficult to go beyond his grief and thought that a change of scene might help diminish his profound sense of loss. "Well, did it help?" I asked. He looked at me with those piercing eyes and answered simply, "Yes."

Ramezooni's father was an architect. Apprenticed at a young age to a master architect, he had gradually developed a remarkable reputation, such that Reza Shah had commissioned him to do several municipal buildings in Tehran, including the Post and Telegraph Office. Ramezooni told of frequent visits to the British embassy when he was a child, where his father had done some remodeling work. There, for the first time, Ramezooni had encountered an intriguingly different world, a fascinating new culture, and the English language. At a time when most of his contemporaries were studying French, he had chosen to study English. Taking every opportunity for exposure to the language, he had gone as often as he could to English-language movies and to the British cultural center, known as the Green Room, where he had also put on plays in their small theater. He had also absorbed American cultural influences when he had joined the Boy Scouts—one of Reza Shah's innovative experiments.

Ramezooni's father, however, had a serious drinking problem. Like my father, he was an alcoholic. "When I was just a little boy," Ramezooni said, "my father would sometimes take me with him on outings. But once when it got very late and we still had not come home, my mother went looking for me and found me sitting on the counter of a bar, where my father had been giving me sips of arrak. She had to rush me to the hospital to have my stomach pumped out." He paused for a moment and then went on. "He was totally irresponsible. My poor mother had to scrounge and scrimp, while he spent all his money on alcohol." I listened attentively, my heart touched by the pain and anger I heard in his voice, sentiments with which I was all too familiar.

Ramezooni not only loved his mother deeply, but obviously admired her as well. She had been one of the first women to venture unveiled onto the streets of Tehran, taking the unprecedented step not long after Reza Shah had banned the veil. Faced with an urgent need to take her sick son to the hospital, she had put on a European-style hat as a token covering for her head and, feeling totally naked, had braved the disapproving stares of passersby to get Ramezooni to the doctor.

A woman of great compassion and boundless energy, she had devoted endless hours to helping the residents of their *mahaleh,* delivering babies, mediating family disputes, arranging marriages, and taking care of the sick and elderly. It was she who had encouraged Ramezooni in his studies. Although some of his relatives had mocked him for his book learning and wondered why he was not getting out into the world and earning a living, she had stood by him and encouraged him to develop his intellectual talents.

I listened wide-eyed as he revealed that his mother had been the second of his father's two wives and the favorite. I was shocked because although the law in Iran, as in other Muslim countries, allows men to marry as many as four wives simultaneously, the custom had almost died out, and I had never before met anyone who had grown up in a polygamous household. The first wife had naturally resented having to share her husband with a cowife, feeling jealous of and hostile toward Ramezooni's mother.

A small yard and gateway had connected the separate but contiguous houses that Ramezooni's father maintained for the two households. He had attempted to allocate his time fairly between them, passing from one house to another on allotted days. He had not been able to hide his preference for Ramezooni's mother, though, and resentment and rancor on the part of the first family had grown to such a pitch by the time Ramezooni was born—a son and the first child of the second marriage—that they attempted to set fire to his cradle. His mother had saved his life by snatching him from the flames and passing him out of the window to the arms of a servant, who held him while his mother put out the fire. It had been a long time before the two households were on speaking terms again. Two more children had followed, both girls.

Not long after Ramezooni's mother died, his father had married again. A simple woman but an excellent cook and housewife, Asiyeh Khanom had done her best to be a caretaker and mother to Ramezooni and his two younger sisters. Eventually they had all grown rather fond of her. Ramezooni confided to me that it was going to be his responsibility to find husbands for his two sisters when they came of age. His father was incapable of taking care of the matter. Once the girls graduated from high school, he, as the elder brother, would have to find suitable grooms for each of them in turn. He did not relish the prospect, for he would have to make sure the men did not have syphilis, did not drink, smoke opium, gamble, or frequent whorehouses, and that they had the means to provide for his sisters. The matter obviously weighed on him.

I was so caught up in Ramezooni's narrative that the time passed quickly, and I was distracted from the discomfort of my cold feet. Having passed Mount Ararat and Lake Van, we spent the night in Erzerum and then finally crossed the border into Iran. Going through customs was a simple matter. Our diplomatic passports helped, of course, but this time we had only a modest amount of luggage. No filmy skirts, no sequined veils, no artificial gems or jewels on pendants, bracelets, or belts for wary customs officials to contend with. Mainly, though, the officials must have had their orders from higher up, and we passed inspection without any difficulty.

In Tabriz we were guests of 'Ali Mansour, the provincial governor, who later would become prime minister a second time. We slept that night in a small hotel where the lights were so dim we could hardly find our way down the hall. Bothered by bugs in the bed, Mummy tossed and turned all night, hardly sleeping at all. The next morning we all went together to pay our respects to our host, the governor of Azerbaijan.

In his office we perched stiffly on straight-backed chairs at some distance from the imposing desk behind which he sat. Making polite conversation, he inquired whether the accommodations had been satisfactory. Such questions were strictly pro forma, of course. Everyone knew the accommodations had been terrible, but we were expected to be polite and say they were entirely satisfactory, which was what Ramezooni and others started to do when up piped Mummy. "*Aqa,*" she said, getting up from her chair and approaching the governor with a piece of balled-up paper in her hand. "Look what I have here." Unfolding the paper, she held it out toward him. "I want you to see this. It is absolutely disgraceful." To our dismay and to the governor's disbelieving eyes she revealed a dead louse. "Look," she said. "It is a louse, and it was in my bed, among the sheets. I saved it to show you."

I cringed and wished the floor would open up and swallow me. Why was Mummy always embarrassing us? Why did she have to laugh out loud at the cinema, or hike her skirts and go wading in the *joob,* or go swimming in her underwear and behave in ways that violated the decorum of the society in which she had chosen to live? The other members of the troupe were struck dumb by her audacity. One does not speak like that to *important* people! One covers up inadequacies of hospitality on the part of one's host.

For a moment there was a dead silence that crackled with tension. Then the governor's face burst into a smile, then a grin, and to our astonishment and relief he started laughing uproariously. He had never before had anyone confront him like that, and here was a Persian-speaking foreigner—a woman at that—who had the effrontery to speak to him boldly and openly. He reached out and took the scrap of paper, carefully wrapped the offending creature in it and laid it on his desk. "Thank you for drawing my attention to this matter," he said and banged his hand down on a bell that sat on the corner of his desk. An attendant entered. "Bring tea for my guests," he ordered. "And tell my assistant to come here." The attendant hurried away to fetch tea, and his assistant entered, bowing to the governor, one hand held across his chest in deference. "Do you see this?" the governor accosted him. "It is a louse, and it was in the bed of Madame, our honored guest. Is that the kind of hospitality we show guests in Tabriz? See to it that this never happens again." He curtly dismissed his assistant, who took the paper gingerly, glowered at Mummy, bowed to the governor, and left the room. Afterward there was some whispering among the members of our group, but I could not hear what they were saying, and I knew it would be no use remonstrating with Mummy. In some ways she would always be a foreigner; nothing would ever change that.

Finally home in Tehran we picked up our lives where we had left off. I returned to school to find myself sorely behind in some subjects, especially geometry. I found a willing tutor in Ramezooni, who came to the house a couple of times a week to help me catch up on what I had missed during most of the school year. I was grateful for his help and somehow managed to squeak through the final geometry exam. Latin also gave me trouble, a subject in which Ramezooni could not help me at all, but I was miraculously able to pass that exam, too—much to my Latin teacher's chagrin. I think she half-wished I could be compelled to take the course again over the summer, for she disapproved of my having gone on tour. The other subjects I caught up with on my own and was happily promoted to the eleventh grade.

Besides helping with my schoolwork, Ramezooni sometimes came over just to visit or to take Mummy or me or both of us to the movies. We sometimes went to a concert by the Tehran Symphony Orchestra. And always he recited poetry in Persian, explaining the meaning of the elegant, beautiful, and sometimes abstruse phrases. And always I was awed by his endless store of knowledge.

Not long after our return I stopped in at Mme. Cornelli's and found myself reinstated in her good favor. Apparently she had heard of my encounter with the Turkish journalist in Istanbul. She graciously asked me to return to ballet classes and talked about giving me a leading part in her next recital in an ensemble with my friends and former fellow dancers, Shuric and Kotic. I was delighted.

I soon discovered, though, that I had been spoiled by the opulence, professionalism, and grandeur of my performances with the Iranian Ballet Company. Our one-night recital seemed trite and inconsequential compared to the two-week runs I was used to, our lighting amateur and inadequate, but I kept my feelings to myself. In school I choreographed and performed a smooth and elegant tango with Shuric and Kotic that elicited much praise. Nothing I did, however, could compete with my memories of colored lights playing on swirling multitiered skirts and of seemingly endless curtain calls. I longed for the thrill of "real" performing. Yet even as I yearned for that thrill again, I knew it would probably never be—at least, not in the same way.

I think I had always known that performing would be a transient phase of my life, that some day I would have to give it up, especially once I married, a notion fostered not just by my own milieu but also by American culture as transmitted through the Hollywood movies of the day. Although I was nowhere near marriage yet, I knew that it could not be far away. I remember going with Aida and her mother to see *The Red Shoes* and hearing Mrs. Akhundzadeh dwelling on the "moral" of the story. "You see, a career is incompatible with marriage," she said, looking pointedly at her daughter. In any case, in the country where I was living the possibilities for a dance career were limited under any circumstances at that particular time, although some years later the Iranian Ballet Company would be revived with Aida at its head, and an opera house would be built that would serve as a performing arts center under Nejad's direction. As for me, the opportunity that had come my way was simply a strange and unexpected twist of fate, a glorious experience that I would look back on with pleasure all my life. In a flash it had come and gone, and now in late 1947, on the brink of turning sixteen, I would have to find other avenues of excitement. I joined the school choir and the debating club, and, of course, flirted madly with any number of boys.

New Horizons

Into this Universe, and *why* not knowing,
Nor *whence,* like Water willy-nilly flowing:
And out of it, as Wind along the Waste,
I know not *whither,* willy-nilly blowing.
                    —Omar Khayyam, *Rubaiyat*

IN THE MONTHS after our return to Tehran I had little news of Mrs. Cook and the troupe, except for snatches of rumor and bits of information that chanced my way: the company had picked up a young girl dancer in Athens to replace me; the company was touring Lebanon; the company was touring India; the company had returned home; Mrs. Cook had suffered a nervous breakdown; the company had broken up. The company had broken up? How could that be? A nervous breakdown—what? Mrs. Cook? I did not know what to think or what to believe. Some of these stories could not be true. Consumed with curiosity, I visited Aida to welcome her home, but also to find out what had really happened.

We sat in her parents' small apartment sipping *sharbat* as she told me of the events of the past few months. The troupe had performed to enthusiastic acclaim in Athens, Beirut, and New Delhi, but while they were in India, something strange had happened to Mrs. Cook; nobody was sure exactly what. "You remember," Aida reminded me, "that before coming here Mrs. Cook had spent some time in India, where, people say, she shaved her head and became a follower of Gandhi. Well, while we were on tour in New Delhi, Mrs. Cook looked up her old guru. She was excited over the prospect of seeing him again, but when she came back from her visit, she was a totally different person. It was all very strange; it was as though she were possessed by demons. Her personality seemed to change overnight: she lost all her self-confidence, her adventurous spirit, her lively sparkle. And, worst of all, she wouldn't speak to any of us." Without warning Mrs. Cook had turned into a tormented, introverted recluse, losing interest in the ballet company, indifferent to her successes and accomplishments, and mired in a deep depression. No one could draw her out or figure out what had happened to her. Bereft of her guidance and leadership, the company was forced to return home and disband. Mrs. Cook herself subsequently seemed to have disappeared from the face of the earth. No one knew where she was—whether she had left the country or gone home or was simply lying low in Iran. It was as though she had evaporated into thin air.

I had trouble believing this news about Mrs. Cook, as though I had been told of a death I could not accept. Was it all really true? Her sudden personality change? Her abandonment of the ballet company just when she was riding a tide of success and acclaim? Her disappearance? What a strange ending to an amazing saga. What secrets were hidden here? What mystery lay behind this abrupt end to an incredible success story? Aida and I talked and talked, but the events remained an unfathomable enigma. Like a whirlwind, this extraordinary woman had blown into our lives, tossed us around like toothpicks, left everything in shambles, and just as quickly vanished. None of the young lives she had touched would ever be the same.

One thing that seemed certain was that Aida's dance career was probably at an end. She had returned to school to find herself set back a year, but said she had no regrets. It had been worth it, for it had been an incredible adventure. What she might have revealed, but did not, was that the adventure had also included romance, and in due time she and Nejad would be getting married. For now, however, she kept this information to herself.

Yes, it had been an incredible adventure. I, too, had no regrets, but clearly a chapter of my life had closed. Although I continued taking classes at Mme. Cornelli's, my dancing now lacked the passion and ardor that had lent me wings and sent me flying into the air as swift as a swallow. There was a gap in my life, and I did not know how to fill it.

I started spending more and more time playing the piano, losing myself in the music, unaware of the passage of time. I was playing without instruction because, disenchanted with the Benedictine nuns and out of favor with them for having sinfully "exposed" my body on stage, I had stopped taking piano lessons from Sister Savina. I simply played on my own whenever I could, walking through the dark halls of Community School at night to reach the unheated assembly room, where there was a piano I had permission to practice on, but where my fingers, numbed by the cold, had trouble functioning. Sometimes I practiced at my friend Toori's home, where a grand piano stood otherwise untouched in an elegant salon. She listened rapturously whenever I played and, being a friend, praised me uncritically. She believed, with misplaced certainty, that I was musically gifted. "But you need a good teacher," she said. "I will speak to my father about it." She knew I could not afford piano lessons.

The upshot was that arrangements were made for me to take free music lessons at the National Conservatory. It was a highly irregular arrangement, but one that amply demonstrated how having the right connections opened doors and accomplished miracles. I was assigned to a teacher who had just returned from studying music in Belgium. An Armenian, Miss Sanasarian was unmarried and lived with her elderly mother in a small house on upper Lalezar Avenue. Once a week I walked over there for a piano lesson, and every day I practiced either at Community School or at Toori's house. Miss Sanasarian's enthusiasm encouraged me to practice with discipline and devotion, and she took great pride in my advancement. Steering me away from my passionate but narrow love of Chopin and the romantics, she enlarged my repertoire, awakening in me an appreciation for the more dissonant music of such modern composers as Jacques Ibert and Bela Bartók. She arranged for me to take the performance part of the final exams at the Tehran Conservatory, where I would play before the judges along with all the other students.

I should have been intimidated because I had had little theory instruction, whereas everyone else taking the exam had totally immersed themselves in musical studies. At the end of the year, however, buoyed by Miss Sanasarian's enthusiastic encouragement, I walked into a huge hall filled with students and faculty, crossed the stage over to a grand piano on which I had never played, and sat down on the piano bench in front of it. The faculty judges were lined up in the front row. I did not look at them. I simply started playing, drawn completely into the music. My hands moved of their own accord. It was as if I were in a trance, and I progressed flawlessly through all three movements of Mozart's Sonata in C major, K. 545. I bowed to the applause when I was finished and walked off the stage, elated. I felt as though I were floating. Why, this was almost as exciting as a dance performance!

At that moment it dawned on me that here was another route to applause, bows, and the adulation of an admiring public. Here was something besides dance worth working for, practicing for, sweating for. Here was another art form to absorb my energies, consume me, thrill me. Here was another way of discovering inspiration and imagination I never knew I had.

Since then I have realized other routes to tapping those inner resources. I have discovered that excelling in academic undertakings, lecturing, giving readings or cooking demonstrations, teaching a class, and even being a hostess share some element of theatricality. One of my students, who is also a friend, says I have an urge to perform before a crowd because I was born under the sign of Cancer, with a little bit of Leo thrown in. People born under such a combination of signs apparently need to show off a little to draw attention to themselves—even if in small ways. She is right, of course. So I still perform in other ways, but I continue to cherish the memory of the exhilaration of standing in the wings, makeup on, my costume aglitter, waiting to perform. I still wonder what happened to Mrs. Cook. The riddle has never been solved.

In the winter of 1948 it snowed frequently and abundantly. The mountains north of the city sparkled white. The snow lay thick on the ski slopes, beckoning us to frolic and play. The closest and most popular place for skiing was Lashkarak, high in the Alborz range. Ramezooni and I went there frequently. Besides plenty of snow, Lashkarak offered gentle as well as steep inclines and brilliant sunshine that made a ski jacket unnecessary most of the time. As far as the eye could see, white-covered mountains curved and bulged upward, bold and massive, their outlines delineated against an aquamarine sky. The air felt buoyant and invigorating. The snow glinted in the brilliant sunlight. I would come home from these outings tanned from the neck up, with unexpected streaks of burnished gold in my dark hair.

Special buses waited in designated areas to take passengers along torturous mountain roads to this scenic playground far from the capital city. Lashkarak could hardly be called a ski resort. There were no ticket booths, no bathroom fa-

Skiing with friends
in Lashkarak.

cilities, no ski tows, no public services of any kind—just the magnificent slopes, a panoramic view, and the opportunity to have some fun. We packed sandwiches for lunch, and when we were thirsty, we bought water from an itinerant vendor who, with the help of a strap over one shoulder, carried a large goatskin pouch from which he poured water into the same tin cup again and again until the goatskin container was empty. He simply rinsed out the tin cup with a small amount of water before offering it to each new customer. Yet we drank from it without hesitating, and no water ever tasted purer.

Neither Ramezooni nor I ever had any instruction on how to ski. Like the village boys who went flying easily over the snow with only rough planks for skis, we simply learned by trial and error. Unlike the village boys, however, we had real skis that we coated with paraffin wax before each trip and buffed repeatedly until they were slick and smooth.

Once we arrived at Lashkarak, we spent most of our time going uphill, a daunting task on the slippery snow. We either had to step sideways up the slope or proceed straight uphill with our skis in a wide V, the tips facing outward and the backs close together. Sometimes we would slip and slide back down for a short distance, laughing at our ineptitude, taking a tumble in the process, and occasionally having to chase a runaway ski all the way down to the bottom of the incline. Today one of those moments is captured in a somewhat faded photograph of Ramezooni, collapsed in a heap in the snow, laughing, while a very young version of myself pelts him with snowballs.

At the end of the day, when the sun started to set, everyone knew it was time

In Lashkarak, pelting
Ramezooni with snowballs.

to start down the slopes toward the parking area, and a mass exodus would begin. With the heat of the sun's rays gone, the temperature would drop precipitously, freezing the snow's surface into an icy crust.

One fateful day I defied common sense by taking it into my head to zip down the slope one last time just as the sun was setting. "Just one more time," I called to Ramezooni, laughing. "We really should go," he called back, "The sun is going down." But I was reluctant to let go of the pleasure of the downhill run and felt irked at being told what to do, so as the sun sank lower and lower behind the tip of the highest peak, I countered, "One more time. I'm going one more time." Digging my ski poles into the snow, I gave a push and started downhill. Unexpectedly gaining rapid momentum over the now icy slope, I found myself hurtling down at a speed that made me catch my breath. "Oh my God," I thought, but it was too late. I went flying down, my skis skimming the frozen surface, the ground coursing past me at a dizzying speed. Straight ahead I could see a crater in the snow, where someone had fallen and created a great gash. Too late I tried to avoid it and went crashing facedown in the packed and hardened snow, with one leg twisted up behind me.

It must have made a funny sight, for Ramezooni stood at the top of the hill doubled over with laughter. I tried to straighten my leg and reposition my skis so that I could get up, but a wrenching pain in my left knee made me fall back in pain. I called to Ramezooni, "I have hurt myself. You will have to come down and help me." He just kept on laughing, but as I persisted in calling for his help, he suddenly realized I was serious and that it was no laughing matter. He came flying down the long slope and stopped next to me, surveyed the scene, and struggled to help me to my feet, but there was no way I could navigate, even with his help. By now I was in excruciating pain. The slightest movement of my leg made me feel like screaming. The tears started rolling down my face as I tried to walk up the steep slope and realized I could not. Several hills stood between us and the parking lot, and there was no one else around to help. How were we going to get back to the bus? We knew the bus driver counted heads before departing; perhaps they would come looking for us, yet perhaps they would not. Somehow we had to get ourselves to the parking area.

We took off our skis and stood them upright in the snow. They stood there facing each other, like partners ready to dance. They were not going anywhere, though; they would stay there, bowing slightly toward each other, until someone came for them, for there was no way Ramezooni could carry both me and the skis. He picked me up in his arms and started up the hill. Without skis on and burdened by my weight, he sank deep into the snow with every step. He struggled and panted. It was excruciatingly slow going. Finally, after what seemed like an eternity, we reached the top of the hill. Had there been anyone around, we might have borrowed a sled with which to coast me up and down the hills, but everyone had left. We were surrounded by a vast empty space of white. It was eerily quiet. All I could hear was his panting and the crunching of the snow under his feet. I was in pain, and I started to shiver. How I hoped the bus had not left.

Then off in the distance we heard shouts and saw two small dark dots against the snow. Gradually they grew larger, and we recognized them as acquaintances from the bus. They had come looking for us after the head count revealed we were missing. "Come on," they shouted, "you are keeping everyone waiting." As they came closer, they realized something was wrong and came forward to help. One of them swooped over the hill, going back for our skis, while the other helped Ramezooni get me to the bus. A number of solicitous hands lifted me on board and made me as comfortable as possible, propping my injured leg on a rolled-up ski jacket.

All the way home I worried about how Mummy would react. She had enough troubles without this accident, and then there would be the medical costs. Perhaps it was not serious, and maybe by morning I would be able to walk again. Everyone on the bus humored me, joked, told stories, and sang songs to distract me from my pain, for I winced every time we hit a bump on the rock-strewn road. From the radio news we learned that Harry Truman had unexpectedly been elected to another term as president of the United States, and there was some discussion of this momentous event.

When Mummy saw me limp into the house leaning on Ramezooni's arm, she turned white, anxiety written all over her forehead and compressed mouth. We reassured her that it was nothing serious, just a mildly twisted knee. By the next day, though, my leg was badly swollen, and the slightest movement caused agonizing pain. Mummy refrained from making any judgmental remarks. Just as she was telephoning for a doctor, Ramezooni knocked on the door, offering to take me to Dr. Mashhoon—a personal friend of his who was a trustworthy and reliable physician and who would not charge us for his services. By now taxis had largely supplanted *doroshkeh*s, and Ramezooni went out, flagged one down, and took me to the doctor. I was diagnosed as having "water on the knee" and torn ligaments, a condition that called for total immobilization of my leg for a long time. After applying a splint, the doctor sent me home with instructions to stay in bed until it healed. It would be a slow process, but he promised to come and check on me from time to time.

It was obvious I was going to be bedridden for quite a while—one more problem for Mummy. I felt guilty for having added to her concerns. These days she often sighed as she went about her daily chores. Luckily, the small first-floor sitting room just off the main entry hall was vacant just then, and she fixed it up for me, placing a bed next to the window so I would have plenty of daylight for reading and a respectable place to receive the friends who inevitably would come to call.

I had a stream of visitors. Classmates brought my homework and took back to school the assignments I had written. I was in my last year of high school, and it was important to keep up with my schoolwork. My textbooks and notebooks were piled within easy reach on a small table next to my bed, and with little else to do I read and studied every book my friends brought me. Sometimes I listened to the radio. Among my visitors were young men. Reclining on my cushions, I would laugh—a little too loudly—at their jokes.

Needless to say, I looked forward to these visits, and from the start my most frequent visitor was Ramezooni. Almost daily he would come over to see if he could make me more comfortable, fetch me what I needed, help me with my homework, or just keep me company. During the hours we spent together he entertained me by reciting poems, and once again I marveled at his erudition. He had pursued the literary branch of studies in high school. Then later, during his first year of law school at the University of Tehran, he had also signed up at the Faculty of Literature.

I learned that Ramezooni's interest in poetry had been stimulated by his life-long friendship with Fereydoon Moshiri, who at this time was already an established poet in spite of his youth and who would later gain great renown. "We used to spend hours walking together, taking turns reciting poems," Ramezooni said. A gentle and sensitive soul, Moshiri had unfortunately contracted tuberculosis and had spent the previous year in a sanitarium recovering from this debilitating disease. Such illnesses were still fairly common.

At other times Ramezooni talked about his legal and political studies. Ever the tutor, he explained the philosophical concepts behind various legal systems, touching on Islamic law, Roman law, and natural law, or discussing why legal defense must be provided even to an apparently guilty criminal. He talked about key players on the political scene and related historical antecedents to current political events, such as the 1905 revolution that resulted in the establishment of a constitutional monarchy. He talked about the 1907 Russian and British partition of Iran into spheres of influence, and told me how threats and flagrant breaches of promise on the part of those two imperial powers had contributed to the overthrow of the Majlis in 1908, thwarting the nascent constitutional movement. I listened, fascinated. He also told me of his great desire to go to England or the United States for his doctorate. He did not know whether he would ever be able to, but he was determined to try.

I found myself looking forward to his visits because they provided a welcome break from the monotony of the days. Besides offering insights on a great variety of subjects, he always managed to make me laugh. He lifted my spirits. One day he brought his sister Mehri over, and I took an instant liking to her. Exceptionally intelligent, thoughtful, and mature for her age, she also had a heart of gold. In time we would become fast friends. She returned several times and taught me how to knit—a happy occupation when time weighed heavily on my hands.

One day Ramezooni seemed in a particularly reflective mood and—to my astonishment—suddenly caught my hand, bent over me, and gently pressed his lips to mine. He gazed into my eyes and, his voice breaking, confessed that he had loved me from the moment he had first set eyes on me and that his love had only grown deeper as our acquaintance grew. He had not meant to declare his love; it had just spilled out. In fact, he had intended to go abroad without ever letting me know how he felt, for he was sure I would not reciprocate his feelings. It was obvious, he said, that I was interested in other young men and thought of him merely as a friend. Besides, he was just a poor student and had neither worldly possessions nor wealth nor prestige.

I was taken completely by surprise. Nothing in Ramezooni's behavior toward me had led me to imagine he was in love with me. Other young men gazed into my eyes, looked at me with adoration or admiration, sought to impress me with their good looks or their dancing skills, or tried in every way to sweep me off my feet. Ramezooni had always behaved like a tutor and like a close and supportive friend. I was deeply flattered. Here was a sophisticated, brilliant, and worldly-wise young man in love with me. Although I was pleased, I did not reciprocate his feelings. This, according to my girlish fantasies, was not how it was supposed to happen. There had been no swaying closely to the pulse of a tango, no sweating of palms, no beating of hearts. He was not tall or fair, as I had imagined the man of my dreams would be. He could not even dance. As far as I was concerned, he was, indeed, just a good friend.

But Ramezooni's confession changed the dynamics of our relationship. From then on it was difficult for me to continue thinking of him in the same way, particularly when he described the depth and fervor of his love in such passionate terms, sometimes quoting the great poets, sometimes pouring out his sentiments in love sonnets of his own composition. In spite of my doubts I was moved by his ardor, although I was slow to recognize my feelings and continued to enjoy and encourage the attentions of other young men, if not their proposals of marriage.

There was George, from the British consulate, whose blue eyes and blond hair were so pale he almost looked like an albino. He desperately wanted to take me to England to meet his mother, of whom he spoke in the fondest terms. "She makes the best plum pudding in England," he said tenderly. Before my skiing accident, he had taken me dancing and introduced me to his British friends, but although I enjoyed the dancing, I was not interested in his offer of marriage.

Then there was Keith, a raven-haired young Briton whose nonchalant puffs on a pipe enhanced, in my adolescent eyes, the masculinity of his handsomely chiselled face. During my convalescence he was transferred to India, and that ended that. Then there was Kotic, dashing and good-looking, for whom I had had a yen for some time, but he contracted tuberculosis and was sent away to a sanitarium to recuperate.

I was bedridden for three long months. When the splint finally came off, I was so weak I had to walk holding onto the walls and furniture, just as I had years earlier after my bout with typhus. It was clear I would not be skiing or dancing again any time soon. A chapter of my life had ended; a new one had begun.

New Beginnings

Don't be like a sparrow
    jumping from branch to branch.
While you look for love here and there
The fire I lit inside you
    will only grow cold.
                    —Jalal ad-Din Rumi,
                        "A Mine of Rubies"

HAD IT NOT BEEN for the skiing accident—that intervention of *qesmat*—Ramezooni and I might well have gone our separate ways. Yet even with fate's helping hand it took me a while to realize that true love need not start with moonlight and a dreamy tune. Love can also be rooted in friendship, in long hours of conversation, and in mutual respect. For a long time, however, I continued to think of Ramezooni only as a close and reliable friend. I went boy crazy and left him totally on the sidelines. I went to every party I was invited to, danced late into the night, and spurned his amorous advances, but like a moth flitting around a candle, he kept coming back. He visited me, took me to the movies, and on long walks discussed politics and philosophy and other interesting matters with me. Gradually, I started calling him by his first name, Ruhi, although it felt awkward at first.

After a time we began to hold hands—not in public, of course, but in a darkened movie theater—and I thrilled to his touch. We kissed—long, passionate kisses that left me weak and breathless. We gazed into each other's eyes and talked about love that would last till the end of time. When we embraced, I felt waves of warmth rising up from the depths of my being. Sometimes I felt giddy and light-headed, like a bubble in a glass of champagne. Yet deep down I still had misgivings. At times I felt a leaden weight in the pit of my stomach. The change in our relationship had catapulted me into an entirely new scheme of events. Was this truly love? Was I ready to commit myself to marriage? Did I want to give up dancing and flirting and going out with other men? Doubt gnawed at me as we talked about finishing our schooling in Tehran and then going abroad to study. Before this point I had not seriously thought about such a prospect. Now I wondered, Did I really want to leave Tehran? Leave Mummy? Leave all that was familiar and throw myself into the unknown? And what would we live on once we got there?

Ruhi, however, had no doubts. He poured balm over my anxieties with soothing words. "Don't worry," he said reassuringly. "We can study and work part-time. It doesn't matter what we have to do—I will be willing to wait on tables or cut hair in a barbershop." Such talk on the part of a young Iranian was remarkable, for most educated Iranians would have considered work of that sort demeaning. He, quite exceptionally, had worked at odd jobs during summers— in a car garage and in a munitions factory—and he did not think of such work as undignified. I found myself quieting the doubts that welled up inside me, going along with his plans. I knew he was an astute and remarkable man, and gradually, very gradually, I started thinking that perhaps he was the right man for me after all. Yet from time to time uncertainty would plague me.

I could not understand why Ruhi was so disenchanted with life in Iran. For me it had always seemed a pleasant enough place to live. Oh, I knew people raved about the beauty of the capitals of Europe, about the amazing skyscrapers of New York, about the attractive displays in the windows, the abundance of goods, and the freedom young people enjoyed. But I already had that freedom, and, anyway, what family and friends I had were all here. *Visiting* Europe or America was one thing, but *living* there was another.

Ruhi, however, saw matters differently. Disheartened at the state of the nation, he was determined to go abroad. He believed that Iran's problems would never be resolved in his lifetime and that trying to change such deeply entrenched problems would only result in failure—and possibly even death.

I myself was still too politically unaware to comprehend why Ruhi was so dissatisfied. In fact, I found his pessimism irritating. But then, what did I know? Before meeting him, I had had little interest in national or international politics and was only vaguely aware of the political eddies swirling around us. How could I judge? Perhaps he was right. Perhaps matters were as bad as he seemed to think.

We often talked about the state of the country while strolling along the broad tree-lined avenues of northern Tehran. Ruhi claimed that although intellectuals were then enjoying unprecedented freedom of expression and were able to discuss politics without fear of reprisal, it was a temporary interlude rooted not in true democracy, but in chaos; no one was in control. He spoke of the tears in the country's social and political fabric caused by foreign occupation and by massive uprooting and dislocation following World War II. He lamented the big landowners' continuing domination of the country and the entrenchment of serfdom. He decried the low literacy rate and the continued hold of fundamentalist religion as well as superstition on the minds of the masses. He spoke of the centuries-old tradition of autocracy, of tribal and familial rather than national allegiances, of the lack of the rule of law. And he spoke of the economy, which was in a shambles and had little prospect of recovery any time soon. Above all it was important to him to be able to speak his mind freely, to write what he thought, and to say what he thought, and he knew that would be impossible here. To prove his point he told me about the assassination in 1945 of a famous historian, Ahmad Kasravi, by a member of a militant Islamic faction called Fadayan-e Islam. The idol of many secular intellectuals, Kasravi was well known for his writings on Iran's Constitutional Revolution and for having spoken out against the clerics.

Now, four or five years later, as if to confirm Ruhi's worst predictions, violence erupted on the campus of the University of Tehran, where hundreds of students had gathered to hear Dean Zangeneh of the Faculty of Law speak. The carefully tended grounds of the university, verdant and cool, seemed an unlikely place for murder. Yet moments after the dean had delivered his opening remarks, two loud shots rang out, and he collapsed in a pool of blood, dying instantly. A left-wing organization was held responsible for the assassination. Ruhi saw it happen. His voice choked with emotion as he told me of the dean falling before his very eyes.

Other disturbances occurred at the university in the waning years of the 1940s. One was caused by the attempt of student members of the Tudeh Party, the best organized communist group in Iran, to steal the elections for the leadership of the student council. "As the ballots were being counted," Ruhi told me later, his voice rising in excitement, "it became increasingly clear they were losing the election, so they simply grabbed the ballot boxes and threw them into the campus reflecting pool, trying to seize by force what they could not win by persuasion. What a bunch of fanatics!"

A few days later Ruhi's prediction of dire consequences for anyone in a leadership position almost came true when he himself came close to being knifed in the back by one of those extremists. As the Tudeh continued to be frustrated in their attempts to seize power, they escalated the level of violence. That morning several thugs eluded security guards, broke windows, and entered the university's basement. During a lecture Ruhi heard a sudden commotion in the back of the hall and turned to see several burly men burst into the room, brandishing knives. Some of the students in the back scuffled with them and tried to throw them out. Within moments there was blood splattered on the wall, torn flesh, and screams of pain. In the uproar that followed the students all poured into the central hallway, where hired strongmen were attacking students opposed to the Tudeh. As one person called out a name and pointed out the targeted person, a thug would attack him with a knife. "There was blood all over the place. Wounded students lay on the floor, where they were trampled as we all ran in different directions, fearing for our lives. Suddenly, I heard my name called out and realized I, too, was being targeted. I started running down the hall, pointing off in the distance, and calling out, 'Ramazani! Get Ramazani! There he is! Get him!' " His ruse worked, for he was soon out the door and down the steps to safety. This incident reinforced Ruhi's sense of urgency about leaving the country.

It was clear to us that there were no limits to how far Ruhi could go professionally if he were to remain. He might some day be a lawyer, a judge, a member of Parliament, or even a prime minister. "But if I stay here, I will be assassinated," he said. "I must leave. Not that I fear death, but as long as I live, I want to be free to speak my mind. Here I will never be able to do that. I will never be able to express my thoughts freely, but will have to watch every word I say, every word I write. I wish I could change things, improve things, but here I will be thwarted at every turn." I thought of the recent assassinations that had taken place. I thought of Grandfather and how hard he had tried to effect changes. In many ways he had succeeded, but in the end it had cost him his life. Perhaps Ruhi was right after all.

It was not until much later, as I came to know Ruhi better, that I began to realize that at some level his assessment of the situation did not arise solely from profound insight into the political turmoil we were experiencing, but from a lifetime of agonizing over the incalculable privation and suffering he had witnessed both in the public arena and within his own home. He spoke of his anguish at seeing a young street urchin, shivering with cold, hugging a dog to his chest so as to keep warm; another picking laboriously through foul-smelling piles of garbage to find food; little girls, as young as seven and eight, being pressed into prostitution so that their parents and their siblings might survive; orphans begging on street corners, their eyes hollow, their limbs often twisted or otherwise deformed; untold numbers of the sick and dying waiting for hours in the halls of government hospitals; his own mother pawning a carpet, a samovar, a silver tea holder so as to put food on the table for him and his sisters while an indifferent father drank himself into a stupor; and, later, his sick mother gasping for breath while inadequate medical care hastened her death. All these inequities and more were seared into Ruhi's consciousness. He tended not to look at the world through rose-colored glasses, as I did, but with skepticism. His political assessments were realistic and completely free of any sentimentalism. It is a wonder he was not cynical, and what is even more surprising is that he could still laugh. We laughed together often.

I graduated from high school in 1949. My graduation picture shows a row of boys standing on the school steps dressed in coats and ties, with a row of girls one step below dressed in white full-length gowns and white gloves—fourteen all together. We are holding diplomas. Many of my classmates I had known since the first grade; many of them I would never see again after graduation.

Meanwhile, Ruhi's sister, Mehri, also graduated from high school. She had received numerous offers of marriage, but had rejected them all as imperiously as if she were the queen of the land. She did not want to get married, but her only weapon to fight the inevitable was to delay it as long as possible. She insisted that her younger sister, Tooran, get married first. Although it was against all the conventions, the family acquiesced to her suggestion, and Tooran was married.

Mehri, however, adamantly continued to hold out, raising objections to every suitor, spurning them all. The matter obviously weighed heavily on Ruhi's mind. He often spoke to me of how concerned he was that the match be a good one. His father was taking no responsibility in the matter, having simply

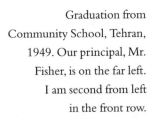

Graduation from Community School, Tehran, 1949. Our principal, Mr. Fisher, is on the far left. I am second from left in the front row.

left it to his wife, Asiyeh Khanom, to find a suitable mate for Mehri, and to his son to make the arrangements. So although Asiyeh Khanom would serve as matchmaker, ultimate approval now lay with Ruhi, the older brother.

Desirable qualifications would be twenty-five to thirty-five years of age, at least a high school education, and, of course, an income sufficient to provide for a wife and family. But Ruhi wanted more. "I will also have to find out whether he has a history of drinking or gambling," he said. "And I am also going to insist on a blood test to make sure he doesn't have a venereal disease. I know my family will be horrified at my demanding a blood test." Like a wary watchdog, he would look out for Mehri's interests in every way he could. For my part, used as I was to the cultural mélange in which I lived, I did not think to question the ironies of the differing courtships of Ruhi's sister and me.

Ruhi knew that Mehri had wanted to pursue a three-year course of study in midwifery, but the only place for such training was at a government-run boarding school near Shah Abdul-azim, and her father would not allow it. "No daughter of mine is going to live in a boarding school and ruin our family's good name," he had shouted. It was inconceivable that a young girl would live away from the family, thus risking her virginity, her reputation, and the family's good name. Neither Mehri nor her brother were able to moderate their father's opposition, and there was little either of them could do to change the course of her life, which now, when she was barely eighteen, stretched unwaveringly before her: marriage was inevitable. Even though Ruhi knew she was a highly intelligent and gifted student, he could not send her abroad for further education; he could not go against his father's and the society's restrictions on young women—restrictions I had happily escaped. He could, however, to some degree influence the choice of a husband for his sister and the terms of the contract that would be drawn up.

Asiyeh Khanom took her role as matchmaker seriously. She made a round of discreet inquiries and came up with the names of several eligible young men, but Mehri kept refusing. The pressure on Mehri to marry was increasing, however, so reluctantly and with many misgivings she finally consented to consider a young man from Abadan, a distant relative whom Asiyeh Khanom described as a good-looking high school graduate with a first-rate job with the Anglo-Iranian Oil Company in Abadan. Asiyeh Khanom joyfully made the arrangements for a preliminary meeting between the two families and the prospective bride and groom—a sizing up.

Next to the bubbling samovar, pastries and sweet delicacies adorned the table—cream puffs and eclairs as well as baklava and *bamieh*. It was, after all, not a time to count costs. Mehri had been primed to wear her best dress and to bring in the tea tray after the guests arrived. "My hands were shaking so hard I was afraid I would drop the tray," she later told me, describing the event. "I knew they were there to look me over. Marriage was the last thing I wanted, but what else could I do?" She consoled herself that it might be easier to pursue a career goal after marriage than as a young girl whose every outing was a source of concern and a possible threat to her reputation. Reputations were a serious matter. Mehri remembered the harsh criticism unleashed when she and her sister Tooran had started going to school unveiled following Reza Shah's decree banning the chador. When the two sisters had first walked to school with their faces uncovered, wearing modern school uniforms, their father's first wife had hurled a veritable storm of imprecations and accusations of "immodesty" at them.

Although their father's two families lived in separate houses, they shared a common courtyard, where the cowives and half-siblings would inevitably run into each other and act out their jealousies and rivalries, like two factions at court vying for power and supremacy. Ruhi and his two sisters had tried their best to avoid the intrigues and to deflect the gossip that the rival family would manufacture in efforts to curry favor with the patriarch of the family. But like webs spun overnight by industrious spiders, innuendo and gossip hung lightly in the air, ready to trap the unwary with the flimsiest of evidence. Thus, Mehri and Tooran had been branded as "immodest," "without shame," and described as having gone out "naked." "May dust cover my head if I ever allow my girls to go unveiled to school," the first wife had declared self-righteously. "I will keep *my* girls at home rather than let them sully their reputations." But, of course, times changed, and eventually even she had allowed her girls to go out with their faces exposed. Before that, however, opprobrium of the most vicious kind had been heaped on Mehri's and Tooran's heads. Their mother, however, had held firm, and the girls had found themselves on the front lines of the movement to unveil, bearing the brunt of the enemy's fire.

Mehri was astute enough to realize that she would enjoy greater freedom once she was married. Staying single, of course, was out of the question. Once she was no longer a virgin under constant surveillance, though, she could use her credentials to teach school. She secretly nurtured that goal in her heart and found in it a source of comfort.

Looking over the prospective *khast-e-gar* was not a comfortable situation, however. "At first, I was so nervous I hardly got a look at him," she said. Then the suitor's sister spoke to her gently, asking her about her studies, setting her at ease, and enabling her to size up the prospective groom, even though she never did speak to him directly. The meeting seemed to go well, for the very next day the suitor's sister came back to say that the young man was interested in making a formal offer of marriage.

Mehri adamantly refused. Although the suitor was presentable enough, well dressed, seemingly clean and tidy, confident and self-assured, she found fault with him, raising every objection she could think of. His front teeth were capped with gold; he was too thin and emaciated; for all she knew he might be an opium addict. Did no one else notice that slight discoloration on his lips? And who knows, perhaps he had a venereal disease. She would have none of him.

Dismayed, Asiyeh Khanom turned to Ruhi. "What shall we do?" she lamented. "Mehri finds fault with everyone. At this rate she will never get married. This man seems to be a really good prospect, and Mehri should accept him." Ruhi respected his sister's reservations and sent word to the suitor's family that the prospective groom must have a blood test to make sure he had no venereal disease. Asiyeh Khanom found the whole exercise highly embarrassing. "We are losing face," she objected. "No one will marry her if you keep laying down such conditions." She was a conventional woman and found the departures from tradition unnerving. But Ruhi stood firm. No sister of his was going to marry unless the groom was certified to be free of venereal disease. To his credit, his insistence won the day, and to Asiyeh Khanom's surprise the suitor's family agreed to a blood test. The young man came back with a certified clean bill of health. Then, through discreet inquiries Ruhi was able to ascertain that the prospective groom did not, in fact, smoke opium. Mehri's objections had been overcome.

As negotiations started between the two families, Ruhi made further demands. Given that polygamy was legal, he took what steps he could to protect his sister from ever having to share her husband with a cowife or wives. Polygamy was an institution he knew firsthand. To Asiyeh Khanom's embarrassment he insisted that when the marriage contract was drawn up, a clause must be inserted—as the law allowed—that if the groom ever married a second wife or if he were found already to have a wife, Mehri would have the right to a divorce instantly if she so chose and to a financial settlement in the event of a divorce. Asiyeh Khanom objected, but to no avail. Although Islamic law provided certain avenues of protection against polygamy and against unilateral divorce and prescribed the standard three months alimony as well as payment of the *mahrieh*, few people availed themselves of such protection, for it was an embarrassment. "What is the world coming to?" Asiyeh Khanom asked. "Such untoward demands, such unthinkable conditions. You will see," she said. "They will never agree to them." But she was wrong. The groom and his family accepted all the conditions. A *mahrieh* was agreed on, and one month later Mehri married, amidst much feasting and merrymaking. Some months after the wedding her husband's gold caps were replaced with natural-looking white ones.

The Garden of the Martyrs

We are Hossein's men, and this is our epoch.
In devotion we are the slaves of the Imam;
Our name is "zealot" and our title "martyr."
—Attributed to Shah Isma'il

BY NOW I WAS SEEING Ruhi almost on a daily basis, and almost daily, it seemed, I was learning from him more and more aspects of Persian history and culture that were totally new to me. As we walked past the Masjid-e Shah, the Royal Mosque, he spoke with admiration of the group of merchants who had taken sanctuary there during the Constitutional Revolution (1905–11) while agitating against the tyranny of the king. As we strolled by the British Legation, he described how thousands of people, protesting against Muzaffar ed-Din Shah's policies in 1906, found sanctuary inside the legation's walled garden, remaining there for eighteen days. As we passed the Majlis, he related in vivid detail how Russian cannons had destroyed Iran's two-year-old parliament building, striking a deadly blow against the constitutionalists of the time. He told me that in that same square, while he and other young students were protesting during the bread riots of 1942, one of his friends was shot and had to be carried, bleeding, to the hospital. Through him I learned of the rising sentiment to nationalize the oil industry and to take charge of the valuable resource now controlled by the British.

I am indebted to the following source for parts of the dialogue in my description of *ta'ziyeh:* M. Rezvani, *Le théâtre et la dance en Iran* (Plan de la Tour, Var, France: Editions d'Aujourd-hui, 1981).

On one occasion I borrowed a chador from Mehri and went with Ruhi to see a religious shrine, with its cut-glass refracted ceiling, its ornately decorated vaults, its crowds of worshipers circling around the saint's tomb, whispering prayers, sighing, crying, and asking for the saint's intercession. And one day I went with him to see a religious passion play.

Walking down Shah Reza Avenue, we chanced upon a religious procession making its way down the road. It was Ashura, the tenth day of the holy month of Moharram, when thousands of Iranians observe the anniversary of the death of the Prophet's grandson, Hossein. We stopped to watch as a *dasteh,* a group of mourners—all men—carrying somber black banners gathered in a circle around the emblem that signified their devotion to the martyr Imam Hossein. They raised their arms and then thumped them down on their chests in perfect time, the pounding getting harder with their rising ardor and passion. Just behind them another *dasteh* lashed their backs with *zanjeer,* short chains clustered at the end of a handle, until their flesh was raw—over the shoulder, left, right, left, right, in exquisitely painful unison. Following them, still another group of penitents rhythmically struck their foreheads with an open palm in a gesture of grief and anguish. All the while, chants of *"Ya Hossein, Ya Hossein"* rang out again and again until both participants and spectators—who were largely women—were in a frenzy of grief and rage. Ruhi and I stood at a distance, for the lamentations were a serious matter and not meant to be objects of the curiosity of outsiders. Although respectful of religious beliefs, Ruhi felt that such public exhibitions of faith were out of step with modern life and demonstrated that the hold of the mullahs on the populace was still strong.

As Ruhi and I talked about religion in Iran, it became abundantly clear that although I had spent most of my life in a land with a largely Shi'a Muslim population, I knew little about the religious practices of the people. Although I did know Hossein was a martyr, I was not really familiar with the historical events that led to his martyrdom and why the populace observed his death with such elaborate and painful rituals.

Ruhi explained to me that this hero of mythical proportions was killed, along with his faithful followers, in A.D. 680 during the Battle of Karbala, while pressing his claim to be the next caliph, the temporal and spiritual leader of all Muslims. Like the flagellants of medieval Europe who scourged themselves in commemoration of the passion of Christ, Shi'a penitents engage in violent physical acts of penance to commemorate Hossein's martyrdom. In imitating the "passion" of a human yet divine hero, they enter into a mystical state that unites them spiritually with the mourned hero. Reza Shah had outlawed some of the more violent forms of self-flagellation some years earlier, such as the use of *qameh*—sharp-edged knives with which penitents struck themselves on the head, drawing blood that ran down their faces in rivulets. Milder forms of self-flagellation continued to be practiced, however.

The mourning would culminate, Ruhi said, in a *ta'ziyeh,* a religious passion play in which the Battle of Karbala and the martyrdom of Hossein would be brought to life in a huge tented arena in the south of Tehran, where many of the processions ended. "Would you like to see it?" he asked me. "I think you will find it an interesting experience. Besides, it is good theater. In fact, it is probably our only truly authentic theater. Men and women sit separately, but I can ask one of my aunts to accompany you so you won't be alone. My aunt is very pious, and I am sure she would be happy to introduce you to the *ta'ziyeh.*" I eagerly accepted the offer.

As we neared the *tekiyeh,* the tented area where the play would be presented, we had trouble pushing our way through the crowd, for the group of spectators surrounding the religious procession had grown into a gigantic mass of mourners, a sea of black-cloaked women, wailing over the cruelty of the oppressors who had killed the innocent Hossein centuries ago. Years later I was reminded of this scene when I saw on my television screen in Virginia large groups of chador-clad women raising their fists and chanting "Death to America" during the hostage crisis that shredded the earlier friendly relations between Iran and the United States.

But now at the *ta'ziyeh* the women were weeping over the inhumanity of the Umayyad caliph Yazid, who more than thirteen hundred years earlier had ordered the blood of their beloved martyr to be spilled. As I watched, the crowds parted at the approach of a magnificent white horse and rider, followed by a band of penitents on foot. The horse was daubed with red streaks. It reared up on its hind legs and whinnied briefly before disappearing with the rider into the covered *tekiyeh.* The crowd followed. The Battle of Karbala was about to begin.

Ta'ziyeh parallels the medieval miracle or morality plays of Christianity, but it is not just religious theater. It is also *national* theater, an annual ritual that reaffirms Iran's cultural identity vis-à-vis the Arab conquerors and symbolizes Iran's independent political existence. It was the death of Hossein that led to the great schism that made most Iranians Shi'a and most Arabs Sunni. The roots of the schism, however, go back to another death—that of the prophet Mohammad.

When Mohammad died in A.D. 632, his cousin and son-in-law 'Ali believed that he had been designated the Prophet's successor. Three caliphs preceded 'Ali's succession to the caliphate, however, all three of whom the Shi'a consider to have been usurpers. 'Ali's followers, the Shi'a-'Ali, or partisans of 'Ali, gave the Shi'a sect its name, one that carries overtones of revolt against injustice. 'Ali, however, was assassinated, and the Umayyad Mo'awiya seized power, declared himself caliph, and designated his son Yazid as his successor. The caliphate thus became hereditary rather than elective.

But 'Ali's son, Hossein, who was also the grandson of the Prophet, believed that he alone was the rightful heir to the caliphate, that his cause was righteous, and that the corrupt Umayyad caliphs were wallowing in luxury at the expense of the poor and the weak. He and his followers set out to overthrow the Umayyads and to establish a caliphate that would champion the downtrodden masses.

Hossein led the revolt against Yazid. With only two hundred partisans and family members he met Yazid's army of four thousand, led by Shemr. Fully aware that he was confronting a superior force and almost certain death, he nevertheless fearlessly insisted on meeting the enemy, on embracing the mantle of martyrdom, and on becoming the champion of the dispossessed.

Karbala, where the battle took place, is located south of Baghdad in present-day Iraq on flat salty plains where water is scarce and the desert heat brutal. The villainous Shemr, the captain of the enemy forces, stood with his men between the river Euphrates and Hossein and his followers. Suffering from thirst and badly demoralized, many of Hossein's followers defected, and their numbers were reduced to seventy-two. In attempting to forge a path through enemy lines to reach the river, Hossein's brother 'Abbas first lost both his arms and then his life. In the end the enemy slaughtered Hossein and all his partisans, placed their heads on pikes, captured his family members—women and children—and took them to Damascus in chains and on foot.

The scripts for the passion plays that dramatize these events are written by anonymous writers. They portray Hossein as heroic and compassionate, his cause as righteous and just. They dwell on the wickedness and cruelty of the enemy, highlighting the injustice and tragedy of their hero's death. Delivering the lines in a sort of *récitatif,* the male actors sometimes hold the written script before them. They can be either amateur or professional, and they play women's as well as men's roles, easily camouflaging facial hair with face veils. The action takes place on a *sakoo,* or raised dais, that serves as a stage. Sometimes a new actor coming on stage suggests a change of scene. An actor whose character is dead, his part finished, might simply get up and walk off, and actors sometimes pass through the audience to reach the *sakoo.* A bucket of water symbolizes the Euphrates River, near which camped the armies of Shemr. Papier-mâché heads stuck on pikes represent the beheaded victims of the battle. The director walks about the stage narrating events and beating his breast at sorrowful moments. The presentation can last for hours. It is theater in the round, neither illusionistic nor suspenseful, for the spectators all know the story line and how the tragedy will end. It is this knowledge and its repetition over the years that sears their souls.

I was elated as I entered for the first time the great tent that covered the *tekiyeh.* It was already filling up. Some spectators had arrived early in the morning to get a good spot. Men, women, children, babes in arms, the elderly, all formed part of the audience. Everyone sat cross-legged on thin, pileless *gelim*s spread over dirt floors. Some had invited friends or family to join them and had arranged for servants to serve their party tea or *sharbat.* The women sat separately from the men, in the upstairs balcony, where they huddled together on a platform, row upon row of shapeless forms, like so many black gunny sacks. They held their chadors tightly over their faces, for, although separate from the men, they were in a public place and sat in full view.

Ruhi's aunt had lent me a black chador and shown me how to wear it. She led me up the staircase to the balcony, her stoutness making her pant. She obviously was proud of the educative role she would play in introducing me to such an important religious event. I struggled to avoid stumbling over the cumbersome garment that covered me from head to toe as we climbed the stairs. Upon reaching the balcony, we sat cross-legged on coarse *gelim*s. The platform was only deep enough for four rows of spectators, but it ran full circle around the arena and was packed. Below us were the men. From a distance the faceless, shapeless women had looked devoid of life, but up close they acquired a living, breathing presence. I smelled the odors of bodies that lacked the luxury of daily showers, breath tainted by garlic, sickness, or rotting teeth. I heard sounds of muttering, whispering, laughing, crying, coughing, cursing, munching, slurping, gulping. I saw women appraising each other, eyes darting looks of admiration, envy, amiability, or contempt. Children—both girls and young boys—were kept strictly under surveillance and control. Mothers, sisters, grandmothers, and aunts sometimes enveloped young children under their chadors, snuggling them close and keeping them quiet. Older boys shared the men's space downstairs.

From where we sat I had an all-encompassing view of the *tekiyeh*. A large *sakoo* had been erected at the center. Huge banners hung from the balcony. Ornate calligraphy in Arabic script snaked across their surfaces in bold white, declaiming over and over, "Allah-o Akbar" (God is great), these words framed by decoratively stylized renditions of the names of 'Ali, Hossein, Hassan, and Qassem.

To allow room for horses to gallop past and for battle scenes to be fought, a wide swath of free space was kept open between the *sakoo* and the audience. There were no curtains, no scenery, and only the faintest attempts at costuming.

Two horses and a camel entered the arena single file, laden with trunks and huge cooking pots. They were led around the *sakoo* a number of times, and Ruhi's aunt explained to me in whispers that Hossein, his family, and followers were making the long and arduous journey to the plain of Karbala—even though Hossein knew what his fate would be. The director of the play walked onto the stage beating his chest and began to narrate the events. Hossein's nephew Qassem, in a passionate tone, predicted the catastrophe awaiting them: "My head will roll like a ball on the battlefield of Karbala. Alas! The hour approaches when the sinister bird of hate will gorge on the flesh of the companion of Karbala." One or two of the women around me started murmuring into their chadors, "Alas, the pity of it." Hossein turned to the spectators: "Hatred and treachery have broken my wings. Through the wickedness of my enemies, I, sad and sorrowful, am separated from the pure tomb of the Prophet and from the mausoleum of Fatemeh, daughter of the Prophet—she who gave me life." Turning to his guide, he said, "Give me a handful of ashes to throw on my head, that the hidden mysteries may reveal themselves." The guide placed a handful of ashes in his hand, saying, "Oh light of Fatemeh's eyes, Imam, Supreme Guide, accept from my hands a fistful of ashes of this earth." Hossein threw the ashes on his own head. "Here on the plain of Karbala, our blood will flow. Here Qassem's wedding feast will be transformed into burial rites, and my head will be separated from my body."

At that, cries of anguish broke from the women around me as they slapped their foreheads with the palm of one hand. "Ah, dust on the head of those who torment you, noble, noble Hossein," they cried out, while from the men below I could distinguish, "May God send death to those who persecute you," amidst the moans and groans. Turning to his brother Abbas, Hossein continued, "Dear brother, let us camp here this night and rest. I know not what ruses and traps await us on this plain under the menacing sky."

The villain Shemr, eager to carry out his superior's orders, appeared on stage flailing a sword and making terrible threats against Hossein and his defenders. "Glory be to Allah. I will be covered with honor and respect when I carry out Yazid's orders and slay the King of Religion. I will be covered with pearls and gold for chopping off the hands of Hossein's brother, the heroic 'Abbas. We will feast and rejoice when the shirt of his nephew, the brave Qassem, is soaked in blood. By Yazid's order we will destroy them all. When I arrive at Karbala, that plain of sorrow, I will cut off their water and will turn their throats into rivers of blood. The wives I will send to Damascus, ripping the veils from their faces. They will walk, their arms bound, through our streets and our bazaars, to the sound of harps and lutes. Bring me my armor. Their faces will swell from the tears they will shed."

By now the murmurs around me were turning to sobs. I could see hands daubing eyes and fists beating chests as the audience's emotions rose to a pitch. Ruhi's aunt was rocking back and forth, tears streaming from her eyes, lamentations pouring from her lips. "Oh Hossein, oh Qassem, oh noble ones. That such innocents should suffer such abuse. May God strike down the tyrant."

A battle followed, with sword clashing against sword and shield. Dust rose from the arena, and the actors were perspiring heavily. Hossein's brother, 'Abbas, lost both arms. He rose from the floor with his sleeves dripping blood. Someone in the audience called out, "Oh, evil ones lacking in faith. May you roast in hell." At that point a warrior from the enemy camp struck the mutilated 'Abbas a death blow; he dropped to the floor.

Hossein appeared on a majestic horse, its white coat splattered with red. He knew the end was near. He got off the horse and, standing before the audience, donned his own shroud, reaffirming his acceptance of imminent martyrdom.

The evil Shemr appeared once again with a group of men and struck Hossein down. At that the entire audience rose to its feet in anguish and horror, some calling on Allah for revenge, some weeping, "The Lord of Mercy is slain, oh woe, oh woe."

Enemy forces carrying papier-mâché heads atop long pikes marched across the *sakoo*. Others paraded a group of women and children around the arena, their hands bound, while the director lamented their fate. In the intense heat of the desert the thirsty children pleaded and begged for water. "Have mercy on us, our throats are parched, our lips cracked, our tongues swollen. Please, give us some water." As the cruel Shemr took a pitcher of water and in front of the children poured it onto the ground, I found myself choking back tears and a sob in my throat. By now tears were flowing freely all around me, accompanied by cries of sympathy.

I was spellbound by the drama. For the first time I understood the importance of the Ashura rituals, realized how they gave expression to the people's suffering, encouraged them to resist and to endure as members of a religious sect. Undoubtedly the women around me who were beating their chests and smacking their foreheads and weeping openly were able to identify with the unfortunate victims of the drama. They, too, had experienced loss of a loved one, a child, a husband, a brother, or a sister; they, too, had experienced tyranny and oppression—most likely at the hands of a bureaucrat or perhaps of a father, a husband, or a mother-in-law. Undoubtedly they gave vent to sorrows arising from personal grief. Most certainly the drama of martyrdom and the persecution of the innocent touched some deep wellspring of recognition within them, providing a cathartic release of pent up frustration and sorrow. But they wept, too, for the collective memory of national suffering that the *ta'ziyeh* dramatized and symbolized. Hossein represented a political as well as religious leader, one who fought against corruption, who defended the *mostaz'afin,* the dispossessed. His martyrdom in A.D. 680 marked the moment when a distinct, discrete sect was born, one with a religiopolitical character rooted in Persian history and culture, stamped with sacrifice, death, and martyrdom. Although ardently embracing Islam, the religion of the Arabs, the Shi'a molded it to fit Persia's unique cultural identity.

Stirred to pity, compassion, and cultural pride by the performance I had just seen, I was unaware that I had allowed my chador to slip back onto my shoulders and that my head and face were uncovered. A woman sitting next to me censored me sharply. Leaning toward me, she hissed, "Cover your face, you shameless woman." I carefully pulled the chador low over my forehead and held the cumbersome garment across my face, with just my eyes showing. I drew closer to Ruhi's aunt.

By the time the event drew to a close I was hungry, thirsty, hot, and tired. Closely veiled women pressed in on us as we made our way down the stairs and out of the *tekiyeh*. Disheveled from wearing the chador, worn out from the somberness and tragedy of the events dramatized as well as from the heat, thirst, and press of the crowd, I must have looked pale and haggard. As Ruhi joined us, his aunt patted me on the back of my hand and, turning to him with much approval in her voice, said, "She, too, wept."

Mummy, along with many foreigners in Iran, looked upon the national preoccupation with mourning as a collective psychosis and considered it strange that so many tears should be shed for someone who had died almost thirteen hundred years earlier. For a long time I shared her views, but watching the *ta'ziyeh* helped me to understand the historical events that had led the Persians to develop national rituals that gave expression to sorrow. As we left the *tekiyeh,* a flood of memories suddenly engulfed me. I remembered, as though it were yesterday, the time when Naneh had taken me to a session of lament, a *rowzeh,* when I had first heard a recitation of these historical events in a private home and watched a group of women weeping in response. I had been perplexed by all the tears I had seen that day. Now I understood the reason for all the grief.

I mentioned to Ruhi that I had gone to a *rowzeh* as a child and was stunned when he elaborated that although the martyrdom of Hossein is a quintessential Muslim Shi'a theme, it actually has its roots in Iranian traditions dating from Zoroastrian times. In Ferdowsi's *Shahnameh,* he explained, two of Iran's legendary heroes are killed through treachery, one of them later becoming the focus of a cult of lamentation that Iranian minstrels accompanied with cycles of songs known as "the weeping of the magi." Centuries later, at the time of the Safavids, a book known as *The Garden of the Martyrs* related the sufferings of the imams, particularly of Hossein, thus blending Zoroastrian and Muslim traditions into a national ritual of public mourning for the martyr Hossein. This ritual gave rise to a tradition of Shi'a preachers known as *rowzeh-khan,* who offer recitations from the book in private homes, even in the *andaroon*s, the women's quarters. Held throughout the year, these *rowzeh* provide women with a sanctioned social activity. It was to such a gathering that Naneh had taken me. As a young boy, Ruhi had been to many.

Pondering matters funerary, I was also reminded of Reza Shah's grand funeral some years earlier, which had turned into a national day of mourning. I remembered having been surprised at the extent of the grief of the populace, for the exiled king had already been dead some years when his body was finally returned to Iran for burial. That waiting period, however, had not diminished the people's lament. Now I understood why, and it suddenly dawned on me what had inspired Mrs. Cook to choreograph a solemnly ritualistic funerary dance. It had no dramatic leaps, no flirtatious mischief, no swishing of skirts or sensuously snaking arms. Instead, it exhibited slow and stately pomp, with controlled and measured movements befitting a somber occasion. Above the mournful dirge that accompanied this dance a rich and resonant voice lamented, "The Shah is dead; alas, alas, the great Shah is dead; where, oh where is he now?" I now realized how skillfully in this dance Mrs. Cook had integrated Iran's history, culture, and rituals into a mournful microcosm of the traditions of martyrdom and lament.

The Gathering Storm

O heart,
Let go of all your worries about the future.
In this friendless world
   come and join *us*.

        —Jalal ad-Din Rumi

"IT'S TIME FOR YOU to find a job," Mummy said. It was the day after my graduation. "With your fluency in English, you could make good money as a secretary." What she did not say was that a big girl like me did not need to be lounging around the house and that if I could bring home some earnings it would greatly ease her burden, but I was oblivious to her needs and had other ideas for myself. With high school behind me I had started thinking about continuing my studies. Exactly what I wanted to study and where I was not sure. I knew I could not attend the University of Tehran because at that time they would not admit students who had not been through the Persian school system.

The only alternative was for me to go to the Ecole Jeanne d'Arc, the school run by French nuns. It was an elementary and high school, encompassing grades one through twelve, but by offering rigorous advanced courses and extra reading assignments, it had come to accommodate an increasingly large number of young women like me, high school graduates who wanted to learn French and pursue further education otherwise unavailable to them. The school's primary mission seemed to be spreading the French language and culture rather than simply proselytizing. When I considered enrolling, anxiety gripped me as I realized how inadequate my French-language skills would be for the task. I had studied French in high school, but could certainly not speak French or write it

267

Turning eighteen in Tehran, 1950.

with a secure knowledge of its grammar, although I could read it without too much difficulty. Like a novice swimmer who shuts her eyes and jumps into the water, I decided to go ahead and enroll anyway. I would simply have to learn the language.

Meanwhile, I felt less and less intimidated by the idea of going abroad for further studies. Ruhi and I were now giving serious consideration to applying to Oxford or Cambridge and had begun exploring ways to come up with the fare. One obvious solution would be for me to tutor private students in English. I should have no trouble finding clients, for English was all the rage. Although the Allied troops, including the Americans, had left the country by now, the United States was sending technical assistance and military advisors to Iran, so the Americans and their language still had a highly visible presence. Furthermore, English had become the principal language of commerce and diplomacy, gradually replacing French as the preferred foreign language. Most of the movies shown in Tehran were American productions, which also helped spur people's desire to speak the language of Hollywood.

So my days were gradually divided between studying and tutoring. I threw myself into my studies with vigor, a strong sense of competition, and a newly awakened curiosity. An intellectual spark I had not known before grew into a blaze and burned brightly. Nothing seemed too difficult or too dull or too strenuous. Stimulated by my contact with Ruhi's prodigious intellect and no longer preoccupied with attracting other men, I found in my studies new avenues of excitement. And several afternoons a week I would ride the bus to the homes of various people to tutor them in English.

My students were an assorted lot—the wife of the Turkish ambassador, a middle-aged businessman and his wife, a young high school girl, a beautiful divorcée, a young mother of three, a university student—all anxious to learn the lingua franca of the day and all with a minimal grasp of that language. Most of them had been taught to read rather than to speak English, so I emphasized conversation. They had a difficult time pronouncing the consonant *w,* the short *i,* and the *th* sound, for none of these sounds exists in Persian. Besides, they were adults, set in their linguistic speech patterns, so my efforts to improve their pronunciation had limited success. Many of them had difficulty grasping how to use definite articles because the Persian language has none, and they were constantly confusing *he* and *she* because all Persian personal pronouns are gender neutral. What is more, as adults with many responsibilities, many of my students frequently canceled their sessions. Tutoring, I discovered, was erratic and not very profitable. I managed to save only a little money.

Ruhi, too, had taken up teaching English, but he had group classes. An elderly relative of his, Mariam Khanom, had a small two-room residence next to a shrine in downtown Tehran where she offered to let him hold classes. She was the *motevalli* responsible for the care of the shrine, which was located off Toopkhaneh (Cannon Square), an enormous plaza bounded by massive municipal buildings, with a reflecting pool at its center and the most imposing statue of Reza Shah anywhere in Iran. Here fountains splashed, exuding a cool freshness amidst the press and noise of peddlers and pedestrians and the fume-spewing traffic hurtling around as if on a racetrack.

Because the square was centrally located, Ruhi and I often met at Mariam Khanom's place, and many a time she poured me an *istikan* of tea and chatted with me while I waited for Ruhi's classes to end. Although she seemed to like me and approved of Ruhi's choice, I knew she must be shocked at the free way we met, considering that we were not even officially engaged, let alone married. We never so much as held hands in front of her, for that simply was not done in front of others, even *after* marriage, but just the fact that we met at her place and went out together unchaperoned was an unbelievable breach of acceptable norms. I could imagine her shaking her head and clucking her tongue in disapproval. To her credit she never said anything and suffered our liberties in silence.

I was now seeing Ruhi more and more frequently, and time spent with him precluded time spent with others. I saw little of my cousins or of my friends and former classmates, and did not really develop new ties at Jeanne d'Arc. I did meet Ruhi's lifelong friend, the poet Fereydoon Moshiri, who eventually became one of the best-loved contemporary poets of Iran. I found him to be a gentle and unassuming young man with sad-looking hazel eyes, a little shy, his head tilted to one side as though the world had struck it a blow. I would listen intently as he recited his latest creations, his husky voice adding drama and pathos to his words, whether lyrical love poems or satirical political diatribes. He knew Ruhi's loyalties were now divided and that I would probably be the wedge that would pry his friend from his side, but he was generous of spirit and approved warmly of our plans for the future. *Qesmat,* he said, had brought us together.

Ruhi never formally proposed to me, never actually asked, "Will you marry me?" Rather, he frequently asked, "Do you love me?" In our minds loving each other necessarily meant eventually getting married. We assumed we would and started making plans accordingly, but when I confided our plans to Toori, her initial reaction was one of dismay, "Oh *no,* you don't really want to get married, do you? Why don't you wait a few years? You are too young." Miss Sanasarian, my music teacher, was equally distressed. It seems she was harboring grand hopes for a music career for me and knew that marriage was incompatible with such a career. She herself had made the decision to remain single and to devote her life to music, a most unusual choice in that time and place. She eventually realized it would not do much good to argue with me, so she dropped the subject and never spoke of it again.

Ruhi and I both knew that some members of our families would be opposed to our getting married, so we chose to say nothing to them at this time. His family would object because I was not a Muslim, and my father would object because Ruhi was not a Zoroastrian. Most important of all, Mummy would object because Ruhi was Iranian. Not wanting me to suffer the same cultural clashes that had brought her so much pain, she had always assumed—as I had—that I would marry a Westerner, most likely British or American. Yet she obviously liked him, thought of him as a good friend, and was amenable to his visits.

These visits were becoming noticeably more frequent, though. It must have been easy for her to read into our looks and gestures a romantic interest, and as she did, her attitude toward Ruhi started to change. "You've become much too serious," she commented as she tried to interest me in going with her to a dance. "There is a ball at the Officers' Club tonight. Why don't you go with me?" she asked in her most persuasive manner. "You might meet a handsome young man there"—a young man, she might have added, whose principal qualification would be that he was foreign rather than Iranian. She started making derogatory remarks about Ruhi, eventually referring to him with some vehemence as "that stinky squirt." Her disapprobation only drove us to meet elsewhere and firmed my resolve not to be swayed by her prejudice. What had happened to her long friendship with Ruhi? He was still the same person. Like a storm gathering force from the changing direction of the winds, her attitude had changed as soon as she sensed our amorous inclinations. Clearly her feelings were not rooted in her assessment of Ruhi's character, but in her own personal experiences with an Iranian husband.

I deeply regretted the rift between us, but knew there was nothing I could do to change her mind. Nor was there anything she could do to change mine. I had to follow my heart, and my heart told me that Ruhi was a man of extraordinary integrity, wisdom, and maturity. Beside him my former classmates and acquaintances faded into vapid, immature caricatures of manhood. Yes, Ruhi and I did have our differences, and sometimes we disagreed vehemently, but I admired him, respected him, loved him. Besides, when he looked into my eyes and recited love poems freshly penned just for me, I would melt. Mummy could do nothing about that. All my life she had urged me to make my own choices. She could not put a leash on me now. Yet how it hurt not to have her approval, not to be able to talk with her about my hopes and plans, which remained bottled within and unshared. More than anything else I wanted her to concur with my choice. It was clear she would not, so I retreated into secrecy and silence. We passed each other in the hallway without greeting; we seldom ate together any more, and when we did, we rarely exchanged a word. It was painful, and we both suffered.

Ruhi and I knew we did not need Mummy's legal consent to be married, but we did need Daddy's, and we anticipated difficulties. It was going to be especially difficult because Daddy was living in the United States with Parvin and their first son. We would not even be able to speak to him face-to-face to discuss any objections he might raise. Our first thought was that perhaps we could circumvent the requirement because I was a British subject. Our visit to the British consulate, however, yielded nothing more than a patronizing lecture from a stern-faced British official who suggested, to our considerable annoyance, that we were too young to be getting married. We left the consulate dispirited.

Ruhi had always done a great deal of writing. For him writing was a passion. Fiction, think pieces, humorous articles poured from his pen and appeared routinely in numerous newspapers and magazines under a variety of pseudonyms. As the nationalist fervor swept the country, however, his writings started taking on an increasingly political color. He picked up the banner of the nationalists, proclaimed the need to shake off the yoke of foreign domination, and used up bottles of ink in support of the nationalization of the oil industry.

But now, suddenly, the need for money entered into the scheme of things, for the two of us hoped to journey across the seas, which required a great deal of money. Abruptly, Ruhi gave up his writing, his political tracts, his satires and poems and diatribes against the big powers, and took a full-time job. Although he was in the last year of his law studies, regular attendance at the university was not required. He could study on his own and simply take the final exams at the end of the year. Still, this decision must have been gut wrenching for him.

He became a translator at Sir Alexander Gibb & Partners, an English firm that had been commissioned to install a piped-water system in Tehran—a task greatly complicated by the haphazard growth of the city and by the numerous cesspools that riddled its substratum. He hated being tied down to the 8:00 A.M. to 5:00 P.M. hours and chafed at the haughty demeanor of his British employers and fellow employees. Although he suffered at not being able to express his opinion when translating conversations between government officials and the British contractors, he held his tongue and transmitted the thoughts and words of others into Persian or English without commentary, riding the waves of necessity like an anchored buoy.

Meanwhile, on every side political tensions were rising rapidly, and street demonstrations and rousing speeches were becoming more frequent and highly explosive. Agitation and pressure were mounting for the government to nationalize the oil industry, which had been run by the Anglo-Iranian Oil Company since 1932. Early demands for an equal share of oil revenues had burgeoned into a single overriding demand for complete national control of the entire industry.

From our house, centrally located near the British and Soviet embassies, Mummy and I could hear loudspeakers booming and crowds roaring as people demonstrated in front of the embassies—by now an almost daily occurrence. Once in a while things would turn ugly; fistfights would break out, and people would be trampled or wounded or even killed.

At home I would sometimes pause in the middle of making my bed or reading a book to listen to the distant rumble of hundreds of voices chanting in unison—a sound menacing yet strangely exhilarating. At other times I would stop on the edge of a curb to watch a group of demonstrators. Their clenched fists, their set jaws, their staccato appeals to honor and nationalism stirred deep emotions in me, like the tapping of drums in a military parade. But with emotions running at fever pitch such demonstrations could abruptly turn violent and dangerous, as Mummy kept pointing out to me, and she warned me to keep my distance. The danger, however, only heightened the excitement. The appeal was irresistible.

While walking home one day, I found my way blocked by a large group of people jammed tightly around a slow-moving vehicle from which a man was declaiming in cadenced, yet urgent tones. Chanting in response to the speaker, whose impassioned eloquence caught my attention, the crowd blocked the road and spilled over onto the sidewalks. I felt my heart pound with excitement. Even as I told myself to back off and take another route to avoid the commotion, I was drawn to it by the fire and urgency of the voice as it proclaimed through the loudspeaker, "After so many years of exploitation we must gain control of our natural resources." The crowd roared its approval, chanting, "Nationalization of oil throughout the land." I could not tear myself away. The speaker's voice sounded uncannily like Ruhi's, but I dismissed that possibility. My view was blocked by a sea of raised fists and angry faces rhythmically repeating, "Death to colonialism." Straining to catch the words, I stood still, oblivious to the dangers posed by the crowd, which was growing by the minute, bringing the vehicle to a standstill. "We must nationalize our oil industry and free our country from the meddling interference of foreign powers," the voice declared, and the crowd responded, *"Azadi, esteqlal,"* clamoring for freedom and independence, expressing sentiments that were spreading across the land like wildfire fanned by the winds of nationalism. As I listened, I felt myself drawn into the mood of the crowd, anger toward the imperialist foreigners welling up inside me as well as pride at the efforts of the people to free themselves of foreign domination. I lingered on until the demonstrators slowly turned down another street.

Later that day when I saw Ruhi, I excitedly shared with him my experience, told him what a stirring speaker I had heard that day whipping up nationalist feelings, and said I wished that he could have been there. Ruhi smiled and took my hand, "I *was* there," he said quietly. *"I* was that speaker." I remembered, then, thinking how much the voice had sounded like Ruhi's. I had not known he was so involved in the struggle. I looked at him with amazement. I felt such pride I could hardly express it in words. I caught him in my arms and kissed him.

At home Mummy and her English friends decried the "impudence" and "audacity" of the Iranian nationalists for trying to take over the oil company when it was *they,* the British, who had invested in it, poured their money and expertise into it, and made it a thriving international business and source of revenue for Iran. "Without us there would be no oil industry," one of them sputtered.

From my Iranian friends I heard the opposing view—of ruthless exploitation of a finite national resource that had benefitted the English and the Western world at the expense of Iran, which received paltry royalties in return. It was time, they felt, for the nation not only to receive more revenues from its increasingly precious resource, but to become equal partners in its control and production. Only by gaining such control could Iran hope to free itself of Great Britain and the Soviet Union's often rapacious interference in Iran's internal affairs. With the ardent conviction of the very young and the newly converted I believed the justice of the nationalists' cause would carry the day. There was no doubt which side of the argument I favored. Just a year earlier I would probably have sided unquestioningly with the British. Now to Mummy's consternation I had been "brainwashed" into supporting the nationalists. The truth is, however, that I was gradually becoming more informed about national and international events. I now followed political discussions attentively and found myself caught up in the arguments and passions that inflamed them. It was heady stuff.

I started reading books on Iran's modern history and learned how brazenly Great Britain and Russia had violated Iran's territorial integrity and independence by partitioning the kingdom into spheres of influence in 1907. For the first time I realized that the Iranian propensity to spin seemingly far-fetched conspiracy theories against the British was in fact rooted in painful historical experience. England had brought to power and deposed kings and potentates, had bought off and influenced many a powerful khan, vizier, and shah, and had actively intervened in Iran's internal affairs. Mummy and her English friends had always laughed at the "preposterous" accusations circulating in Iran that saw "the British hand" in every failure of government action or policy. Yet more and more I was convinced from reading accounts by such writers as Morgan Shuster, the American financial advisor to Iran from 1911 to 1912, that England, my country of birth, had in fact selfishly implemented imperial policies that helped thwart Iranian efforts to establish a constitutional monarchy, a modern financial system, and a modicum of representative self-government. I started to question the opinions I read in the British embassy newsletter delivered to our door once a week in which Great Britain's policies were cast as noble and beneficent. I started to see these policies instead as self-serving and exploitative. Now along with my Iranian friends and acquaintances I became ardent in my belief that the new leadership of Mohammad Mosadeq represented the brightest hope for Iran's political independence and for the people's aspirations for democratic participation.

Mosadeq was already a well-known figure on the political scene. Born into a prominent, elite family, he had begun his political career while still in his teens and had earned his first political stripes by opposing the accession of Reza Khan to the throne in 1925, making him Reza Shah. He had spent time in exile and in jail for political reasons. In 1944, elected to the Fourteenth Majlis, he had vociferously condemned Reza Shah's tyranny, spoken out for a more democratic form of government, and waged a successful battle against the granting of any further oil concessions to any foreign power. By now his name was a household word. At a time when corruption in high places was rife and politicians lined their pockets by selling out the interests of the country, he was a sterling model of integrity. His shrewd protection of Iran's postwar independence and political autonomy had gained him many followers.

Mosadeq was now the leader of a minority group of Majlis deputies, known as the National Front, who professed liberal nationalist goals, opposed foreign intervention in Iran's affairs, and had a vocal following among educated and middle-class Iranians. The National Front was calling for the nationalization of the oil industry "throughout the land," with the goal of wresting control from Great Britain in the south and denying the Soviet Union oil concessions in the north. The cause of independence from foreign control seemed within grasp, and support for the National Front grew, along with calls for full nationalization. As such goals were more clearly defined, however, they gradually became slogans, and extremists on both the left and the right became more determined to gain their ends by any means. Eventually a member of the extremist Fadayan-e Islam gunned down Premier Ali Razmara, who was among those who had sought remedies to the crisis short of full nationalization. Although shocked by the assassination, we cheered from the sidelines when, not long afterward, the Shah reluctantly appointed Mohammad Mosadeq as the prime minister, and the National Front finally came into its own. Then, on May 1, 1951, following the Majlis's unanimous approval, the Shah promulgated the law that nationalized the oil industry, to the acclaim of many Mosadeq followers, including Ruhi and me.

Britain's condemnation of Iran's action was predictably swift and harsh, but its counterproposals were considered to be too little and too late. Terms that might at one time have appeared attractive, such as an equal sharing of profits, now appeared unacceptable. In my burgeoning nationalist fervor I wondered at the British leaders' seeming obtuseness.

In the midst of the increasingly tumultuous events of that spring, having completed three years of studies in two, I graduated second in my class from Ecole Jeanne d'Arc, ruing the two weeks of illness that had prevented me from graduating first. At the same time Ruhi graduated first in his class from University of Tehran Faculty of Law, Political Science, and Economics. For his thesis he had translated into Persian a book on British criminal law.

Because Ruhi's exemption from military service was predicated on his being a bona fide student, our preparations for the future now took on greater urgency. He had only one year's grace period to enroll for further studies. If within a year of graduating he did not have an acceptance from a foreign university, he would be conscripted, his head would be shaved, and he would face two years of compulsory military service—a prospect he did not relish. Military service would mean a major interruption in his education, a brutalizing subjection to harsh discipline at the hands of often uneducated and inept superiors, and, as he saw it, a total waste of time. We would have to put our minds quickly to getting university acceptances and scraping up the necessary travel expenses; otherwise, the opportunity to leave would slip away. We would worry about the rest of the details later. Because it was conceivable that I might have to work full-time and postpone my own further education, I enrolled in a typing class—an idea that I somehow found more acceptable now than when Mummy had first suggested it.

We assumed that if we were accepted at either Oxford or Cambridge I would surely find work in England with little difficulty because I was a British subject. Just how I was going to combine work with study was not clear to me. I only knew that in order for Ruhi to get his doctorate, I would have to find work, whether part-time or full-time, but first I would need a work permit if we were to go to England.

Our trip to the British consulate was brief. The consular official who received us was courteous enough, but he quickly disabused us of the idea that I could find work in England. Yes, I could get a work permit, but unemployment was high in England, and jobs were scarce. There was little likelihood we could put ourselves through school there without substantial help from our families. We would certainly be well advised not to count on it. By the time the consular official closed the door behind us, he had already effectively closed the door on our consideration of going to England. We were deeply disappointed. For the first time the magic of my English birth had not worked miracles.

So we turned our thoughts to the United States, whose universities were less well known to us. We would have to make inquiries. Of course, jobs were more abundant in the States, and if I could qualify for an immigration visa, perhaps I could find work there.

In the back of a meandering alley behind a small wooden door a single American consular employee sat in a sparsely furnished office advising students on how to go about applying to American universities. Later that day we pored over the literature he had given us, finally figuring out that a Ph.D. was the same thing as a "doctorate," vaguely comprehending the meaning of a "major," and pinpointing several universities on the map. We decided to go ahead and apply, and to deal later with how we would support ourselves. Time was getting short, and unless Ruhi had an acceptance in hand by the spring of 1952, he would be drafted, and all our plans would collapse like a house of cards.

How I wished I could talk openly to Mummy about our plans, but I could not. I knew she would be opposed not to my going abroad, but to my marrying Ruhi. When I let her know only about our plans to study in America, my heart ached over the coolness that now marked our interaction.

Meanwhile, political tensions around us were mounting by the day, for the British and the Iranians remained at loggerheads. The two governments were caught up in name-calling, and the citizens on either side felt outraged and offended. Iranian grievances rose to the boiling point when, in March 1951, British destroyers made a show of force in the Persian Gulf. In May Iran rejected the jurisdiction of the International Court of Justice in the case brought by the British government against Iran on behalf of the Anglo-Iranian Oil Company. In June Iran defiantly proceeded to take over the operations of the oil company; three thousand British paratroopers arrived in Cyprus ready for action in Iran; and the British oil company staff began evacuation. Soon thereafter tanker masters started refusing to take on oil, leaving Iran without means of exporting its oil. By the end of July 1951 the gigantic oil refinery in Abadan had closed down. Iran faced financial ruin and political isolation. Mummy had difficulty concealing her "I told you so" attitude regarding the entire matter, and I was deeply offended by her smugness.

For my part I expected America, with its lofty ideals, to be fair and impartial, to protect the weak and the oppressed. How was it possible that America could not see the obvious justice of Iran's cause? How could it side with the British? Although initially the United States had maintained neutrality in the dispute between Iran and Great Britain, it was gradually drawing closer to the British position.

In July, in spite of American attempts to mediate between the two parties, negotiations broke down. In October Britain took its case to the United Nations Security Council, and soon thereafter Mosadeq appeared in person before that body to reject the council's jurisdiction. He presented Iran's case with unusual skill and pleaded ill health or fatigue whenever he considered it strategically helpful to be absent from a meeting. Even as Mosadeq was ridiculed in the foreign press for his "pajama-clad" diplomacy, his weeping, his outbursts, and his seeming intractability on the issue of nationalization, he was more and more revered at home.

Here at last at the helm was a man of unimpugnable integrity, a charismatic leader who had been educated abroad yet had not lost touch with his own people and their native culture. Here was a man from the traditional land-owning aristocracy who put the interests of the people above his own, who was not increasing his personal wealth at their expense, who could defy the Shah and the Soviets and the British. Here miraculously was a man so fearless as to tweak the tail of the British lion and make it roar with anger. His ill health, his tears, his bedside conduct of diplomatic negotiations, which so offended foreigners, only endeared him to his own people.

Rumor held that Mosadeq had ordered all government offices to sell their fine carpets to help sustain the nation in its battle for justice and independence. What integrity! What courage! No matter that no one could actually verify the account. It was the perception that was important, and such anecdotes enhanced the man's already mythical standing in the minds of his followers.

Many of Mosadeq's supporters were convinced that he would bring about land reform, taking ownership of huge tracts of land and many villages out of the hands of absentee landlords and distributing it among the peasants. Others were skeptical because Mosadeq was himself a member of the landed aristocracy. But that was not the reason for Ruhi's circumspection. "Even if Mosadeq does bring about land reform," Ruhi said, shaking his head, "that will not solve the country's problems." He was right, of course. In a land rife with corruption in high places, where bribery was widespread, where a swollen bureaucracy effectively strangled governmental services, where disparities between the rich and the poor grew ever larger, where a lack of adequate financial resources assured the continuation of intolerably high illiteracy, where earlier attempts at reform had caused much social dislocation, and where even the well-off middle classes were unable to participate in the political process, land reform was not the panacea some thought it would be. Yet I clung passionately to the hope that enlightened leadership on the part of the National Frontists under the benevolent guidance of Mosadeq would lift Iran out of its miasma of problems and set it on the path to independence and prosperity.

As the U.S. position hardened into one of uncompromising support for the British, politically aware Iranians felt betrayed by the United States, a great power that had until then championed Iran's struggle for self-determination. It was American diplomacy that had nudged Churchill and Stalin into signing, with Roosevelt, the Tripartite Declaration of December 1, 1943, which pledged economic assistance to Iran and renewed commitments to the withdrawal of British and Russian forces after the cessation of hostilities. A reciprocal trade agreement in 1944 had raised hopes that American assistance would help the country get back on its feet.

The public had always held in high esteem the American Presbyterian missionaries who had established schools as well as a widely lauded hospital and who had conducted philanthropic work throughout the country. Everyone knew of Miss Doolittle, who had worked hard to improve the plight of orphaned girls abandoned in the capital city. Until now Americans had always been the champions of the weak and the downtrodden.

Iranians in the early 1950s therefore found it difficult to understand why the United States was backing Great Britain when Iran's cause was so clearly just. "Can't the Americans see we are fighting for our independence?" a young nationalist exploded, exasperation showing in every word. "Oil is our lifeblood. We should be in charge of its extraction and sale." Ruhi, drawing on his legal training, pointed out that as a sovereign nation, Iran had the right to control its natural resources. It was not confiscating the Anglo-Iranian Oil Company, for it had declared all along that it would pay compensation. But what was so clear to us and to much of the nation seemed, at best, murky to the British and to their friends the Americans.

What Iran's anguished citizens did not quite comprehend was that although the United States had championed Iran's political independence in the past, its ties with Great Britain were woven of stronger threads. What is more, the United States now feared that the dispute might lead to a shutdown of the flow of oil to its European allies. It worried that the act of nationalization might set a bad example for other oil-producing states of the Middle East, all of whom might get uppity and make outrageous demands that would hurt American oil interests. But above all it was alarmed by the increasing strength of the Tudeh Party. Much against my inclinations, I found myself agreeing with Ruhi that the United States was acting not on principle, but out of pure self-interest, which, realistically, was how most nation-states behaved. I found that idea difficult to swallow.

Ultimately, the emerging cold war and the U.S. fear of a communist takeover proved pivotal in the downfall of the Mosadeq government. Convinced that the United States wished mainly to strengthen the position and influence of American oil monopolies in Iran, the Tudeh Party sought to exploit the nationalization crisis with a view to substituting a communist regime for the nationalist one. Although to the United States a communist takeover seemed imminent, to most Iranians a successful Tudeh takeover seemed highly unlikely. Yet we were all acutely aware that the political edifice was collapsing around us.

More than ever Ruhi was convinced that he and I must leave—and soon, for Iran's economy had slowly ground to a halt, and the government faced a staggering array of technical, administrative, economic, political, and diplomatic problems. Great Britain had banned the export of sugar, iron, steel, and other goods to Iran. Iran had retaliated by transferring deposits from the British Bank of Iran and the Middle East to the Bank-e Melli-ye Iran. Later, all British consulates and all foreign cultural institutions would be ordered closed, and on October 22, 1952, Iran would break off diplomatic relations with Great Britain. But all that was still in the future.

Although for a while Iran seemed triumphant in its resistance to foreign domination and on the verge of establishing a more democratic political system, the initial euphoria quickly dissipated, to be replaced by uncertainty and anxiety. The country now seemed on the edge of economic, political, and social collapse. A sense of hopelessness permeated the social structure. Like an ominous storm slowly gathering strength, the political impasse darkened all facets of our lives and threatened to unleash its destructive force over our heads.

Leap into the Unknown

Leap like a flame thru the sky,
Scatter the dark spirits
and become the pillar of heaven.
—Jalal ad-Din Rumi,
"Only Through This"

LATE THAT FALL OF 1951, as turmoil and uncertainty engulfed us and threatened to sabotage all our plans, Ruhi and I received from the University of Georgia not only admissions for both of us for the spring semester of 1952 but scholarships as well. We laughed at the news and felt by turns elated and anxious. The University of Georgia had not been our first choice, and its law school did not offer the doctoral program Ruhi wished to pursue, but once in the United States we would be able to transfer to another university.

We composed letters of acceptance, unsure of the correct terminology or appropriate form. Ruhi relied heavily on me for the right syntax and turn of phrase, although this was all new territory for me, and I was not sure of the right terminology either. We applied for student housing and quickly sent off the entire package of papers, for we could afford to wait no longer. If we did not leave soon, Ruhi would be drafted, two precious years of his life would be frittered away, and all our plans would be ruined.

We had no way of knowing, of course, that student housing in Athens, Georgia, would consist of a dilapidated mobile trailer with no hot water, only a communal bathhouse we would share with several other couples, barely functioning cooking facilities, and little protection from the suffocating, humid heat. Even if we had known, it would have made no difference. We were intent on seizing the opportunity that would help us shape our future. We were leaving our homes and families and everything that was familiar not for a more comfortable life, but for a freer one, no matter what the cost. The knowledge of inadequate, dilapidated housing would not have deterred us.

Mummy's face remained composed when I gave her the news. I knew she was happy for us, but wary of what else other than study these plans might represent. She must have felt torn, for her only daughter would be leaving her and going far away. As always she kept her emotions under control. She would not, I knew, stand in the way of my going abroad to study, but she wanted to know more. I was evasive, for I was certain she would not be happy to learn that marriage with Ruhi was in the picture.

We set about obtaining visas. The U.S. immigration quota system, then based on the applicant's country of birth, had a very small quota for Iran and a large number of applicants. It would be impossible for Ruhi to get an immigration visa, so he would have to apply for a student visa. England's quota, on the other hand, was very large and the number of applicants small. Obtaining an immigration visa for me would be easy and quick, allowing me to work.

In filling out the requisite forms, I answered such offensive questions as "Are you now or have you ever been a prostitute?" and "Are you now or have you ever been a member of the Communist Party?" with an indignant *NO* in bold letters. I then went to a hospital to have X-rays taken to certify I did not have tuberculosis, for I would not be allowed to enter the United States without them.

Yet another hurdle loomed—we would have to declare all our financial assets and, because these assets were negligible, would have to provide a guarantee of financial support by a relative, friend, or acquaintance to assure we would not become "public charges." We did not, of course, expect anyone else to support us while we were in the United States, but the official requirement had to be met. Fortunately, the codes of obligation governing personal relationships would make it incumbent on relatives or friends to help us out if we asked them to. Ruhi asked Dr. Mashhoon, his old friend who had taken care of my injured knee, to become our guarantor. He readily agreed, and we submitted the completed forms to the American embassy.

Looking back, I marvel at what a far-reaching impact my place of birth had on our destiny. How odd that just because I was born in Manchester and not Tehran, I could acquire an immigration visa within a few weeks of applying.

And how lucky. Some weeks later Ruhi received his student visa, and we were able to proceed with our plans.

As these events unfolded, mixed feelings plagued me. I was troubled over leaving Mummy all alone. After all, I was the only close family she had in her adopted country. No matter how long she had lived here and how well she spoke Persian, she was still a foreigner. Besides, I realized there was much about Iran I would miss, and I feared the unknown. Now that departure was near, I was no longer absolutely certain it was what I wanted. I raised my concerns with Ruhi. "What about Mummy?" I asked. "She will be all alone here." But Ruhi spoke with assurance, "Perhaps we will come back after we get our degrees," he said. "Who knows? If we don't and decide to stay in America, then we will send for her to come and live with us." A heavy weight seemed to lift off my shoulders. Reassured, I started to feel more at ease with the idea of leaving my mother, my home, my friends.

Meanwhile, Daddy's family, with whom I had had little contact ever since my parents' divorce, now felt entitled—no, *obliged*—to meddle. Uncle Aflatoon, Father's eldest brother, had heard rumors and gossip that Ruhi and I were seeing each other and planning to get married. Because Daddy was abroad, my uncle felt it was his duty to interfere. He objected to our marriage on grounds of religion. What did Ruhi, a Muslim, think he was doing trying to marry a Zoroastrian girl? He objected on grounds of social status. How dare Ruhi, an impecunious student, even think of marrying a girl from such a respectable and reputable family? A marriage between us would violate all the social codes. He sent a message to Ruhi. "You must stop seeing Nesta. If you don't, I will have you knifed in the back and your body thrown to the vultures." Although Ruhi dismissed the threat as nothing but overblown rhetoric, I was dismayed. I didn't think Uncle Aflatoon might really carry out the threat, but I realized that feelings still ran deep in the Zoroastrian community against marrying outside the religion. What hypocrites, I thought. No one had ever made any effort to teach me about Zoroastrianism, and my uncle's generation was the one that had first deviated from the code and married outsiders. My own father had married a foreigner. Anyway, who had made up the rules that forbade young men and women from different religions to marry each other? It was absurd. Neither of us was a practicing Muslim or Zoroastrian, although we firmly believed in the importance of spirituality in modern life.

But I worried and fretted because I knew that we had to have Daddy's permission to be married; the law required it. A trickle of anxiety quickly gathered into a powerful wave that washed away my self-assurance. What if Daddy raised the same objections? After all, he had at one time, like a traditional patriarch, entertained the notion of an arranged marriage for me. Getting his consent now loomed as a major obstacle. It would take all our ingenuity to persuade him to see things our way. If we failed, all our plans would collapse. In an old and dusty box somewhere in our basement in Virginia I still have the letter that Ruhi wrote to Daddy. It came into my possession many years later, after my father died. In this eloquent and persuasive missive Ruhi tried to anticipate the arguments Daddy might raise about our different religions, Ruhi's lack of financial standing, his not having important family connections, and the fact that I might instead marry into a family of considerable wealth and social standing. Ruhi elaborated on his educational accomplishments and aspirations, his future prospects, our devotion to each other, and his undying commitment to me. "You can rest assured," he wrote, "that I love her with every fiber of my being, that I promise to take care of her all the days of my life, and that I will spare no effort to provide adequately for her."

To our surprise gaining Daddy's approval was easier than we had expected. Before long we received a reply in which my father not only gave us his formal written permission to get married, but also his promise to provide my transportation expenses to New York. We were overcome with relief and joy.

The moment of truth was at hand. It was time to inform Mummy of our plans. I trembled inwardly. So far I had told her only that we were planning to go to the United States to study. Although she obviously guessed that Ruhi and I were serious about each other, neither she nor I had up to this point said anything about it. She just kept making derogatory remarks about him.

Just a few days earlier I had seen lying open on Mummy's desk a letter she had written to Aunt Stella complaining that my close friendship with Ruhi had made me reject my English heritage, which hurt her deeply. But it was not true, I thought to myself, full of regrets over the rift between us. It was not that I was rejecting my English heritage, but that I was starting to better understand my *Persian* one. Clearly we stood at opposite ends of the political and personal divide, and I could not even talk to her about it.

By now Mummy's hostility toward Ruhi was so intense that she hardly spoke to him and obviously was not going to give us her blessings. Yet so badly did I want her approval that on two separate occasions I tried to talk to her about our plans. "Mummy," I started hesitantly, "Yesterday Ruhi and I were talking and . . ." She whirled on me, "You spend far too much time talking with that miserable little wretch," she exploded. The exchange quickly spiraled into an argument, followed by more hurt feelings, more chagrin, and less and less openness. What had happened to our frankness with each other? Our intimate closeness? Our mutual sympathetic understanding? Would we ever be able to recapture any of that former relationship? It seemed unlikely.

It was obvious that Mummy would have a tantrum if Ruhi and I told her we were getting married. We would have to go ahead without her consent. We would have a simple civil ceremony, witnessed by two friends, as required by law, and inform her afterward. We bought a wedding ring and a large boxful of pastries. We would present Mummy with a fait accompli and then offer to celebrate the occasion with her—*after* the fact. Surely she would accept our union once she knew we had signed the marriage contract. After all, she herself had once done the very same thing. She could hardly blame me for following in her footsteps. In any case I knew I was going to marry Ruhi no matter how much she objected.

I kept wishing she and my husband-to-be would recapture their earlier warm relationship, but she now seemed to see him only as an Iranian suitor to her daughter. Personal and historical emotional baggage warped her attitude. After a lifetime of suffering she seemed to have concluded not that she and Daddy had had personal differences or that many of their problems could be blamed on his alcoholism, but—with a patronizing touch thrown in—that East and West could never meet amicably. Ruhi and I had no alternative other than to go ahead without her consent. I did so with a heavy heart. For me the word *elopement* had lost all its romantic connotations.

We arrived at the registration office without ceremony or fanfare, accompanied by Dr. Mashhoon and another friend to serve as witnesses. It was February, and a blustery wind was blowing. I wore not a bridal outfit but my warmest winter clothing. A turbaned mullah sat behind a simple table in an otherwise bare office devoid of any furnishings other than the two straight-backed wooden chairs on which we would sit. Our witnesses stood. The building was unheated, so none of us removed our overcoats. The mullah scratched my name into a ledger with a quill pen that he kept dipping into an inkwell. He asked my name, and I watched him write it in the ledger in the ornate, decorative Persian script that goes from right to left. He asked my religion. "Zoroastrian," I said, for my lineage automatically made me a member of that community, whether or not I practiced the faith. He put his pen down. "Is this to be a permanent or a temporary marriage?" he asked, looking up at me over the rim of metal glasses that made him look like an owl—an omen of bad luck. I was taken aback, for temporary marriages, *mut'a,* although allowed by the religious law, were contracted largely by poor and uneducated women, for whom a marital contract that lasted for one or two years was better than none at all. I responded with some vehemence that this marriage was to be a permanent one, of course. What does he imagine, I thought to myself, that a girl such as *I* would agree to become a *sigheh?*

But the mullah went on. "Because you are Zoroastrian and not Muslim, I cannot make this marriage a permanent one unless you convert to Islam." Startled, I looked at Ruhi questioningly, who also looked up in surprise and started to say something. The mullah interrupted him, saying, "No problem. All you have to do is to repeat after me, 'There is no God but Allah, and Mohammad is His Prophet,' and that will make you a Muslim, and then I can make it a permanent marriage." Before anyone could intervene, I repeated after him, *"La-illaha el-Allah, Mohammad-an rasool-ollah."* It was done. I had become a Muslim. The last barrier to our marriage had been removed.

This simple formula for conversion to Islam had been streamlined over centuries and utilized by thousands of Zoroastrians after the Seljuk and Mongol conquests, when the choice had often been between conversion and privation or even death. For me the choice was much easier; I was not, after all, a practicing Zoroastrian. Now I would simply be a nonpracticing Muslim.

I learned later that the mullah had erred in requiring my conversion and that Muslim men can marry Zoroastrian women under Islamic law. Even though Zoroastrians are not considered to be "people of the book" in the same way that Christians and Jews are, the reported tradition, hadith, holds that both Mohammad and the leading Shi'a imam, 'Ali, viewed Zoroastrianism as monotheistic and therefore as a legitimate religion. A Muslim man is thus permitted to marry a Christian, Jew, or Zoroastrian. However, a non-Muslim man wishing to marry a Muslim woman must first convert to Islam. Clearly, our mullah was misinformed, but I was not troubled by my hasty conversion, for I had been exposed to too many religions in my lifetime to have allegiance to any single one. Ethical and spiritual life were what counted, not allegiance to one creed or another.

Squinting and bending close to the ledger, the mullah scratched some more information on it, and then Ruhi, our witnesses, and I each in turn signed our names. Ruhi placed the gold ring on my finger. We did not kiss. After the witnesses had congratulated us, Ruhi and I headed to my home to break the news to Mummy and to celebrate with tea and pastries. I should have felt elated, but was instead in a somber mood. This was not how I had imagined my wedding would be. I felt an icy band around my heart. I felt like crying. Not that I minded so much the absence of a festive celebration or fancy wedding gown, but I would have liked for those closest to me to have participated in the event. I wished Mummy could have been there—and Ruhi's sister Mehri. I wished I could have had my mother's approval for this very important day of my life. Instead, I braced myself for our confrontation.

We came home to find Mummy taking a big bite out of a chocolate eclair. Ruhi laughed and said, "Now wait a minute. Don't start without us. That pastry is meant to sweeten our wedding day. We . . ." Mummy's face turned ashen. She put the pastry down and turned to us with a stony stare, her jaw tight. "Wedding?" she said coldly. "Why rush into marriage? Why don't you wait until after you have arrived in the United States and been there a while?" My heart sank as I heard her words, and I quietly slipped my brand new wedding ring off my finger and dropped it into my pocket. Somehow, I had expected that, faced with the facts, Mummy would come around, but she had interpreted Ruhi's words as announcing our imminent marriage, not our recently enacted one. "I have no objections to your going to America together," Mummy said. "Why don't you wait and see how things work out and then, in good time, you can get married?"

I knew what Mummy was thinking. She was hoping that when we went to the United States, I would meet someone else whom I might find more attractive than Ruhi and end up marrying an American instead of an Iranian. There was something condescending in her belief that no Iranian husband could accommodate to a Western woman, as though Iranian men were all primitive and uncivilized brutes. She should have more confidence in my judgment and in my ability to handle the cultural differences, I thought with some resentment. She seemed to forget that I had grown up largely in Iran, not England, and was more in touch with Iranian mores. No one had to tell *me* not to hike up my skirts and go wading in the *joob!*

Mummy knew well that youthful desires played a powerful role in decisions about marriage, but she had no hang-ups about virginity, and she continued to encourage us to travel together, but to postpone any talk of marriage. Her proposal—at that time and in that culture—was so unorthodox that the brazenness of it still takes my breath away. Ruhi and I quietly let her have her say. We could not bring ourselves to tell her that we had already sealed our pact. Our dance of love had not worked out quite as we had planned. We had thought we would draw circles around her. Instead, we had stumbled in our pas de deux and bungled our attempts to leap lightly over her opposition. For the moment, on the day of our wedding, she thought we were simply traveling together to the United States, where we would continue our studies. I hated myself for having to put up a pretense.

We waited anxiously to hear from Daddy regarding my travel fare, and even as the days passed and there was no word, we did not waver in our belief that he would send it, sooner or later. Mummy, however, scoffed at our confidence that he would fulfill his promise, for she knew better. She knew there was not a chance in the world that he would make good on his word. His intentions were always good, but he had broken too many promises for her to have any faith in him. Still, we clung to the hope that this time he would come through. I was, after all, my father's only daughter. I had made few demands on him in my lifetime and had cost him little. It was not too much to ask. He could consider it a wedding present, I reasoned.

We waited in vain. Just weeks before our departure, timed for us to arrive at the University of Georgia for the spring semester, we finally received a letter from Daddy in which he expressed his profound regret that he could not come up with the money after all. He had done everything he could to borrow an adequate sum from friends or acquaintances, but they had all turned him down. He himself was in severe financial straits, what with living in New York with Parvin and their young son, and another baby was on the way. He was already deeply in debt, and there was just no way he would be able to help us.

In the end it was Mummy who helped us. From her meager savings she lent me the money for my fare. She agreed I should repay it gradually, whenever I could. I still feel pangs that during the next few years, at a time when she was so financially strapped that she felt compelled to take a part-time secretarial job for the first time in her life, I was unable to repay more than a fraction of the loan. Then, when I was finally able to pay off the balance, she was gone.

By the time of our departure Ruhi and I had managed to save only a small sum, barely enough to serve as a hedge against the initial expenses we would encounter as we got started in the New World, not enough to pay for an airplane ticket. So Ruhi's eldest half-brother, Hajji Dadash, a wise and gentle man of some means, agreed to lend him a sum large enough to cover his travel expenses. Hajji Dadash had the loan signed and sealed before a notary public to make it official. The term of the loan was indefinite and without interest, but it would have to be repaid ultimately. Sixteen years later, however, when Ruhi tried to repay his debt, Hajji Dadash took the contract out of a drawer and tore it up. "Your debt has been paid," he said.

As we were engrossed in our plans to leave the country, a power struggle was developing between the Shah and Mosadeq. The generous U.S. aid policy toward Iran had changed, and now in early 1952 the Iranian government's request for financial aid was met by a rebuff and a warning that Iran would receive no help from the United States unless and until it reached agreement with Great Britain on the oil nationalization question. Thus, Mosadeq was severely undercut in his attempts to play the United States off against Britain and both Western powers off against the Soviet Union and the Tudeh Party. Opposition to him was mounting in the Majlis, and the country seemed on the verge of financial ruin and political chaos. Even so, we could not possibly have predicted Mosadeq's fall from power.

As it turned out, Ruhi and I would read about his overthrow from a great distance, in our mobile trailer in Georgia, disbelieving at first that the United States could or would have engineered such a coup, shocked at the vitriolic hostility the prime minister evoked in the American press, and dismayed at the turn of events.

Eventually the historic and momentous oil nationalization crisis would constitute the subject of Ruhi's doctoral dissertation, but before we left the country, it was the main event at the heart of the rising tide of chaos that threatened to engulf Iran and us with it. As the crisis built, we prepared for departure.

We called on a few people to say good-bye. I visited Aida, who was not dancing anymore, but making plans for her marriage to Nejad. She said that

Departure for America from Mehrabad Airport, March 1952. Mummy is on the left; Ruhi Ramazani, my newlywed husband, is in the center; and Dr. Mashhoon can be seen in the back.

Mrs. Cook's whereabout were still unknown. Mehri wept when we said good-bye. She had just had her first child and was still bedridden. She rightly guessed it would be a long time before we would be reunited, and her tears fell freely. She would not be seeing us off at Mehrabad Airport.

Among those who did, however, was my new father-in-law, whom I met there for the first—and last—time. Although he was wizened and slightly stooped, he had a firm handshake and a strong voice as he greeted me and then bade me farewell.

Mummy was there, too, stoic as usual. In an old photograph taken just before our departure she is wearing a white scarf and carrying a lambskin muff. Her face looks drawn, her eyes distant and sad. But, of course, she is shedding no tears. I, on the other hand, have tears streaming down my face. I kissed her good-bye, and Ruhi and I started up the ramp to board the plane. I turned and waved. I would never see her again.

Epilogue

THE LAST NEWS I ever had of Mrs. Cook depicted her living alone on a remote Greek island, writing poetry. As far as I know, her poems remain unpub-
lished. She never again undertook a major organizing endeavor or ever returned
to Iran.

Some years after Ruhi and I departed for America, Mohammad Reza Shah
Pahlavi ordered a command performance from our disbanded troupe. Aida as-
sembled those troupe members whom she could, extracted costumes from
mothballs, performed for the Shah, and eventually managed to revive the company. Under her direction and her husband Nejad's management, her folkloric
dance company flourished. Much like Mrs. Cook's enterprise, it highlighted the
rich tribal and ethnic diversity of Iran. In 1979, however, the Islamic Revolution
swept away the entire endeavor and scattered the dancers to the far corners of
the earth.

But the seeds of the enterprise thus tossed on the winds took root elsewhere.
There exists now in California, under the direction of Anthony Shay, a Persian
dance group comprising first generation Iranian Americans who, deprived of a
full command of their Persian linguistic and literary heritage, have found in
dance a means of maintaining their ties with their unique cultural legacy.

What is more, dance in Iran itself continues to grow, both underground and
overtly. In a private home in Tehran a former dancer without fanfare teaches
tribal and ethnic dancing to young students eager to retain this aspect of their
heritage. In village and countryside celebratory dancing continues, adding vi-
vacity and gaiety to otherwise drab lives.

Even more surprising, dance as a *performing* art form has made a tentative comeback in the Islamic Republic, this time through the agency of an Iranian woman, Pari Saberi, who returned to her homeland after spending some years studying theater and cinematography in France and the United States. Rediscovering her roots, she—like Mrs. Cook—was inspired by Iranian literature to blend together mysticism, poetry, music, acting, and dance to create not a ballet company but a unique form of indigenous Iranian theater. She established in 1998 the Ayeneh Theater Group as a vehicle for training young students in the field of dramatic arts and for professional performances. She has produced a wide array of plays, ranging from a tragedy based on Ferdowsi's *Rostam and Sohrab* and a love story based on his *Bijan and Manijeh* to musical and lyrical plays based on famous verses from Attar, Rumi, and Hafez. She also draws on the *ta'ziyeh* and *zurkhaneh* traditions, as Mrs. Cook did. Her company draws packed houses night after night. Not long ago, in January 2001, in a theater in Tehran I watched her play about the life of the great Sufi poet Jalal ad-Din Rumi. A vibrant swirl of color, intricate musical rhythms, intoxicating recitations of Rumi's poems in song, modest dance steps, and imaginative staging plaited the Zoroastrian, Islamic, and Western strands of Iran's cultural history into a triumphant tribute to its enduring richness. Although even the minimal dancing in this play was controversial and condemned by some traditionalists, Pari Saberi did not strike it from her play and was not compelled to do so. So we see that dance has endured against all odds and holds out the promise of flourishing further in the Islamic Republic of Iran.

In 1955 Mummy, anxious to see her two new grandchildren, made preparations to come to Virginia to visit us. She was to have some "minor surgery" before coming, recommended for symptoms associated with the onset of menopause. She died of the ensuing hysterectomy.

Daddy and Parvin wandered back and forth between Iran and the United States for a number of years, finally settling in Iran. Eventually Parvin was reconciled with her father and inherited much wealth. For a while Daddy lived in luxury, indulging his artistic inclinations, building houses, designing gardens, recording classical Persian music, and writing, until Parvin divorced him. He thereafter sank into a deep depression from which he never recovered. He died a few years later.

My brothers remained in California, where Parviz became a chemical engineer, was married, and had four daughters, and Iraj became a lawyer, married, and had three children. We do not see each other very often, but whenever we do, it is a sweet reunion. We stay in touch.

Mehri was able to fulfill her ambitions to become a teacher, eventually rising to the rank of high school principal. She had five children. In 1983, at the height of the terror and counterterror of the Islamic Revolution, one of her daughters was mercilessly executed for opposing the tyranny of the revolutionary regime and for refusing to reveal the names of antiregime dissidents to prison officials. Eventually Mehri and the rest of her family settled in California.

After one semester at the University of Georgia Ruhi and I moved to Charlottesville, Virginia, where Ruhi earned a doctoral degree in the science of jurisprudence at the University of Virginia. He joined the faculty there in 1954, the same year our first son was born, and went on to have an illustrious career in teaching and writing, pioneering the study of Iran's foreign policy. We eventually had three sons and a daughter.

I took up dancing again, exploring new and dynamic dance forms—jazz, tap, and theater dance—and started teaching ballet and dance-exercise classes. Eventually, I was able to pursue my literary studies and earned a master's degree in English literature at the University of Virginia. I discovered the joy and excitement of writing and lecturing, and published a book on Persian culinary arts as well as many articles on women of the Middle East.

Ruhi and I still believe in the power of *qesmat*. How else can one explain the good fortune that brought us to, of all places in this vast North American continent, Charlottesville and the University of Virginia, where we found a second home as well as abiding freedom to think what we wish and write what we will without fear of reprisal?

Glossary

ab-anbar: an undergound cistern for storing water for general household use in the days before a piped water system was installed

ab-e roo: reputation, dignity, honor, face (as in saving face)

ab-e shah: At one time Tehran's drinking water was drawn from underground springs, one of which was located near the premises of the British embassy. This potable water was distributed by horse-drawn carts, each loaded with a large barrel of water.

ab-e goosht: a thick soup made with beans, garbanzos, potatoes, and a soup bone or a very small amount of meat

abi: one who delivers drinking water

ab-shan: oregano

aftabeh: a water pitcher with a long spout used for washing the lower extremities

Ahriman: the god (or power) of evil

Ahura Mazda: the god (or power) of good

ajeel: a mixture of roasted, salted nuts and dried fruits—usually watermelon seeds, pumpkin seeds, almonds, filberts, dried chickpeas, mulberries, and raisins

"aleikom-o-salam": "and unto you be peace" (loosely translated)

anbar: cellar

andaroon: the interior part of a house designated as women's quarters

Aqa: Sir or Mister

'aqd: the religious or civil contractual exchange of nuptial vows, often separate from the celebratory wedding *(aroosi)* when consummation takes place

arrak: an alcoholic beverage similar to vodka

aramgah: Zoroastrians apply this term, literally meaning "a place of rest," to their graveyards

arbab: lord (loosely translated); originally a title ascribed to persons of high rank or nobility, it eventually became a mark of respect, such as in Arbab Kaykhosrow Shahrokh

aroosi: wedding festivities, following which consummation takes place, as distinguished from *'aqd*

Ashura: the tenth day of the holy month of Moharram, when Shi'a Muslims observe the anniversary of the martyrdom of Imam Hossein, third imam of the Shi'a sect and the Prophet Mohammad's grandson; the day is marked by mourning, self-flagellation, and passion plays that reenact Imam Hossein's tragic death

atesh-charkhoon: small wire baskets attached to long wire handles used to help start a charcoal fire; after being lit, the baskets are swung around and around to fan the coals

Avesta: the holy book of the Zoroastrians

ayd-e shoma mobarak: "Happy New Year"

azadi: freedom

baba-joon: literally means "dear father," but customarily designates a grandfather

baghcheh: a small symmetrical garden plot usually surrounded by dwarf boxwood in the European style

bakhshesh: a bribe

Bakhtiaris: a large nomadic tribe

baklava: a sweet pastry made of paper-thin buttered dough layered with ground walnuts, almonds, or pistachios, sweetened with syrup

ballal: corn on the cob

"ballal-e dagh daram": "I have hot corn on the cob"

bamieh: sweet, syrup-drenched pastry

band-andaz: a professional depilator of body hair who uses coarse thread to pluck hair out by the roots

baqali pollo: rice flavored with dill weed and mixed with green fava beans and lamb or chicken

"befarmaeed": used in many different ways as a polite expression when offering hospitality or courtesy to another, ranging from "after you" to "please come in" to "please have some" (food) or "please sit down"

beshkan: a loud cracking noise made by rubbing the index fingers together

biroon: outside, specifically the outer, male quarters of a house

bolbol: a nightingale

bolbol zaban: one whose "tongue" is like a nightingale's; one who speaks well

boqcheh: before the advent of suitcases, it was customary to carry goods or clothes wrapped in a large cloth and tied into a bundle

borek: a Turkish specialty made with phyllo and filled with chicken, meat, spinach, or cheese

boteh: a shrub

caliph: a temporal and spiritual political successor to the Prophet

chador: an all-enveloping veil that covers a woman's body from head to toe and that can also be pulled across the face

chah: a deep pit, a well

Chahar Shambeh Soori: the eve of the last Wednesday before Norooz (the New Year that takes place on the vernal equinox), when Iranians celebrate by jumping over large bonfires while reciting a poem that transmits one's pallor to the fire while taking from the fire its rosy color

chai: tea, usually black

"chai biar": "bring some tea"

chello kabab: a national dish comprising fluffy mounds of buttered rice served with skewers of barbecued lamb with a sprinkling of sumac

cummerbund: although in English usage this word signifies a wide belt, in Persian *kamarband* simply designates a belt

dakhmeh: a Zoroastrian funerary tower on top of which are placed the deceased for the vultures to strip away the flesh

dallak: a professional bath attendant who scrubs, shampoos, massages, and sometimes depilates customers in public baths

Dari: an old Persian dialect with Median roots, spoken by Zoroastrians

darkand: the opening or "mouth" of a *qanat*.

dasteh: a group of mourners who beat their chests or otherwise flagellate themselves during Ashura to commemorate the martyrdom of Imam Hossein

dhimmi: non-Muslim "people of the book"—that is, Christians, Jews, and, by extension in Iran, Zoroastrians

dishlameh: method of sipping tea with a sugar cube held between the teeth

div: a supernatural being, usually evil

dohol: a wind instrument that is a cross between a horn and a recorder

dolma: known in Persian as *dolmeh*, this is the Turkish word for stuffed grape leaves, cabbage, eggplant, tomato, or squash

dooley: affectionate term for a young boy's penis

do-rageh: having two bloodlines; the offspring of a mixed marriage

doroshkeh: a horse-drawn carriage

erfan: the Sufi mystical belief that through the special devotion of love, one can meet the Divine Beloved in the present world, a union that brings ecstasy and esoteric knowledge

esteqlal: independence

Fadayan-e Islam: the Devotees of Islam, an extremist religiopolitical group

farangi: European, Western, derives from the word *Frankish*

farman: an edict

Farsi: the Persian language

fesenjoon: a dish of braised lamb or fowl (duck or chicken) smothered in a rich, dark sauce of ground walnuts and pomegranate syrup

fes–fes: a word used to describe a slowpoke, a dawdler

gavah-giri: the Zoroastrian term for the formal signing of the wedding contract, known among Muslims as *'aqd*

gawd: the pit wherein *zurkhaneh* exercises are held

gaz: a sweet white nougat filled with pistachios or almonds

geeveh: shoes with leather soles but cloth upper parts

gelim: the Persian word for *kelim,* a handwoven, pileless rug

goor: the wild ass

gul: the floral designs in a Persian carpet, from *gol,* the Persian word for flower

hadith: reports of the sayings, practices, and silent approval of the Prophet Mohammad, which were compiled and became one of the sources of Islamic Law

haft-seen: seven *s*'s, referring to the table set with seven items that start with the Persian letter *s* as part of the celebration of Norooz, the Persian New Year's Day

halvah: a honey-colored sweet confection

hamam: a bath, a public bath

imamzadeh: a shrine that commemorates the burial place of a saint or holy person

istanbolli pollo: a rice dish made with lamb, tomatoes, and green beans

istikan: a small, narrow-waisted tea glass

jaziyeh: a tax on non-Muslims

joob: a water conduit or channel

Kaffir: Anglicized version of *kafar,* a nonbeliever

kaka siyah: a performer in blackface

keeseh: a mitt-shaped washcloth made of rough goat hair used in baths to slough off dead skin

"Khaleh-sooskeh": "Aunt Roach"

khanom: lady, Mrs., a term of deference toward women

khar: heaven-sent glory that united with a young woman, who then gave birth to the Prophet Zoroaster, who was from then on surrounded by a divine radiance

kharab: spoiled goods, a term of opprobrium applied to young girls suspected of having had premarital relations

khast-e-gar: suitor

khaymeh sayeh-gardoon: a shadow play in which wooden or tin forms were silhouetted against a large cloth, a mode of entertainment that has died out

khaymeh shab-bazi: a marionette or puppet show

khazineh: a pool in a public bath used for the final rinse

khoresht: braised or stewed meat or chicken dishes meant to accompany rice

kolah-e namadi: a felt hat

koocheh: a narrow lane or side street

koozeh: a clay jug of variable size and shape used for storing water, milk, yogurt, or pickles

korsi: a heating system; a brazier of hot charcoals placed under a low table covered with quilts, around which family members sit with their legs under the table to keep warm

koshti: a ceremonial cord used in Zoroastrian prayers and worn by members of the faith

"la-illaha el-Allah, Mohammad-an rasool-ollah": "there is no God but Allah, Mohammad is His prophet"

lavash: a paper-thin flat bread

longue: large cloth wrap worn in public baths

lork: a mixture of seven dried fruits and nuts, usually peaches, apricots, mulberries, raisins, walnuts, pistachios, and almonds

ma'bad: a Zoroastrian place of worship

madreseh: a school, specifically a school where the instruction is largely in Koranic studies

magi: Zoroastrian wise men

mahaleh: neighborhood

mahrieh: a sum of money promised to a bride by the groom, often considered as security in the event she is divorced

mahzar: registration office

Majlis: Iranian Parliament

maktab: school

mashallah: praise be to God

meze: Turkish word for hors d'oeuvres

mosha'ereh: a game in which members of a group take turns reciting poems, the aim being for each person to start a line that begins with the last letter of the previous participant's last line

mobed: a Zoroastrian cleric

mohr: a small disc made of clay from the holy sites of Mecca or Karbala; a person praying will touch his forehead to the disc at prescribed times

moj-pa: a wave step; an ancient dance step

moqanni: a professional cleaner of *qanat*s and *chah*

morshed: spiritual guide, sheikh, elder

mostaz'afin: the downtrodden

motevalli: the custodian of a religious shrine

motreb: a performer, a hired dancer or singer

mullah: a Muslim cleric

mut'a: temporary marriage

najess: unclean

naqareh: a drum held upright with a cord looped around the neck of the player, who can then beat the drum with sticks on either side

noql: a white confection consisting of a slivered almond covered with a sweet, white, hard coating, used at weddings, Norooz, and other special occasions

Norooz: New Year's Day, the principal Iranian national holiday that celebrates the arrival of spring; its roots go back to ancient Zoroastrian times, long before the advent of Islam

ood: incense

osool-e din: the tenets or principles of the faith, peculiar to Shi'a Islam, not to be confused with the Five Pillars of Islam; these principles are *towheed, adl, nabovat, imamat, ma'ad-e rooz-e qiamat:* unity (of God), justice, prophethood (of Mohammad), the institution of imams, and the day of resurrection

pambeh-zan: a professional mattress refurbisher who plumps up the cotton fillings of mattresses

pardis: ancient Persian word for heaven

pari: angel

pide: Turkish for pita or pocket bread

qaba: a long cloak

qahveh-khaneh: a teahouse, although the word literally means "a coffeehouse"

qalam-kar: hand-blocked cloths, tapestries, or fabric

qameh: short-handled knives used in rituals of self-flagellation commemorating the martyrdom of Hossein *qanat:* subterranean canals that for centuries carried fresh water down from the mountains to the parched plains, cities, and villages of Iran

qesmat: Persian for kismet, fate, destiny

raqs-e dastmal: handkerchief dance

reng: music that is lighthearted and has a rhythmic beat suitable for dancing

rooband-bazi: a theater of masks, a form of entertainment that has died out

roo-hosy: entertainment in the form of music or dance, performed on a boarded-over pool

rowzeh: lamentation session held in a private home to commemorate and mourn the martyrdom of Hossein

rowzeh-khan: a reciter of lamentations bewailing the persecution and death of Hossein

sabzeh: sprouted greens symbolic of renewal and rebirth, customarily placed on the *haft-seen* table for Norooz

sabzi: a side dish of fresh herbs, usually basil, tarragon, and watercress

sakoo: a raised, tile platform in a *hamam*; also a raised dais that serves as a stage

"salaam": "greetings," "peace be upon you"

"salaam aleikom": "may peace be with you," a greeting

salak: a large sore that, before the days of penicillin, left deep scars

sangak: a flat bread that derives its name from the fact that it is cooked directly on hot gravel

sang-e saboor: a patience stone

Saoshyant: the Zoroastrian messiah, the Savior

sar-sheer: the solidified cream that forms on top of unhomogenized boiled milk

Sassanian, also Sassanid: pre-Islamic Persian dynasty (A.D. 224–641)

sedreh: a Zoroastrian white ceremonial shirt

seerabi: a stew made from the entrails of sheep

seerok: a sweet bread fried in oil served at the Zoroastrian temple on special occasions

seezdah be-dar: the thirteenth day after Norooz, when people picnic and throw spouted greens into running water for good luck

"shab-be-khayr": "good night" or "may the night go well"

shahada: bearing witness, during prayers, to Allah and to his prophet Mohammad

shahi: a tenth of a rial, this coin is no longer in use

shahr-e farang: a portable nickelodeon; for a small fee spectators could look through peepholes and watch the rotation of beautiful pictures

sharbat: a sweet cold drink made from fruit syrup mixed with water; the origin of the English *sherbert*

sheer-khesht: purgative manna

sheer-mal: a sweet gateaulike bread

sigheh: a temporary wife

Siyah: Blackie

sofreh: a tablecloth spread on the floor

sopoor: a cleaner of streets, whose job in the old days would include sweeping up horse dung

taftoon: a flat bread

tah-deeg: the crusty rice that forms on the bottom of the pan in the Persian method of cooking rice

takht: wooden bed frames

takhteh-hosy: a pond covered with wooden boards to form a platform suitable for *roo-hosy* performances

tar: a stringed instrument

ta'ziyeh: a Persian religious passion play that commemorates the martyrdom of Hossein, the grandson of the Prophet Mohammad

tekiyeh: a large tent where the *ta'ziyeh* is held

termeh: a handwoven paisley brocade

tudeh: literally "the masses"; the Tudeh Party was the name of the Soviet-supported Communist Party of Iran

vajebi: a white paste used as a depilatory cream

vozoo': the ritual ablutions Muslims perform before saying their prayers

"Ya-Allah": "in the name of God," often abbreviated to *yallah*

yakhee: the iceman

zanjeer: a chain; during religious processions several short chains clustered on one handle are used for self-flagellation

zurkhaneh: the House of Strength, in which martial arts exercises are practiced to the accompaniment of singsong recitations of epic poetry; also refers to the martial arts themselves